Collins

CAMBRIDGE IGCSE® ENGLISH
REVISED EDITION

Series editor: Julia Burchell

Authors:
Claire Austin-Macrae, Julia Burchell, Nigel Carlisle, Mike Gould and Ian Kirby

**Complete coverage of the
Cambridge First Language English syllabuses 0500 and 0522**

Published by Collins Education
An imprint of HarperCollins Publishers
77–85 Fulham Palace Road
Hammersmith
London W6 8JB

Browse the complete Collins
Education catalogue at
www.collinseducation.com

© HarperCollins Publishers Limited 2013
10 9 8 7 6 5 4 3 2

ISBN 978 0 00 752073 2

Claire Austin-Macrae, Julia Burchell, Nigel Carlisle, Mike Gould and Ian Kirby assert their moral rights to be identified as the authors of this work.

All rights reserved. Any educational institution that has purchased one copy of this publication may make duplicate copies for use exclusively within that institution. Permission does not extend to reproduction, storage in a retrieval system, or transmittal in any form or by any means, electronic, mechanical, photocopying, recording or otherwise, of duplicate copies for loaning, renting or selling to any other institutions without the publisher's prior consent.

British Library Cataloguing in Publication Data.
A Catalogue record for this publication is available from the British Library.

Commissioned by Catherine Martin
Edited and project-managed by Lucy Hobbs and Hugh Hillyard-Parker
Design by Hugh Hillyard-Parker
Cover design by Paul Manning

With thanks to Caroline Green, Grace Glendinning and Jackie Newman.

The Publishers would like to thank the IGCSE teachers and students of the following schools for their contributions to Chapter 10:

VIBGYOR High, Mumbai, India
The Perse School, Cambridge, UK
The British School of Rio, Rio de Janeiro, Brazil.

This text has not been through the Cambridge endorsement process.

ACKNOWLEDGEMENTS

The publishers gratefully acknowledge the permission granted to reproduce the copyright material in this book. While every effort has been made to trace and contact copyright holders, where this has not been possible the publishers will be pleased to make the necessary arrangements at the first opportunity.

p. 179, from www.wildernessdiary.com. Reprinted with kind permission

p. 183, from 'Mountain Goat Kills Hikers' by Alex Robinson, *Outdoor Life*

p. 184, from 'Why do men love dangerous dogs?' by Robert Crampton, *The Times*, July 5th 2008. Reprinted with permission of NI Syndication

p. 206, from *Set In Stone* by Linda Newbery copyright © 2006 by Linda Newbery. Used by permission of David Flickling Books, an imprint of Random House Children's Books, a division of Random House Inc, Any third party use of this material, outside of this publication, is prohibited. Interested parties must apply directly to Random House Inc, for permission.

pp. 222–3, from 'The Snake' by D. H. Lawrence, 1921

pp. 228 & 230, 'Is the Giant Panda really worth saving? Yes, says Chris Packham' by Leo Benedictus, *The Guardian*, 23 September, 2009 © Guardian News and Media 2009. Used with permission

pp. 233–4, from 'Brady's Bad Bite: in his own words' by Brady Barr, from http://channel.nationalgeographic.com/series/dangerous-encounters#tab-python-encounter. Reprinted with permission of *National Geographic*

p. 250—1 from 'Chilean miners: A typical day in the life of a subterranean miner' by Jonathan Franklin, *The Guardian*, 10 September, 2010. © Guardian News and Media Ltd 2010. Reprinted with permission

p. 265, from 'Not all gaming is bad – it can be as engrossing as a novel or chess' by Nigel Kendall, *Times* game reviewer, *The Times*, 27 March, 2008. Reprinted with permission of NI Syndications

The publishers would like to thank the following for permission to reproduce pictures in these pages:

Cover: Shutterstock
PPT 1.6a, Nenad.C/Shutterstock; Harsanyi Andras/ Shutterstock
PPT 3.14g, Artur Bogacki/Shutterstock; elvensou1/Shutterstock; FuzzBones/Shutterstock; artcphotos/Shutterstock
PPT 5.2e, ArindaMBanerjee/Shutterstock
PPT 7.2a, Radiokafka/Shutterstock

Contents

Introduction ... 4

Lesson plans

SECTION 1 Building Key Skills
Chapter 1   Key reading skills ... 6
Chapter 2   Key technical skills ... 24
Chapter 3   Key writing skills ... 40

SECTION 2 Applying Key Skills in Examinations
Chapter 4   Summary questions ... 70
Chapter 5   Comprehension and writer's effects questions ... 78
Chapter 6   Extended response and directed writing questions ... 90
Chapter 7   Composition questions ... 98

SECTION 3 Applying Key Skills in Written Coursework
Chapter 8   Approaching written coursework ... 110

SECTION 4 Speaking and Listening
Chapter 9   Approaching speaking and listening ... 120

SECTION 5 Exam Practice
Chapter 10 Practice exam-style papers and advice ... 144

Worksheets

Chapter 1   Key reading skills ... 150
Chapter 2   Key technical skills ... 161
Chapter 3   Key writing skills ... 176
Chapter 4   Summary questions ... 195
Chapter 5   Comprehension and writer's effects questions ... 200
Chapter 6   Extended response and directed writing questions ... 208
Chapter 7   Composition questions ... 213
Chapter 8   Approaching written coursework ... 222
Chapter 10 Practice exam-style papers and advice ... 233

Appendices

Appendix 1   Summary questions: exam focus ... 279
Appendix 2   Writer's effects questions: exam focus ... 280
Appendix 3   Extended response and directed writing questions: exam focus ... 281
Appendix 4   Composition questions: exam focus ... 282
Appendix 5   Written coursework focus ... 283
Appendix 6   Speaking and listening: exam focus ... 284
Appendix 7   Speaking and listening: coursework focus ... 285
Appendix 8   Two-year scheme of work ... 286

Introduction

Welcome to the Collins Cambridge IGCSE English Teacher Guide. Our popular first edition has been fully updated to support the teaching of the syllabus for first examination in 2015. We hope it will provide invaluable support to teachers worldwide, as they prepare students for the freedom, challenge and enrichment offered by the Cambridge IGCSE in First Language English (syllabuses 0500 and 0522).

Using the Student Book

The Student Book is structured so that it builds the fundamental skills that underpin IGCSE success before explaining the specific blend of skills necessary to tackle each type of examination question and coursework assignment, and offering opportunities to practise and consolidate these tasks.

The book opens with three chapters that systematically cover the basic Reading and Writing skills required by all IGCSE English students. These are divided into:

- Chapter 1: Key reading skills
- Chapter 2: Key technical skills
- Chapter 3: Key writing skills.

It then focuses on each of the question types set in the exam:

- Chapter 4: Summary questions
- Chapter 5: Comprehension and writer's effects questions
- Chapter 6: Extended response and directed writing questions
- Chapter 7: Composition questions.

It then moves on to cover each written coursework assignment and the requirements of the Speaking and Listening exam and coursework tasks:

- Chapter 8: Approaching written coursework
- Chapter 9: Approaching speaking and listening components.

The book closes, in Chapter 10, with resources for exam practice. These can be used in stages as each exam question type is covered, or could be set together as a 'mock' examination to provide a formative assessment opportunity.

In our opinion, the best way to approach the course would be to work through Chapters 1, 2 and 3 early in the course, or even before it begins. This said, it would be perfectly acceptable – desirable even – to mix and match content from all three chapters rather than work through each in isolation.

Alternatively, it would be possible to work through Chapter 1 and then tackle the summary and writer's effects questions chapters (4 and 5). However, it is not advisable to use the extended response and directed writing, composition or coursework chapters (6–8) until students are familiar with the skills introduced in Chapters 2 and 3. The exam tasks in Chapters 6–8 require a blend of skills with which students need to be confident before tackling these tasks. Please see the suggested **Two-year scheme of work** on pp. 286–7 of this Guide.

Features of the Student Book

The book offers lively approaches to exciting texts and ensures that students have access to a wide range of fiction and non-fiction.

Standards are exemplified throughout: for example, by shorter sample responses demonstrating clearly the differences between Band 3 and Band 1 and by the longer sample responses at the key boundaries of Band 4/3 and 2/1 in the **Exam-style questions and sample responses** and **Coursework-style responses** sections that end each chapter.

The **Top tips** given will allow students to see the examiner's viewpoint, and the **Checklists for success** summaries will help to consolidate students' learning.

Core and/or **Extended content** is clearly signalled by these icons at the start of each lesson. Further regular differentiation points and peer- and self-assessment opportunities are provided by the **Sound progress** (aiming for Grade C) and **Excellent progress** (aiming for Grade A) boxes at the end of lessons, and by the **Check your progress** pages at the end of each chapter.

Using the Teacher Guide

Each two-page (or occasionally four-page) section in the Student Book is intended to provide work for one lesson, or occasionally two lessons, and is supported in the Teacher Guide by a two-page lesson plan, plus worksheet(s) and Power Points (PPTs).

The Teacher Guide is designed to help you with the following.

Planning

- Key references to the specification are listed at the start of each lesson plan, with the **Assessment objectives** and links to **Examination papers** and **Coursework assignments** identified so that the wider application of learning is clear.
- Detailed, ready-to-use **lesson plans** offer all you need to teach: these are divided into sections that match the Student Book – *Exploring skills*, *Building skills*, *Developing skills* and *Applying skills* – ensuring progression and pace as well as opportunities for consolidation. Often, the *Developing Skills* section focuses on the extra skills needed for the higher grades.
- **Worksheets** and **PowerPoint slides** (PPTs) supplement and extend activities in the Student Book and are itemised in each lesson plan, meaning that time-consuming preparation is kept to a minimum.

Differentiation

- Each lesson plan begins with **Learning outcomes** differentiated by grade.
- Further differentiation opportunities are provided in the **Extra support** and **Extra challenge** boxes, ensuring all students are stimulated.
- **Worksheets** and **PPTs** offer additional activities to suit a range of learning styles and abilities.
- **Towards A/A* advice** at the end of each lesson plan (apart from those aimed specifically at Core-level students) gives a specific tip or activity suggestion for students aiming for the highest grades.

Assessment

- A complete suite of exam-style practice papers is provided in Chapter 10, as well as marking guidance, sample answers and detailed analysis of how marks could be allocated. Video clips of series editor, Julia Burchell, advise students on how to tackle the most challenging exam questions.
- Peer- and self-assessment is regularly used to help students understand how to progress towards their target grade.
- **Appendices 1–7** can be used as revision aids, as they provide a brief summary of the major exam question types and coursework assignments.

Our resources are designed to enhance performance so that candidates can work towards IGCSE grades they can be proud of. We hope you enjoy using them.

Julia Burchell
Series Editor

1 Locating information: skimming

Assessment objectives

AO1 Reading

R1 Demonstrate understanding of explicit meanings

IGCSE examination
- **Paper 1** all questions
- **Paper 2** all questions
- **Component 4** Coursework portfolio (Assignment 3)

Differentiated learning outcomes
- **All students must** be able to gain some understanding of a text and select sections of a text that are relevant to questions (Grade E/D).
- **Most students should** gain a good understanding of a text, make relevant annotations and be able to find appropriate information in a text (Grade D/C).
- **Some students could** quickly understand the focus of a text, make precise annotations and select a full range of the most appropriate information from a text (Grade B/A).

Resources
- **Student Book**: pp. 8–9
- **PPT**: 1.1a–d

Exploring skills

As a class, read through this section of the Student Book and ensure that the class understand the term 'skimming'. Copy and complete the table for the longer skimming exercise in **Q1**. Take feedback as a class. Responses will include:

- Text type: a novel.
- Setting: Africa (Kgale Hill, Botswana) – strong sense of setting.
- Action: no action.
- Description: yes, lots of description.
- Character: Mma Ramotswe is introduced with some larger-than-life features.
- Attitude/message: one message is that she is a strong character.
- Purpose: to describe and entertain.
- What might happen next: expect a client/problem to be introduced; might get a sense that the agency is in trouble (the mention of assets and inventories).

As an extension, use **PPT 1.1a–b** to develop the skill of skimming with some quick pair challenges. After each activity, discuss how easy it is to gain a quick understanding and why some information seems more important than other details.

In **PPT 1.1a**, students should note the aunt's age and old-fashioned ways. In **PPT 1.1b**, they should pick up on the writer's attitude towards London, the range of things to do, sighting David Beckham and the pros and cons of city travel.

Building skills

Read through this section with the class. For **Q2**, ask students to work in groups of four. Test the effectiveness of their skimming by reading out questions (a), (b) and (c) one by one, with the students pointing to the relevant area of text as quickly as they can.

If students are finding the tasks so far quite difficult, repeat them using the opening paragraphs of any novel and get them to complete the same table. Then ask them three text-specific questions about where information is located. This could be done as a small group, with one group member challenging the others to find certain information from the text.

Developing skills

Read this section of the Student Book and complete **Q3**.

For the first paragraph, ideas might include: describing the agency; introducing Mma Ramotswe; who and what.

For the second paragraph, ideas might include: the surroundings (vegetation); the view from the door.

PPT Students complete **Q4** in pairs, deciding what information is held in the different sentences of each paragraph. You can display the text of the passage from Student Book p. 8 using **PPT 1.1c–d**. To aid this discussion **PPT 1.1d** is already annotated to show where information on 'vegetation' can be found in the second paragraph.

Applying skills

For **Q5**, ask students to write up answers to questions (a), (b) and (c) from **Q2** of the 'Building skills' section, as if for Question 1 on the Core exam paper. Remind them of the importance of putting the ideas into their own words and of using appropriate quotations as evidence.

> **Give extra support** by helping students to find relevant sections again or appropriate quotations. Help could also be given with sentence starters, such as: *Some of the vegetation looks quite big and harmful...* or *The phrase 'great white thorns' makes the vegetation sound...*
>
> **Give extra challenge** by encouraging students to be detailed yet concise. Remind them that it is good practice to refer to any relevant techniques, such as the effect of using adjectives or metaphor.

Class feedback might include:

- Vegetation – big, harmful looking acacia trees ('great white thorns'); the trees look unusual because, in contrast, their leaves seem pretty ('so delicate'); it seems dry rather than lush ('scrub bush').
- Staff – one member of staff ('her secretary').
- Mma Ramotswe – unique ('only lady detective', or 'no inventory...'); polite, generous or down to earth (she brews tea for her own secretary); clever or skilful ('human intuition and intelligence', or 'in abundance').

After feeding back as a class, invite students to share their work in pairs and – using the **Checklist for success** on Student Book p. 9 – to assess how well they have done and what they need to do to improve.

| **Towards A/A*** | To achieve the highest marks for reading, students need to skim texts for quick understanding. They should quickly find the most appropriate information for the question being asked. They also need to do this in order to quickly select the 'best' quotations that will allow them to analyse the effects of a writer's language choices. Encourage students to practise the skill of skimming on a regular basis in order to sharpen their abilities. |

2 Locating information: scanning

Assessment objectives

AO1 Reading
- R1 Demonstrate understanding of explicit meanings
- R2 Demonstrate understanding of implicit meanings and attitudes

IGCSE examination
- **Paper 1** all questions
- **Paper 2** all questions
- **Component 4** Coursework portfolio (Assignment 3)

Differentiated learning outcomes

- **All students must** select different sections of a text in order to show their understanding (Grade E/D).
- **Most students should** select a range of relevant information from a text that displays a good understanding (Grade D/C).
- **Some students could** quickly select a full range of the most appropriate information, suggesting insight into a text (Grade B/A).

Resources
- **Student Book**: pp. 10–13
- **Worksheet**: 1.2 Locating information: scanning

Exploring skills

As a class, read through the opening sections on Student Book p. 10 and ensure that students understand the term 'scanning'. In pairs complete **Q1**. Take feedback, eliciting the following answers: 1G, 2D, 3F, 4A, 5B, 6C, 7E. In each case discuss the features that matched the text type and what made them easy to scan for.

Ask the students if they can think of any other real-life situations where they have used scanning skills (such as reading a bus timetable, finding out what time a television programme starts, searching for something on Google, checking food labels for an allergy-causing ingredient).

Building skills

Read through **Q2** with the class on how to unpick a question and scan for appropriate information. For **Q3**, hand out **Worksheet 1.2** and ask students to discuss the extract from *Q & A* in pairs and then complete the table.

Give extra support by asking students questions that help them to explore the different phrases in the table. For example:

- Why isn't artificial light as nice as 'natural light'?
- Why would you want 'ventilation'?
- What do you think of when you imagine 'corrugated metal'?
- What does the adverb 'violently' add to the roof image?
- What would a train 'passing overhead' be like?
- What do you need 'running water' for?
- What does it mean by 'no sanitation' and how would this affect the house?

Give extra challenge by encouraging students to consider the connotations (implied meanings) of specific words. This is getting them to consider *how* and *why*, not just *what*.

Take feedback on the extract as a class, focusing on the unpleasant words that students found and how other phrases implied something unpleasant.

Developing skills

As a class, read this section and complete **Q4**, discussing with students what they can tell about migrants from the whole sentence given. Explain the importance of using context to gain full understanding of certain meanings. Responses might include:

- 'destitute' shows they are poor and suggests homelessness
- 'from all over the country' suggests migrants move away from their home towns, presumably for economic reasons
- 'jostle' suggests there are lots of migrants
- 'their own handful' suggests they are grateful for what they can get
- 'slum' suggests they are in extreme poverty and have to put up with a lot of hardship.

As an extension, ask students to scan the extract to select the 'best' word or phrase to describe the following things. Encourage students to explain their choices by thinking about how the language suggests or enhances meaning. For example:

- not having much room ('cramped', 'million ... packed', 'squabbles over inches')
- the surrounding landscape ('swampy urban wasteland')
- suggestions of aggression ('jostle', 'squabbles', 'turn deadly')
- lack of self-esteem ('live like animals', 'die like insects').

Applying skills

Ask students to use the extract from *Q & A* to complete **Q5**: 'How does the writer suggest that life is not easy for the narrator?'

> **Give extra support** by reminding students to use the information they have already gathered. Help students with sentence starters, such as: *The writer suggests life is not easy for the narrator by describing a lack of hygiene...* or *The phrase, 'no sanitation' implies that life would not be easy because...*
>
> **Give extra challenge** by encouraging students to be detailed yet concise, grouping their ideas and considering the connotations of the words that they select and their context. Advise them to refer to specific techniques, such as use of adjectives or simile.

Feed back as a class, taking examples of the points that they identified, the phrases that students selected, and how the choice of language within their phrases conveys that life is not easy. Responses might include:

- the state of the house (as already explored in **Q3**)
- the narrator's lack of money (emphasised by the short sentence) and people's desperation ('inches of space ... bucket of water')
- the local area ('packed ... swampy urban wasteland')
- his feeling of being unvalued (the simile, 'live like animals')
- the sense of danger (the simile 'die like insects', and the reference to 'daily squabbles ... which at times turn deadly').

After feedback, ask pairs to share their work and – using the **Checklist for success** on Student Book p. 13 – to assess how well they have done.

Towards A/A*	To achieve the highest marks for reading, students need to scan texts and quickly find the most appropriate information for the question being asked. They also need to do this in order to select quickly the 'best' quotations that will allow them to analyse the effects of a writer's language choices.
	Encourage students to practise this skill with a variety of forms of writing that they encounter, such as newspapers, leaflets, or their favourite magazine.

3 Selecting information

Assessment objectives

AO1 Reading

R1 Demonstrate understanding of explicit meanings
R3 Analyse, evaluate and develop facts, ideas and opinions
R5 Select for specific purposes

IGCSE examination

- **Paper 1** all questions
- **Paper 2** all questions (in particular, Question 3)
- **Component 4** Coursework portfolio (Assignment 3)

Differentiated learning outcomes

- **All students must** be able to select some key information from a text (Grade E/D).
- **Most students should** differentiate between what is and is not relevant in a text, according to different questions (Grade D/C).
- **Some students could** select the most appropriate and useful information for their response to a range of questions (Grade B/A).

Resources

- **Student Book**: pp. 14–15
- **PPT**: 1.3a–i

Exploring skills

As a class, read through the opening section of the Student Book on p. 14 and ensure that students understand how skimming and scanning lead on to selecting the most relevant information for their answers.

For **Q1**, use **PPT 1.3a** to show the two alternative answers. Either through teacher-led discussion, or through individuals coming up to the board, highlight the less relevant information that could be removed.

Make sure students understand why, for this question, they only really need two points from this list: Petchey wanted people to experience walking on the beach, swimming in the sea or the view.

Building skills

For **Q2**, read through the two sample answers. Ask students to discuss which is more effective and, using the three bullet points, why.

During feedback, use **PPT 1.3b–f** to illustrate what the different pieces of unnecessary information are in the first sample answer, and how this extra detail has been summarised to make a clearer response in the second sample answer.

As an extension, ask students to complete the activity on **PPT 1.3g**, explaining what Uncle Howard is like. They should extract that he is in his sixties, is bald, likes music, is nostalgic, is sociable, and has difficulty walking. During the activity, ask students to explain how they know what is and isn't important to select; encourage them to highlight the specific examples, descriptive detail and unnecessary additional information that they decide to remove. Encourage them to summarise points where appropriate too.

Developing skills

As a class, introduce the purpose of the anecdote on p. 15 of the Student Book, and discuss **Q3**. Students should pick out that the writer is conveying why he hates cats. The anecdote starts with the phrase, 'It all started...' and ends, '...even louder than it had'.

Pairs should then complete the rewriting task in **Q4**.

> **Give extra support** by helping students to select alternative words. For example: looked (seemed, appeared), harmless (innocent, docile), cuddly (sweet, furry), kind (friendly, considerate).

Applying skills

Ask students to use the text on cats to answer **Q5**: 'How does the writer feel about cats and why?'

> **Give extra support** by helping students with sentence starters, such as: *The writer finds cats...* or *The phrase, 'I hate our furry friends', shows...*
>
> **Give extra challenge** by encouraging students to also consider the effectiveness of the language, for example the use of irony in the phrase 'our furry friends'.

Take feedback as a class, discussing the different feelings that students came up with and how these are made clear by the writer's language choices. Ideas should include:

- He/she hates cats.
- He/she is scared of cats.
- He/she finds cats mysterious.
- He/she was clawed across the face by a cat when he was a child.

After feedback, get students to share their work in pairs and, using the **Sound progress** and **Excellent progress** criteria on Student Book p. 15, to assess how well they have done.

As an extension, ask students to answer one of the following questions about the cat extract:

1. What features of a cat doesn't the writer like and why?
2. What animal does the writer like and why?

PPT This can be supported using **PPT 1.3h–i**. Share and mark their responses, using the grade criteria on Student Book p. 15. For the first question, responses should include:

- the way they look and move ('slinky, panther-like frames')
- they aren't friendly ('mysterious, aloof creatures')
- their claws ('swiped me across the cheek, 'they scare me').

For the second question, responses should state 'dogs' and refer to aspects such as:

- the fact you can tell what they're feeling ('one look... and you know it all')
- they interact ('yes, yes, yes, let's play now')
- their gentleness or friendliness ('soppy canine').

Towards A/A*	To achieve the highest marks for reading, students need to filter out any irrelevance and select the most appropriate information for the question type. Encourage students to practise this skill of summarising key ideas and selecting only the most relevant information in the different forms of writing that they encounter.

4 Explicit meaning

Assessment objectives
AO1 Reading
R1 Demonstrate understanding of explicit meanings

IGCSE examination
- **Paper 1** all questions
- **Paper 2** all questions
- **Paper 3** Section 1 (Directed writing)
- **Component 4** Coursework portfolio (Assignment 3)

Differentiated learning outcomes
- **All students must** be able to select some key explicit information from a text and comment on the meaning of words (Grade E/D).
- **Most students should** select appropriate information, and consider how the meaning of words affects the text (Grade D/C).
- **Some students could** select the most appropriate and useful information, and analyse its effect on the reader (Grade B/A).

Resources
- **Student Book**: pp. 16–19
- **Worksheets**:
  1.4a Explicit meaning (1)
  1.4b Explicit meaning (2)
- **Dictionaries**

Exploring skills

As a class, read through Student Book p. 16, ensuring students understand what 'explicit information' means.

Then read the extract from *The Salt Road* (going through any difficult words in the Glossary) and set students the five comprehension questions in **Q1**, which ask for explicit information.

During class feedback, ensure that students do not include any comments that are either irrelevant or inferred (rather than explicit). Responses should include:

(a) wigwam in the back garden (paragraph 1)
(b) boxes of yellowed papers, ancient artefacts, dusty objects (ninth line of paragraph 2)
(c) wild, loud, messy, unbiddable (last line of paragraph 2)
(d) the past, archaeology, artefacts, objects, ancient civilisations (seventh to ninth lines of paragraph 2)
(e) going to the cinema on Saturday morning (paragraph 1); spending time in her tent (paragraph 2); playing outside, mutilating and burying dolls (paragraph 3).

Give extra support by guiding some students where to look for specific information.
Give extra challenge by encouraging students to put answers in their own words.

As an extension, students could then be asked to work in pairs on selecting explicit information to show how Izzy is different from her parents.

During feedback, responses might include:
- she is imaginative while they are scientific and studious (paragraph 2)
- she is energetic while they are sedate (paragraphs 2 and 3)
- she is loud while they are quiet (paragraph 2).

Building skills

As a class, run through this section on Student Book p. 18 and reread the extract. For **Q2**, arrange students in groups of four. Then hand out **Worksheet 1.4a** to one pair and **Worksheet 1.4b** to the other pair (the examples are the same on both worksheets, but the words that each pair need to explore are different). Using the glossary entries and dictionaries, ask students to complete the exploration of the words in their chart then feed back to the other pair in their group. (This offers possible differentiation, as the vocabulary on the second worksheet is a little more difficult.)

Developing skills

Return to Student Book p. 18 and read the sentence starters leading into **Q3**. Ask students to use the sentence starters to write up their findings about three of the words from **Worksheet 1.4a or b**. For each chosen word, students should use either starter 1 and 2, or starter 3.

> **Give extra support** by helping students to begin with starter 1 (referring to the first two columns of their table), and then use starter 2 (referring to the word again, followed by the last two columns of the table).

Applying skills

As a class, read through p. 19 of the Student Book, including the sample question types. Ask students to complete **Q4**.

> **Give extra support** by helping students with sentence starters, such as: *The girl likes to go outside because...* or *The phrase, 'felt small and suffocating' shows that the girl likes to go outside in order to...*
>
> **Give extra challenge** by encouraging students to select information carefully, use their own words, and support their point with a quotation. As an extension, they could also complete the fifth (summary) question.

Feed back as a class, making sure that students' ideas are supported by quotations. Responses should include this information:

1. to escape parents' arguing; because the house felt oppressive; as a place to let her imagination free
2. beheaded or scalped them; buried them
3. going to the cinema; imagining things; being loud and messy; playing outdoors games; mutilating her toys
4. parents are unsociable; out of step with the rest of the world; self-absorbed; pay little attention to their daughter; trapped.

It may be good to discuss with students why the second type of question is more difficult than the first type: explanation involves the skill of 'translating' explicit meaning into your own words.

After feedback, ask students to assess their work in pairs, using the **Sound progress** and **Excellent progress** criteria on Student Book p. 19 to see how well they have done.

Towards A/A*	To achieve the highest marks for reading, students need to select a range of the most relevant explicit information. It is important that they can recognise when they are being asked for this explicit information, so that they restrict themselves to it and consider its purpose. Students will need to pick out the 'best' quotations and analyse their effects on the reader.

5 Implicit meaning: character

Assessment objectives

AO1 Reading

R2 Demonstrate understanding of implicit meanings and attitudes.

R4 Demonstrate understanding of how writers achieve effects.

IGCSE examination
- **Paper 1** all questions
- **Paper 2** all questions (in particular, Question 2)
- **Paper 3** both sections
- **Component 4** Coursework portfolio (Assignment 3)

Differentiated learning outcomes
- **All students must** be able to select some key implicit information from a text and comment on what it suggests about character (Grade E/D).
- **Most students should** select appropriate information and use it to infer meaning about character (Grade D/C).
- **Some students could** select and link the most appropriate information and analyse how it conveys meaning about character (Grade B/A).

Resources
- **Student Book**: pp. 20–3
- **Worksheet**: 1.5 Implicit meaning: character

Exploring skills

As a class, read through this opening section of the Student Book on p. 20. Make sure that students understand the five bullet points about character.

Check understanding of the term 'implicit meaning' and explain that 'inferring' is a skill we use every day. Then ask pairs to complete the spider diagram task in **Q1**.

Afterwards, ask the students what other things they have inferred today, for example:
- how your family and friends are feeling
- what the weather might be like later
- what a passer-by might be like from how they dress, move, etc.

Building skills

Revisit the five bullet points about character. Then ask students to complete **Q2** on implicit meaning.

Give extra support by selecting a certain phrase (for example: 'the photographs of elaborate cakes') and asking students what it might suggest about Sasha or her mother.

Invite class feedback. Responses may include:
- It appears that Sasha's mother has been trying to convince her.
- Sasha clearly doesn't like the unnamed girl.
- Mother wants to be nice to her daughter but is disturbed by her behaviour.
- Mother is going to invite the unnamed girl anyway.
- Sasha appears to have a short attention span; she also seems greedy.
- Mother has been planning her party for a long time.
- Sasha is spoiled and used to getting her own way.

Encourage students to explain which particular words or phrases suggested the implicit meanings that they have written down.

Developing skills

As a class, read through the extract from *Great Expectations*. Then hand out **Worksheet 1.5** and ask students to complete the character table for Pip and Magwitch in **Q3**. During class feedback, responses on each character might include the following:

Pip	Magwitch
• 'you little devil' suggests Pip is young • 'sir' implies Pip is quite respectful • 'terror' shows how scared he is • 'nothing in them but a piece of bread' might suggest poverty • 'not strong' suggests he doesn't exercise or is badly fed • 'expressed my hope that he wouldn't' conveys that he doesn't understand the man is not speaking literally.	• 'you little devil' suggests he doesn't like children • 'cut your throat' shows he is violent and immoral • 'coarse grey... great iron' indicates that he is an escaped convict • 'soaked in water', etc., implies he has been sleeping rough and travelling across country • 'limped and shivered' suggests he is ill and injured • 'glared and growled' makes him sound mentally ill • 'Show us where you live' and other orders convey his dominance • 'turned me upside down' demonstrates strength • 'ravenously' suggests he hasn't eaten for a long time • 'Darn me if I couldn't eat em' suggests that the man is not well-educated or of a high class.

Ask students to complete **Q4**, using their notes from **Worksheet 1.5** to write a paragraph about each character.

Give extra support by giving students sentence starters, for example: *Magwitch seems like a violent person when...* or *The phrase 'ravenously' suggests that...*

Give extra challenge by encouraging students to link phrases together and comment in detail on the effect of Dickens's language choices.

Applying skills

As a class, read through this section of the Student Book. Ask students to complete **Q5**, answering the two questions. Remind them to make use of their notes from **Worksheet 1.5** and to comment on the effects of the language being used in the text.

Give extra support by giving students sentence starters, for example: *It is clear that Pip is scared when Dickens writes...* or *When Dickens describes Magwitch as a man who 'limped and shivered, and glared and growled' this makes the character seem...*

Give extra challenge by encouraging students to explore implied meanings, not just select literal ones. Students should try to group their ideas, link phrases from the text together, and comment on the effect of specific features of language, such as the use of verbs and adverbs.

Feed back as a class, encouraging students to build on any underdeveloped points about the effects of language. Then ask them to assess their work in pairs, using the **Sound progress** and **Excellent progress** criteria on Student Book p. 23 to see how well they have done.

Towards A/A*	To achieve the highest marks for reading, students need to select a range of the most relevant implicit meanings. They need to link information together and analyse how language is being used to create different effects that convey information about character.

6 Implicit meaning: setting

Assessment objectives

AO1 Reading

R2 Demonstrate understanding of implicit meanings and attitudes

R4 Demonstrate understanding of how writers achieve effects

IGCSE examination

- **Paper 1** all questions
- **Paper 2** all questions (in particular Question 2)
- **Paper 3** both sections
- **Component 4** Coursework portfolio (Assignment 3)

Differentiated learning outcomes

- **All students must** be able to select some key information from a text and comment on what it suggests about setting (Grade E/D).
- **Most students should** select appropriate information and use it to infer meaning about setting and mood (Grade D/C).
- **Some students could** select and link the most appropriate information and analyse how it conveys meaning about setting and mood (Grade B/A).

Resources

- **Student Book**: pp. 24–7
- **Worksheets**:
  1.6a Implicit meaning: setting (1)
  1.6b Implicit meaning: setting (2)
- **PPT**: 1.6a–b

Exploring skills

As a class, read through this section on Student Book p. 24, making sure that students understand the term 'inferring'.

Then ask students to complete the spider diagram in **Q1** before sharing their ideas in pairs. Ideas might include:

- reference to other senses (such as smell)
- how many people are around (and what they are like)
- what time of day it is
- the temperature
- the age/history of the place
- its upkeep, etc.

Building skills

Introduce the first extract on p. 25 and ask students to talk generally about the atmosphere created. Class inferences will include that the text is describing some kind of party, that people are enjoying themselves, and that the atmosphere is happy and upbeat.

Give extra support by selecting a particular phrase (for example: 'The room buzzed with energy'), or just a single word (such as: 'balloons'), and asking students what it might suggest to them about what is going on and what the mood is.

In **Q2**, students are asked to choose three words to sum up the atmosphere in the room. During feedback, ensure that students give evidence to support their ideas. Words chosen may include:

- Excited: 'buzzed with energy'; 'everything appeared to be moving'; 'couples danced or chatted animatedly'; 'dresses swept by'.
- Relaxed: 'cheerful voices'; 'gently swayed'.
- Happy: 'cheerful voices'; 'balloons'; 'bunting'; 'couples'; 'brightly patterned table cloths'.

Invite students to suggest the effect of these descriptions on the reader and why the author may have done this. For example: to make you feel positive about the setting; to make you like any characters involved; to make you anticipate an exciting event; or even to surprise you by then making something bad happen.

Next, introduce the concept of pathetic fallacy using the glossary and then discuss how phrases like 'the room buzzed', 'balloons swayed gently', and 'bunting swished' are examples of pathetic fallacy in the extract. For **Q3**, encourage students to create their own examples of the technique to extend the extract. Share examples as a class.

PPT After discussion, use **PPT 1.6a** to develop the students' understanding of pathetic fallacy by inviting them to discuss the different emotions reflected in each setting. Ask students to consider use of place, lighting, colour, background, etc.

As an extension, discuss with students the different verbs, nouns and adjectives being used. Ask them to think of any other verbs, nouns and adjectives for a party that could suggest excitement, relaxation or happiness. Develop this with **Worksheet 1.6a**, by inviting students to alter the atmosphere of a piece of writing.

Developing skills

As a class, read through the second extract from *Set in Stone* on p. 25, and ask students to complete the setting chart for **Q4** using **Worksheet 1.6b**. Other phrases the students might add include: 'the mist clung', 'vaporous swamp', 'my heart pound and my nerves stretch taut', 'wailing shriek', 'the shadow of the wall', 'a sound of terrible distress', 'I felt the hairs prickle', 'some creature yowling'. During feedback, take ideas in the order of the chart: time of year, time of day, weather, landscape, objects, actions, what is said/sounds.

Use the end column of the setting chart from **Worksheet 1.6b** to complete the vocabulary task in **Q5**, considering how the piece could be made exciting and optimistic.

Applying skills

As a class, read through this section on Student Book p. 27. Ask students to complete **Q6**, making use of the notes from their table.

PPT Use **PPT 1.6b** to provide a sample answer for part of the first question. Explain how the answer is attempting to fulfil its requirements, using both the question and the **Sound progress** and **Excellent progress** criteria on Student Book p. 27.

> **Give extra support** by helping the students with a sentence starter (for example, *One phrase that suggests he is afraid is...*) or a phrase to be working with (such as, 'The metal bit into my hands as I clung onto the gate').
>
> **Give extra challenge** by encouraging students to select a variety of phrases and to use technical language (such as verb, adjective, personification, metaphor, etc.) as part of their explanation of effects. Advise students to link phrases together in order to show how mood is built up by a writer.

Feed back as a class, then ask students to assess their work in pairs – using the **Sound progress** and **Excellent progress** criteria in the Student Book to see how well they have done.

Towards A/A*	To achieve the highest marks for reading, students need to show they can select a range of the most relevant implicit meanings. They also need to demonstrate that they can link information together and analyse how language is being used to create different effects that convey information about setting and mood.

© HarperCollins Publishers 2013

7 Emotive language

Assessment objectives

AO1 Reading

R3 Analyse, evaluate and develop facts, ideas and opinions

R4 Demonstrate understanding of how writers achieve effects.

IGCSE examination
- **Paper 1** Question 1
- **Paper 2** Question 2
- **Paper 3** both sections

Differentiated learning outcomes
- **All students must** be able to pick out and acknowledge the intensity of some emotive language (Grade E/D).
- **Most students should** select a range of emotive language and consider its effect on a text (Grade D/C).
- **Some students could** select a full range of emotive language, analysing how it is being used to create a specific effect on the reader (Grade B/A).

Resources
- **Student Book**: pp. 28–31
- **Worksheets**:
  1.7a Emotive language (1)
  1.7b Emotive language (2)

Exploring skills

As a class, read this section of the Student Book on pp. 28–9, ensuring that students understand the terms 'emotive language' and 'connotation'.

Ask students to complete **Q1** in pairs. Feed back as a class, discussing the emotional effects of each word. Encourage students to identify where a word is relying on connotation to create a reaction. Responses should include:

- 'sullen' suggests misery and might create sympathy or annoyance in others
- 'sunset' is more complex and might link to peace, romance, or even tiredness
- 'red rose' suggests love again, especially Valentine's Day, but this might be interpreted differently by someone who sees this as clichéd
- 'irritable' suggests someone who is bad-tempered, gaining little sympathy.

Building skills

For **Q2**, ask students to discuss the words in pairs then share ideas with the class. Move on to **Q3**; either invite students to place the feeling words on the scale of intensity in pairs or recreate it at the front of the class (four students represent the emotions and the rest of the class arrange them). To make the latter more interesting, add the words (and extra students): appreciate, be fond of, admire, cherish. This can also be presented through using a piece of string as a washing line with students pegging the words on paper to the line in the order they choose.

Repeat the activity with the 'dislike' words in **Q4**. Again this could be written in pairs, or done physically by small groups or as the whole class. Words might include: abhor, averse to, detest, disgust, dislike, displease, hate, loathe, put off by, scorn.

Developing skills

As a class, read through this section on Student Book pp. 29–30. To introduce how we choose words to express our feelings or provoke a reaction, discuss how the students might use the like/dislike words they explored. For example, ask them how they honestly feel about a food they don't enjoy (such as Brussels sprouts or pineapple) and then how they would say they felt about that food if their parents tried to make them eat it. This could be linked to the writing styles of inform and argue/persuade. **Q5** will reinforce understanding of a piece of writing's purpose.

To develop the students' understanding of how we choose words to provoke a reaction, write these two headlines on the board: 'Football Player Has Car Accident' and 'Football Hero in Car Smash Horror'.

Ask the students, in pairs, to decide which is the better headline and why. During feedback, encourage them to consider the effects of 'hero', 'smash' and 'horror'. Then ask students to complete **Q5** on p. 30.

As a class, read the Animal Aid extract on p. 31. Use **Worksheet 1.7a** to complete **Q6** (**Worksheet 1.7b** is a differentiated version for students needing extra support). During feedback, draw out the effects of the words and how they are being used by the writer. Basic responses on the connotations of the words might include:

- 'victims': suggests vulnerability; creates sympathy
- 'dying': final; creates sympathy
- 'horrific': extremely horrible; a thing you would not want to witness
- 'suffer': intense, lingering pain
- 'plough': thoughtless; destructive
- 'fragile': implies delicacy and vulnerability
- 'devastating': destruction; the shock of those who witness it
- 'contaminated': disease; death.

Applying skills

Ask students to answer **Q7** on p. 31, using the bullet point prompts and their notes from **Worksheet 1.7** to help them. Remind them to keep focusing on the purpose of the writing (to make the reader feel concerned).

> **Give extra support** by helping the students with a sentence starter. For example: *The writer makes the reader concerned for the sea by using the phrase...* or *The phrase 'suffer horrific injuries' creates concern for sea creatures by...*
>
> **Give extra challenge** by encouraging students to select the most powerful language for analysis and to use technical language (e.g. verb, adjective, metaphor) as part of their explanation of effects. Advise students to group their ideas together (for example, images of pain, images of death, suggestions that the oceans are doomed).

Students will find that some of their ideas could appear under more than one bullet point. This is not a problem; it is the breadth of ideas and detailed analysis that is important. During feedback, responses might include:

- how the scale of the problem is made clear: intensifiers ('greatest'); rhetorical questions; emotive language ('brink of collapse'); statistics; lists of species affected
- how the writer uses facts and examples: numbers to create shock and sympathy ('hundreds of thousands of marine animals die'); examples to explain (the fate of the albatrosses) and to show the different things affected (whether specific creatures or the ocean floor)
- how the writer uses comparisons: to shock and disgust ('sewage produced by 9.4 million people'); to show the problem of farming fish ('three to five tons... to produce feed for one ton')
- how the writer uses emotive language: to shock ('stripped bare... dying'); to create sympathy ('horrific injuries'); to worry ('brink of collapse'); to accuse/condemn the fishing industry ('plough... devastating').

Take feedback as a class. Then ask students to assess their work in pairs, using the **Sound progress** and **Excellent progress** criteria on p. 31 of the Student Book to see how well they have done.

Towards A/A*	To achieve the highest marks for reading, students need to select a range of the most powerful emotive words and phrases. They need to link words and phrases together and analyse how language is being used to create a specific effect on the reader.

8 Sensory language

Assessment objectives

AO1 Reading

R3 Analyse, evaluate and develop facts, ideas and opinions

R4 Demonstrate understanding of how writers achieve effects

IGCSE examination
- **Paper 1** Question 1
- **Paper 2** Question 2
- **Paper 3** both sections

Differentiated learning outcomes
- **All students must** be able to name the senses and find evidence of these in a text (Grade E/D).
- **Most students should** select a range of different senses and use them to infer meaning within a text (Grade D/C).
- **Some students could** select and link sensory descriptions, tackling complex usage and analysing how meaning is being conveyed (Grade B/A).

Resources
- **Student Book**: pp. 32–3
- **Worksheets**:
  1.8a Sensory language (1)
  1.8b Sensory language (2)

Exploring skills

As a class, read through this opening section of Student Book p. 32, checking that students understand the importance of appealing to the senses in writing and the meaning of the word 'connotations' (refer back to **Key terms** on p. 28 if necessary).

For **Q1**, hand out **Worksheet 1.8a** and instruct students to complete the sensory connotations flowchart.

> **Give extra support** by helping students to think about what sense the phrase links to, how the narrator would react, and what mood or atmosphere it creates.

Feed back as a class, drawing out the different sensory connotations and effects on the reader of each phrase.

Read through the extract about a summer's day. Ask students to work in pairs on **Q2**, again using **Worksheet 1.8a** to make their list of different words or phrases that use the senses. Feed back as a class, collecting ideas for each of the five senses.

Building skills

Set students the **Q3** writing task and give them ten minutes to try to use each of the senses in an effective way.

> **Give extra support** by helping students to select sense words, or by giving them sense pairs to include (such as: sun, hot; girls, laughing).
>
> **Give extra challenge** by encouraging students to use the full range of senses. Use the last sentence of the extract to show students how the senses can be used in quite unusual ways.

Either get pairs to swap their work and spot each other's use of senses, or feed back as a class. If doing the latter, for fun, perhaps divide the class into five and allocate them one of the senses; each time they spot that sense being used in someone's writing they have to stand up. This could lead to discussion of why some senses are used more than others.

Developing skills

As a class, read through this section on Student Book p. 33. Discuss the use of the adjective 'slush-grey' and encourage students to consider the connotations of 'slush' (suggesting a dirty grey, perhaps – thinking about snow – a sense of something being spoiled or horrible). Check students understand the meaning of noun, adjective, verb, and adverb before they undertake **Q4**.

Ask students, in pairs, to complete the table exploring the impact of using different word types in **Q4**, using **Worksheet 1.8b**. Take feedback as a class, asking students to explain and explore the effects of the words they have selected.

As an extension, introduce students to the idea of 'nuances': subtle differences in meaning. Ask students to revisit the beach extract in pairs, exploring how the language and senses used in the first paragraph create a more positive mood than those in the second paragraph. Share ideas and discuss students' findings as a class, trying to draw out the different effects of language and senses. Responses might include:

- see – 'toddlers wrestle over plastic spades' suggests play and togetherness, while 'stray flip flops' suggests desertion
- hear – 'giggling carelessly' suggests happiness and freedom, whereas 'there is no laughter in my mouth' uses a lack of sound to suggest unhappiness
- touch – 'the warm wind' sounds nice and comforting, but 'water sucks at my feet pulling me inwards' seems threatening
- smell and taste – 'sweet smell of candyfloss' sounds innocent and pleasurable, whilst 'salt spray lingers' sounds harsh and difficult to get rid of.

Applying skills

Ask students to answer **Q5**, making use of their notes from **Worksheets 1.8a** and **b**.

> **Give extra support** by helping the students with a sentence starter. For example: *The writer makes the beach seem...* or *The phrase 'sticky toddlers wrestle' suggests that the beach is...*
>
> **Give extra challenge** by encouraging students to select a variety of phrases that cover all the senses, and to use technical language (such as verb, adjective, personification, simile, etc.) as part of their explanation of effects. Advise students to link phrases together in order to show how mood is built up by a writer.

Feed back as a class, paying particular attention to the quotations that students have selected and their accompanying analysis. Encourage students to add depth to their comments by asking them focused questions about how specific words or techniques create an effect upon the reader.

Invite students to assess their work in pairs, using the **Sound progress** and **Excellent progress** criteria on Student Book p. 33 to see how well they have done and how they can improve.

Towards A/A*	To achieve the highest marks for reading, students need to select a range of the most effective sensory words and phrases. They need to link information together and to analyse how senses can convey different moods and ideas.

9 Synthesis

Assessment objectives

AO1 Reading

R1 Demonstrate understanding of explicit meanings
R3 Analyse, evaluate and develop facts, ideas and opinions
R5 Select for specific purposes

IGCSE examination

- **Paper 1** (in particular Question 3)
- **Paper 2** (in particular Question 3)
- **Paper 3** Section 1 (Directed writing)
- **Component 4** Coursework portfolio (Assignment 3)

Differentiated learning outcomes

- **All students must** be able to pick out relevant information and make some links between ideas (Grade E/D).
- **Most students should** select a range of information and group it successfully (Grade D/C).
- **Some students could** select, sort and order a full range of information from more than one text (Grade B/A).

Resources

- **Student Book**: pp. 34–6
- **Worksheet**: 1.9 Synthesis
- **PPT**: 1.9a–d

Exploring skills

As a class, read through this section on Student Book p. 34, checking that students understand the term 'synthesis' and asking them to come up with other examples from everyday life. Read the **Top tip** and get pairs to complete the sorting task in **Q1**, checking their understanding via class feedback.

Building skills

Read through this section of the Student Book then hand out **Worksheet 1.9** for **Q2**. As a class, read through the extract and ask students to underline and number all the different statements about the problems caused by extreme weather conditions. Tell them to be as thorough as possible, highlighting each idea when they come to it and not worrying about any repetition of information. Tell students that they should be able to underline and number about 20 phrases from the main extract.

Conduct feedback and, as you go through the answers, ask students to underline and number any that they missed. (It doesn't matter if their numbers are in a different order to the ones here.) Students should have found:

- 1) can overturn caravans
- 2) tear off roofs
- 3) topple trees
- 4) causing extreme distress to many people
- 5) and financial hardship to whole communities
- 6) some of the strongest tornadoes can demolish houses completely
- 7) leaving people homeless
- 8) and vulnerable to disease
- 9) and criminal harm
- 10) people may be knocked down or struck by debris
- 11) and many places may lose electricity
- 12) flooding and storm surges can destroy buildings
- 13) and [destroy] roads
- 14) contaminate water supplies
- 15) halt other essential services
- 16) and drown people
- 17) large hail stones can damage cars and roofs
- 18) and destroy crops
- 19) but rarely kill people
- 20) heat waves can lead to drought
- 21) which causes crop loss
- 22) as well as health issues
- 23) and death from dehydration.

Developing skills

Explain that by grouping ideas together when making notes from a text, students can save valuable time. Discuss how this can be done after all the ideas have been selected, but that it is much more efficient to do it while they are selecting their ideas.

For **Q3**, ask the students to reread the text from **Worksheet 1.9** in pairs. As they read, they should put the phrases that they have numbered under different headings in the boxes supplied. These headings should be written in the boxes provided. They need to decide whether each of their numbered phrases needs a new heading or goes under a heading that they have already created. Come up with between five to nine headings.

Feed back and discuss the different headings that the students have come up with. Some groupings might include:

- destruction of property (1, 2, 6, 12)
- damage to nature (3, 18)
- other dangers to people (10, 16, 17, 19)
- problems with health and hygiene (8, 14, 22)
- short-term effects on communities (4, 7, 11, 13, 15)
- social problems (9)
- wider effects on communities (5, 20, 21, 23).

These can be shown to students, to compare with their own ideas, using **PPT 1.9a**.

> **Give extra challenge** by asking students to order their points within their headings and consider whether any points overlap (for example, dehydration could be a health problem as well as a wider effect after possible heat waves).

Applying skills

As a class, read through the sample directed writing task in **Q4** and ask students to complete the note-making task. Students' notes might include:

Problems arising:

- injury or loss of life
- damage to, or destruction of, homes
- financial hardship
- flooding, but also drought
- loss of infrastructure
- spread of disease
- crop damage
- crime.

What can be done in advance:

- have stockpiles of supplies, fresh water, medicines, tents, pipes
- individuals to take out private insurance
- have trained and equipped rapid response teams.

What needs to be done after the disaster:

- rapid response teams search for survivors, treat injured and remove debris
- set up temporary homes
- distribute emergency supplies
- fix broken water pipes and ensure clean water
- deploy extra police to deal with looting
- warn locals of how to deal with heat waves, including support for the vulnerable.

Feed back as a class; the points above can be shown using **PPT 1.9b–d**. Ask students to share their work and use the **Sound progress** and **Excellent progress** criteria on Student Book p. 36 to assess how well they have done.

> **Towards A/A*** To achieve the highest marks for reading and directed writing questions, students need to select and sort a full range of information from multiple sources. They need to be able to arrange their information in a cohesive and highly convincing manner.

1 Sentence types, functions and varieties

Assessment objectives
AO2 Writing
W5 Make accurate use of spelling, punctuation and grammar

IGCSE examination
- **Paper 3** both sections, or **Component 4** Coursework Portfolio
- **Papers 1** and **2** will also award some marks for the quality of writing

Differentiated learning outcomes
- **All students must** use sentences that are mostly accurate, demarcating single sentences correctly and attempting different types of sentences (Grades E/D).
- **Most students should** use a variety of types of sentence, demonstrating accurate use of punctuation (Grades D/C).
- **Some students could** use a full range of appropriate sentence structures to create meaning and to have an effect on the reader (Grades B/A).

Resources
- **Student Book**: pp. 38–9
- **Worksheets**:
  2.1a Sentence functions
  2.1b Types of sentence
- **PPT**: 2.1a–d

Other Student Book pages
- Conventions of diaries and journals, pp. 70–1
- Conventions of speeches, pp. 62–5

Exploring skills

As a warm up, ask students to work in pairs to answer the question: *What are sentences for?* (2 mins). Take feedback and group the answers into four: making a statement, asking a question, stressing a point, giving orders. Write these headings on the board.

Explain that these 'functions' are often indicated to the reader by a punctuation mark and check that students can allocate the punctuation mark for each one.

Recap on the different sentence functions using **PPT 2.1a**.
(Answers A = imperative; B = declarative; C = interrogative; D = exclamatory.)

Use the grid on Student Book p. 38 to confirm each sentence function and associated punctuation mark. Explain that functions are used to create meaning in texts – sometimes the meaning is obvious and sometimes it is implied, suggested or can work at a range of levels. Then ask students to complete **Q1** individually (5 mins). Take feedback and share examples of each sentence type on the whiteboard.

> **Give extra support** by starting the three sentences with 'What...?', 'Turn...', 'Wow...!' Explain that imperative sentences often start with a verb, missing out the subject ('Go left at the end', 'Leave your coats and bags outside').

Try to draw out the meanings that are literal and implied. For example: *Turn right here and look round the corner carefully before crossing the road.* Literally, the instruction is telling the reader to be careful, but there is also an implication that a danger might be present and that drivers are not too careful at that junction. Link the skill of using apt sentences in your writing to the **Excellent progress** success box on Student Book p. 39.

Building skills

Use **Worksheet 2.1a** to make cards about the size of playing cards marked Dec, Int, Imp, Ex. Hand out the sets of four cards to each pair. Use one pair to model the activity using the example on Student Book p. 39 so the two students play card Imp when saying *'Turn left out of my house...'*, Dec when saying *'It's a very busy road'*, Int when saying *'Really?'* and Ex when saying *'I can't see a single car!'*

24 • Lesson 1 © HarperCollins Publishers 2013

For **Q2**, invite pairs to describe how to get to their school from home using all the cards like playing cards, so every time they use a declarative, they put a 'Dec' card down and so on until all their cards are used up (10 mins). You could hand out extra cards to pairs that are working quickly. Explain that sentence functions can be repeated, but discourage students from using sentences that they cannot define.

Developing skills

Explain the difference between 'function' and 'type' of sentence. Read the opening section, up to the end of the examples of simple sentences. Make sure that everyone understands 'subject' (who performs the action), 'verb' (act of doing, being or feeling something) and 'clause' (part of a sentence containing subject and verb).

> **Give extra support** by using straightforward, familiar sentences: *Jacob plays tennis; Marjane reads her emails; Felix listens to music.* Explain to students that the simple sentences *Jacob plays, Marjane reads, Felix listens,* are the same 'type' as the sentences above as they still contain the two essential ingredients – subject + verb = clause. A simple sentence contains one clause.
>
> **Give extra challenge** by using less straightforward example sentences, e.g. *The boy with black hair called Jacob plays the game requiring two racquets and a ball called tennis.* Ask students what is the subject here. Explain that a subject can be long and detailed, and the verb can be joined to other words such as an object, but they still represent one subject and one verb so are 'simple'.

Next, work through the paragraphs on compound and complex sentences. Many students struggle to differentiate between these, so be prepared to spend time on this.

Hand out **Worksheet 2.1b** and spend 5 mins on Task 1. The first three sentences are those in **Q3**. Use Task 2 to extend **Q3** by assessing students' confidence with the key terms *subject, verb, subclause, connective.* Then introduce how implied meanings are conveyed in sentences via Task 3 – for example, 'They seemed to be smiling!' implies a good-humoured sense of danger whereas 'I could see just how many teeth they each had' does not.

> **Give extra challenge** by eliciting extra layers of meaning. For example, the simple sentence 'I simply had to leave' could convey impatience; the compound sentence 'The rain was pouring and the wind was howling, but we still soldiered on through the forest to the campsite' could convey frustration. Either use the worksheet to support particular students to do this or **PPT 2.1b** to support whole class teaching.
>
> **Give extra support** by asking students to pick out writers' use of simple, compound and complex sentences in a class novel. Recap on the definitions using **PPT 2.1c**.

Applying skills

Ask students to complete **Q4** independently using their table as guidance (15 mins). Display the success criteria on the whiteboard using **PPT 2.1d**. Students then mark their work (one mark for each function, type and punctuation mark, five marks for an example of a sentence that is constructed to convey more than the literal meaning).

Pairs then share their writing explaining how they have used appropriate sentence structures and a variety of sentence types (10 mins). Exemplify the difference between Grade A (full range and variety of sentence types and functions to convey subtle layers of meaning) and Grade C (basic but correct sentence types and functions). Refer to the **Sound progress** and **Excellent progress** criteria on p. 39 to illustrate this.

Towards A/A*	To gain the highest marks for writing, students need to create sentences where the structure is imaginative, precise and accurate. Look at a range of extracts from classic texts and ask groups to assess the numbers of words in sentences, the range of punctuation marks and the variety of sentence types and their effects.

2 Sentences for effect

Assessment objectives
AO2 Writing
W5 Make accurate use of spelling, punctuation and grammar

IGCSE examination
- Paper 3 both sections, or Component 4 Coursework Portfolio
- Papers 1 and 2 will also award some marks for the quality of writing

Differentiated learning outcomes
- **All students must** use sentences that communicate in a way that is fit for purpose and audience (Grades E/D).
- **Most students should** construct sentences appropriately in ways that are likely to engage the reader (Grades D/C).
- **Some students could** use a full range of sentence types fluently to create a range of effects that sustain the reader's interest (Grades B/A).

Resources
- **Student Book**: pp. 40–1
- **Worksheets**: 2.2 Using sentences to create an effect
- **PPT**: 2.2a–c

Other Student Book pages
- Writing to analyse, pp. 80–3
- Writing to describe, pp. 98–103

Exploring skills

As a warm up, ask students to work in groups of four with each group member describing the events of the day so far using sentences with four words or fewer (5 mins). Take feedback from each group evaluating the narrative in this format – ask: *What are the advantages and disadvantages of speaking in this way? What advice would you give to someone who wanted to improve on this?*

Ask students to look at Student Book p. 40 and to work in pairs to complete **Q1**. During feedback, draw out the links between the advice they gave for improvement to each other and the improved paragraph.

Use **PPT 2.2a** to focus attention on the connectives 'which' and 'although'. Explain that the comma tells the reader that extra information is coming and that it is often this detailed information that will stick in the mind, even though it is a clause that cannot stand alone. Invite pairs to work from the PPT screen to turn the sentences into the simplest form (i.e. *The car swept past them, The dogs were placid*).

Explain that the difference between the simple form and the complex form can be what is meant by 'make some attempt to engage the reader'. Elicit that *comma which* and *comma although* are straightforward triggers for signalling added detail to engage the reader. Then use the example in **Q1** to check that students recognise that 'although' signals an alternative point of view is being presented.

Use **Q2** to recap on the different sentence functions and types and link to the lesson's learning objective: 'to understand and use the full range of sentences for deliberate effect'. Explain that it is this *use* of different sentences for effect that makes writing stand out and achieve higher marks.

Building skills

Read the example simple sentences that create tension on Student Book p. 40 and ask pairs to continue this with at least three more sentences. Take feedback on how this felt then ask what the reader needs next to release the tension and ask students to suggest what might come next in terms of sentence types. Model this change of pace with 'He dragged himself up the stone stairs, despite the pain from his wounded leg', and sentence invite students to come up with alternatives and to evaluate the impact of their choices. Then ask students to complete **Q3** individually.

Give extra support by offering the writing frame for **Q3** in **Worksheet 2.2**.

Give extra challenge by asking higher attainers to invent their own dramatic opening paragraph to a short story using different types of sentences. They could choose from these genres: science fiction, horror, contemporary, romance.

Developing skills

Working with the whole class, recap on the structure of compound sentences and how generally they offer detail rather than tension or layers of meaning. Explain that compound sentences can present two balanced or contrasting points or ideas. Then use the advice writing example on **PPT2.2b** to discuss the advantages of using subordinate clauses rather than linking two or more clauses with commas and 'and' or 'but'.

As part of **Q4**, evaluate the *complex-complex-simple* paragraph structure as a whole class using the text on **PPT 2.2c** and elicit from students what they can infer about what the old man does next. Draw out what effect the long sentence has at the start of the paragraph. Does it suggest that things were happening quickly or that the day was dragging? Ask the same question of the second and third sentences.

For **Q5**, revisit the learning objective, explaining that all of the techniques involved here in constructing sentences are having effects on their reader. As part of this, draw attention to the **Key terms** box about minor sentences.

Give extra challenge by asking targeted students to rewrite the paragraph starting 'He walked towards me' and to convey sympathy for the old man rather than frustration. This may not require the short simple sentences but would need more detail about the old man (compound sentence) and recollection about the past (complex sentence).

Applying skills

Consider **Q6** on Student Book p. 41 as a whole class and decide together on the success criteria for the task. These may include:

- establishing a clear tone or mood (positive, negative, tranquil, troubled)
- the sentence choices match the tone and create appropriate pace
- an appropriate blend of simple, compound and complex sentences
- creating effects with exclamatory or minor sentences.

Students should discuss their ideas briefly before starting. Check that everyone is focused on the 'how' of the task, i.e. using a variety of sentences, as much as the 'what', planning the content.

Towards A/A*	Highest achievers will demonstrate assurance, using sentences that are entirely appropriate throughout (see **Excellent progress** criteria on Student Book p. 41). To work toward this, students could collect sentences used in different texts for different audiences and purposes, for example: • from a website explaining the help available for older people with filling out forms • a flyer for a sports club in the school holidays for under 10s • an advertisement for a playgroup for mums and toddlers • the description of a character from a Dickens novel. The different types of sentences used and the tones conveyed could make interesting comparisons.

3 Punctuation

Assessment objectives
AO2 Writing
W5 Make accurate use of spelling, punctuation and grammar

IGCSE examination
- **Paper 3** both sections, or **Component 4** Coursework Portfolio
- **Papers 1** and **2** will also award some marks for the quality of writing

Differentiated learning outcomes
- **All students must** use basic punctuation (full stop, comma, apostrophe) competently (Grade E/D).
- **Most students should** use punctuation accurately to communicate with their readers in specific ways (Grade D/C).
- **Some students could** use punctuation fluently to have deliberate effects in their writing (Grade B/A).

Resources
- **Student Book**: pp. 42–5
- **Worksheets**:
  2.3a Getting commas right
  2.3b Getting apostrophes right
  2.3c Punctuation of speech
  2.3d Colons, semi-colons, brackets and dashes
- **PPT**: 2.3a–e

Other Student Book pages
- Conventions of diaries and journals, pp. 70–1

Exploring skills

Recap on use of commas and apostrophes by asking students to read the opening section on Student Book p. 42. Also, remind them that all sentences should start with a capital letter and end with a full stop, question mark or exclamation mark. Then ask pairs to explain to each other any rules they were unsure of. Make a list of misunderstandings and confusions on the whiteboard – for example, 'a comma indicates a pause in a long sentence' or 'all words ending in –s need an apostrophe'.

> **Give extra support** to targeted students using **Worksheets 2.3a** and **2.3b**. Direct students to the rule they are having particular trouble with – for example, commas in lists, separating parts of a sentence, adding more information, apostrophes of omission or possession.

(PPT) Then ask students to complete **Q1** individually. Working with the whole class, use **PPT 2.3a** to explain all the punctuation that was missing in **Q1**. Then use **Worksheet 2.3a** and **2.3b** to support students who are still not quite secure in one or more of the rules.

Building skills

Ask students to work in groups of three to share the knowledge they have about punctuation of speech. If students have a novel with them, encourage them to use it to inform their discussion. Then, if you have a visualiser or scanner, you could share a fiction extract on the whiteboard. Show students what direct speech looks like and start to elicit the rules. Ask each group to come up with five rules to then be written on the whiteboard, nominate a spokesperson in each group and take feedback.

(PPT) Then ask students to read the direct speech on Student Book p. 43 to check that none of the rules have been overlooked or confused. You can also display the five rules using **PPT 2.3b**.

Pairs should next complete **Q2**. One student writes and the other checks the punctuation using the five main rules, then students swap over for each speaker. Alternatively you could support this activity using **Worksheet 2.3c**. Students first rewrite the text using more appropriate description of speakers and then extend it following all the conventions for punctuating speech. Refer to the **Top tip** on Student Book p. 43 to help.

Developing skills

Work as a whole class through the first part of this section on Student Book p. 44, recapping on the use of colons and semi-colons.

Explain that a colon signals to the reader 'and I'm going to tell you why'. Demonstrate this by reading the two example statements and replacing the colon with 'and I'm going to tell you why'. Then ask students to work in pairs using colons to complete the following sentences: *Sports Day was a disaster... If only we had something to do in this village... Having a pet is a big responsibility...* Share some student examples with the class.

Now explain that a semi-colon signals to the reader 'and I'm going to tell you a little bit more about that'. Use the example sentence to demonstrate, then ask students to work as above with semi-colons to extend: *Today the sky was blue... Our new car is stunning... Energy conservation is not an option in this school...* Check that the description is still valid by sharing examples from the class.

Ask students to complete **Q3** and use **PPT 2.3c** to share ideas about how the punctuation could have been improved. Warn against overusing these punctuation features though, even if they are correct. It might be useful to explain what is meant by 'judicious' usage here.

Read through the text on Student Book p. 44 about brackets and dashes and ask groups of four to come up with a description for each punctuation mark. Brackets could be 'don't forget that' and dashes might be 'know what I mean?' An example of over use of dashes is given on **PPT 2.3d**. Ask students to work in pairs to complete **Q4** and use **PPT 2.3e** to share ideas for changes.

> **Give extra challenge** by asking targeted students to work in role as a politician, a comedian, a charity worker or a TV presenter using **Worksheet 2.3d**. Students write a speech to persuade an audience to agree with them. The topic might be global warming, rights for young people, improved transport systems or the rise of celebrities. Encourage use of the punctuation marks that are most fit for purpose for their character.

Applying skills

Read through the checklist for using punctuation on Student Book p. 45. Then ask students to select one piece of advice that they think will be particularly important to them and to write it at the top of the page before they start to write. This could be highlighted so that it is easy to refer back to whilst writing. Ensure that everyone understands the bullets in **Q5**, explaining 'a humorous aside' (a throw-away comment, like someone talking to the camera) then ask students to complete the article-writing task.

You could assess how effectively students are using their own advice by checking the statement at the top of their writing page. Offer reminders about planning, checking and proofreading as they write. After everyone has completed their two paragraphs, ask students to assess their work in pairs, using the **Sound progress** and **Excellent progress** criteria on Student Book p. 45.

Towards A/A*	High-attaining students will show they can discriminate between opportunities for using a punctuation feature and a place where there is a real need for emphasis. They will also understand which kinds of punctuation are appropriate to the purpose, audience and form. Encourage students to question their decisions on use of punctuation – *Was there a pressing need? Does it have the desired effect? Have I used this feature carelessly elsewhere?*

4 Paragraph cohesion

Assessment objectives

AO2 Writing

W5 Make accurate use of spelling, punctuation and grammar

IGCSE examination
- **Paper 3** both sections, or **Component 4** Coursework Portfolio
- **Papers 1** and **2** will also award some marks for the quality of writing

Differentiated learning outcomes
- **All students must** use paragraphs to order their ideas even if this is not done accurately (Grade E/D).
- **Most students should** use paragraphs in order to make their writing clear for the reader (Grade D/C).
- **Some students could** use paragraphs to achieve particular effects in their writing that are suited to purpose and audience (Grade B/A).

Resources
- **Student Book**: pp. 46–7
- **Worksheets**:
  2.4a Structuring a paragraph
  2.4b Using connectives
  2.4c Constructing an argument
- **PPT**: 2.4a–b

Other Student Book pages
- Writing to persuade, pp. 88–9
- Writing to argue, pp. 90–3

Exploring skills

As a warm up, ask students to work in groups of three to answer the question, *When and why do you start a new paragraph in your writing?* Take feedback and dispel all myths about length of paragraphs. Reinforce the idea that as a writer you must have a good reason to start a new paragraph. Ask students to read the opening section on Student Book p. 46, which explains what these reasons might be.

Run through the annotations on the text on p. 46 or use **PPT 2.4a** as an aid to annotation. Ensure understanding of terms such as *topic sentence (what the paragraph is about), connective (linking word to make ideas flow well, often linked to time or feeling).*

Explain that paragraphs need to be cohesive – they need to fit together so that ideas follow logically. Pairs then discuss cohesion in the text using the three prompts in **Q1**.

> **Give extra support** with **Worksheet 2.4a**, which starts with straightforward paragraph structuring. This might be a helpful preparatory exercise prior to this lesson as well as support for a targeted group. Acknowledge that cohesion needs to be more sophisticated than the *topic–this–it* trail, to avoid writing becoming too formulaic, but that this is a good place to start. Introduce the phrase used by examiners, 'in an orderly way', to describe how ideas need to be structured in students' writing.

Building skills

Signalling that you are starting a new topic within a larger subject that is linked to the previous paragraph is an essential writing skill requiring competent use of connectives. Ask students to remind themselves of how time can connect paragraphs by telling the story of their weekend. You could model the structure on **PPT 2.4b**:

> *On Friday night... Then on Saturday morning we... Later that day we... That evening.... Sunday morning was... And finally by Sunday night, I...*

Then ask students to complete **Q2**, which requires them to write a follow-up paragraph to the text on Student Book p. 46.

> **Give extra challenge** by asking students to link their follow up paragraph by mood (for example, *despondency*) rather than time. This paragraph might begin: *'The sky clouded over and rain began to fall'*.

Developing skills

Explain to the class that cohesion needs to be evident *within* and *between* paragraphs and that the best way to show this is to use connectives appropriately. Ask students to read the bullet points on Student Book p. 47 then to work in pairs to complete **Q3**.

You could use **Worksheet 2.4b** to support students in practising their use of connectives. There is a list of connectives, which could be cut out as small cards and tried out by students in the paragraphs. Encourage students to try a range of connectives for each and to group them as a 'definite match', 'possible match', 'complete contradiction'. For example,

[.....................................] it was incredibly busy at the airport.

[.....................................] there were long queues up to my desk.

Try 'Yesterday', 'On the other hand', 'Therefore', 'Moreover', 'Furthermore', 'Tomorrow'. Decide which are a 'definite match', 'possible match', 'complete contradiction' for each, then make your choice.

Model a bad choice (but unfortunately typical) by using 'On the other hand' to start the second sentence. Explain that this mistake often happens when students write an argument. It is therefore beneficial for the students to weigh up their choices when writing and to consider their options carefully even if they find a match straightaway.

> **Give extra support** by inviting pupils to play 'argument dominoes' using the connectives cards on **Worksheet 2.4b** and the argument on **Worksheet 2.4c**. Hand out the connectives and the cards with the series of points for and against the building of a new power station. Ask students to take turns in laying appropriate cards to make a cohesive argument.

Applying skills

Explain to the whole class that paragraphing is given considerable weight in the success criteria for writing. It is worth about a fifth of the marks and so it is well worth getting it right. Writing typical of the highest mark bands demonstrates careful choice of connectives and subtle trails of ideas that flow smoothly towards the end.

Read the example plan on Student Book p. 47 then ask each individual to plan a piece of writing for **Q4**. They could jot down a quick *aide memoire* prior to starting writing (*choose connectives that link paragraphs at the start carefully, use a topic sentence to start each paragraph, ensure that subsequent sentences are linked to the first one*). Run through the **Checklist for success**, ensuring that the relevant technical vocabulary is secure.

When students have finished their writing, encourage self-assessment using the checklist for success. You could award marks for each connective used correctly, each topic trail, each original link word (not from the selection provided in Q3).

Towards A/A*	Students who show confidence in using paragraphs to experiment with different ways of conveying information or ideas are often given the highest marks. These paragraphs are not formulaic and often use original linking words, unusual pronouns, unconventional connectives yet keep an appropriate tone and cohesion. For example, a paragraph about a football match might begin: 'Thus began the onslaught'. The following paragraph might begin: 'With cumulative force, the team drew on the substitutes for the final attack'.

5 Vocabulary

Assessment objectives
AO2 Writing
W3 Use a range of appropriate vocabulary
W4 Use register appropriate to audience and context

IGCSE examination
- **Paper 3** both sections, or **Component 4** Coursework Portfolio
- **Papers 1** and **2** will also award some marks for the quality of writing

Differentiated learning outcomes
- **All students must use** some vocabulary that suits the need of their intended audience and purpose (Grade E/D).
- **Most students should** use a range of vocabulary chosen to meet a particular need (Grade D/C).
- **Some students could** use vocabulary that is highly appropriate for the circumstance and achieves a range of appropriate effects (Grade B/A).

Resources
- **Student Book**: pp. 48–9
- **Worksheet**: 2.5 Vocabulary choices
- **PPT**: 2.5a–e

Other Student Book pages
- Writing to describe, pp. 98–103
- Narrative writing, pp. 104–7

Exploring skills

Choosing my words carefully is a well-known phrase in English. It suggests that out of a range of options, a particular choice was made in order to not hurt someone's feelings (you might say *There was plenty of space at the meeting* rather than *Hardly anyone turned up*). As writers, we can make choices constantly to carefully control the impact we have on the reader.

As a starter ask students to work with a partner to change the words in the following sentences in order to alter the likely impact of the sentence on the reader. Display the sentences on **PPT 2.5a**.

> The house was dilapidated and would need completely renovating before we moved in. *[With a bit of work the house would be fine]*.

> The painting was destroyed by the stain that happened when the house was flooded. *[That painting would be lovely in the dark corner of the hall]*.

> The bride was absolutely devastated when she picked up her dress only to find it was much too long. *[A quick hem is all that is needed to make the dress perfect]*.

Explain that taking time to consider your choice of words is time well spent both in an English examination and in life outside school.

Read through the text in **Q1** on Student Book p. 48 with the class and use **PPT 2.5b** to annotate the word choices made by its writer. Discuss the thoughts and intentions that the writer might have had when the text was written.

Building skills

Explain to the class that they are going to be learning how to make an impression as a writer in this section. They need to decide for themselves if they would rather be described as 'nice', 'OK' or 'all right', or as 'inspirational', 'innovative' or 'unique'?

Read through the text on Student Book p. 48, and then ask students to work in pairs to complete **Q2** and **Q3**. During class feedback discuss the replacement choices they have made and the likely impact of their changes. You could use the example on **PPT 2.5c** to model or generate ideas for **Q3**, if necessary.

Give extra support by ensuring targeted students are secure in their understanding of word classes and by using **Worksheet 2.5** to support students in making choices about more unusual words in their writing.

Developing skills

Use **PPT 2.5d** to engage students with the decisions they need to make as writers. Discuss the route to achieving a low mark (choosing dull, clichéd vocabulary), an acceptable mark (choosing some interesting words but some dull) and an excellent mark (going the extra mile – making considered vocabulary choices tailored to audience and purpose). Make sure that students do not equate word choice with volume, i.e. they should focus on quality rather than quantity.

Look at the text on p. 49 together and ask students to describe what the improved writing contains (precision and detail) before completing **Q4**. Then share students' improved sentences as a class. There is a model for this on **PPT 2.5e**.

Invite small groups to come up with examples of imagery to expand descriptions of:

an enormous insect (it was ...)
a skilful sportsman (he was ...)
a famous pop band (they were like ...).

Then read through the text on Student Book p. 49, recapping on similes, metaphors and personification at an appropriate pace. Encourage originality in comparisons and try to steer students away from hyperbole.

Give extra challenge by asking students to choose which they prefer from the following simile, metaphor and use of personification, giving a detailed explanation for their choice:
- a biting wind
- an ocean of frozen air
- as aggressive as an army of locusts seeking their next feed.

Applying skills

Remind students of the skills that have been using: precise choice of vocabulary; inclusion of detail; use of imagery. Allow plenty of time for students to plan their response to **Q5** and ensure that the **Sound progress** and **Excellent progress** success criteria are fully understood by all. Give students an opportunity to review and change their first draft before evaluating their final pieces of writing using peer assessment.

Ask students to work in pairs to assess each other's work, making comments on WWW (what works well) and EBI (even better if).

Towards A/A*	Sophisticated and pertinent choice of vocabulary can be quite minimal, a fact that can often surprise students working towards A*. It can be appropriate to use one well-chosen word where 20 had been used in an early draft.
	Encourage students to find words they have never heard before by reading high-quality editorial writing then use them in similar or contrasting texts. Typical words to be used appropriately at this level could be *copious, arcane, subterfuge, obtuse, plethora, verbose.*

6 Audience: formality and informality

Assessment objectives
AO2 Writing
W4 Use register appropriate to audience and context

IGCSE examination
- **Paper 3** both sections, or **Component 4** Coursework Portfolio
- **Papers 1** and **2** will also award marks for the quality of writing

Differentiated learning outcomes
- **All students must** use some features of formal and informal language that is fit for purpose (Grade E/D).
- **Most students should** use a variety of language features that have been adapted to suit different purposes or audiences (Grade D/C).
- **Some students could** make pertinent choices of language in order to create a tone in their writing that is fit for purpose and meets the needs of a particular audience (Grade B/A).

Resources
- **Student Book**: pp. 50–3
- **Worksheets**: 2.6 Formal and informal language
- **PPT**: 2.6a–c

Other Student Book pages
- Writing to inform, pp. 94–5
- Conventions of letters, pp. 78–9

Exploring skills

Ask students to work in pairs with one in role as a student just starting secondary school. The other student needs to give advice on how you need to speak to your teachers, your classmates, the head teacher and visiting parents.

The student in role needs to ask for examples of what kind of conversations might be had and then make notes to feed back to the whole class. Try to encourage a focus on language, grammar and gesture. Take feedback, drawing out key features of formal and informal language on the whiteboard. Explain how talking formally can be a useful rehearsal for writing formally.

Now read the opening section on Student Book p. 50, which gives examples of formal and informal texts. Cross reference the features on the whiteboard to the features annotated on the examples. Then hand out **Worksheet 2.6** and ask students to annotate examples A and B for **Q1**.

Building skills

As a warm up to **Q2** and to support students' peer/self-assessment skills, arrange students into groups of five and provide each with a blank sheet of paper. Use **PPT 2.6a** to outline the task:

- Each student starts a letter to a local businessman using the appropriate salutation [1]. Then they need to fold over the top of their paper so that their writing cannot be seen and pass it to the next person.
- Once students each have a folded letter, they continue without reading what is written and ask if there are any vacancies for Saturday work [2]. Then they fold their piece of paper over again so that their work cannot be seen and pass it to the next person.
- Next, students write the reason why they should be employed, [3] then fold the paper over again and pass it to the next person.
- Then they need to add advice on how the businessman can contact them [4].
- Finally, they should close the letter appropriately [5].

This should mean that all five members of the group have contributed to each letter. Each student should read out the letter they have at the end and as a group evaluate the letters' use of appropriate formal language.

Next, turn to Student Book p. 51 and read through the formal letter discussing the similarities and differences between this one and those they have written. Students then complete **Q2** in pairs. Remind students that this text should not contain any of the features they have been using in the formal letter writing but warn them of taking informality too literally – referring to the **Top tip** about avoiding rudeness.

> **Give extra support** by providing examples of phrases that are informal rather than that rude or disrespectful *(I could help you out – informal; You could sit on your backside and watch me do all the work – rude)*. Remind students that informality in talk can easily be managed and changed to suit the appropriate level of formality whereas in writing a bad impression can stay for a long time.

Developing skills

As a whole class, discuss what is meant by 'tone' in writing *(attitude, manner or stance of a text – how you are being spoken to in a piece of writing)*. Consider how the following tones might be conveyed: sly; aggressive; innocent; distracted.

Read through the text on Student Book p. 52. Then for **Q3** and **Q4**, allow students to annotate the differences between the active and passive voice on **Worksheet 2.6**. Elicit from the active text: the use of personal pronouns, the vagueness about measurements of time or space, the simplicity of the language. Read to the end of the section, checking that understanding of active and passive forms is secure. Reinforce how the 'ownership' of the verb changes – *Macbeth killed Duncan* becomes *Duncan was killed* – so no one owns the verb and the culprit remains unnamed and free.

> **(PPT)** **Give extra support** using **PPT 2.6b–c** to help students with **Q5**. The subjects of the sentences are highlighted in **2.6b** and then removed with the use of the passive in **2.6c** but the verbs remain. Use **Worksheet 2.6** to recap on use of active and passive voice.
>
> **Give extra challenge** by asking students to change the tone of the report slightly, to increase the level of suspicion about what had happened to the ship. Make sure that students still adopt the impersonal stance and make subtle comments rather than outright accusations, for example: *'The shipwreck was discovered abandoned as night fell'* rather than *'Everything had been ransacked by thieves'*.

Applying skills

Read through the explanation on Student Book p. 53 of the features of informal language – contractions, tags and idioms – and ask students where they have encountered this kind of language. Provide more examples of idiomatic slang – *You never know what's round the next corner, look what the cat's dragged in*. You could touch on new words added to the dictionary, such as *lol*, and words with flexible meanings, such as *wicked (evil or good)* or *lame (injured or rubbish)*. Remind students that these features would be considered informal and inappropriate for formal texts.

Recap on the features of formal and informal language discussed in this section and then ask students to complete **Q6** independently, demonstrating their flexibility in use of language to create appropriate tone in their writing.

| Towards A/A* | Students working towards A* need to be able to establish or change the tone of their writing quickly, often by using a single word, phrase or punctuation feature not used previously. Confident students need to make clear signals to their readers that this is what they are doing and ensure that they do not overdo it. So if a writer is trying to introduce the legal side of an argument about litter in the town centre, it might be appropriate to say *'Of course, failure to comply would automatically result in litigation'* rather than *'If you drop litter, you could get a fine of £2000 and you might have to go to jail.'* |

7 Choosing the right style for your audience

Assessment objectives

AO2 Writing

W3 Use a range of appropriate vocabulary

W4 Use register appropriate to audience and context

IGCSE examination
- **Paper 3** both sections, or **Component 4** Coursework Portfolio
- **Papers 1** and **2** will also award some marks for the quality of writing

Differentiated learning outcomes
- **All students must** attempt to use content, structure and language that is suitable for different audiences (Grade E/D).
- **Most students should** match content, structure and language to a range of audiences and be able to produce writing that is fit for purpose (Grade D/C).
- **Some students could** use appropriate content, structure and language fluently to create styles that match a wide range of audiences (Grade B/A).

Resources
- **Student Book**: pp. 54–5
- **Worksheets**:
  2.7a Different language for different audiences
  2.7b Matching content to audience
- **PPT**: 2.7a–g

Other Student Book pages
- Conventions of news reports, pp. 74–7
- Conventions of letters, pp. 78–9

Exploring skills

As a warm up, use **Worksheet 2.7a** and ask students to role play in groups of three, where one is the host and two are guests.

- The first scenario offered is a birthday party for 5-year-olds. The host needs to welcome two young guests and take them to the room where food is being served.
- The second scenario is a dinner party. The host needs to welcome the two guests, who are senior colleagues from work and take them through to the dining room checking that Italian cuisine is acceptable to both.
- There are two further scenarios provided that could also be explored.

Take feedback, asking students how straightforward the changes that they made were. Ask the class where else they would expect to find language modification. Emphasise the need for language to be fit for purpose.

Now turn to Student Book p. 54 and read through the text, ensuring that students are thinking about content, structure and presentation, and language in relation to audience. Explain how structure refers to the organisation of the text in terms of words, sentences and paragraphs. Then ask pairs to read the news report and complete **Q1**, steering them toward speculative discussion rather than making declarative statements. (For example, *the target audience **might** be educated adults with an interest in animals* rather than *it's for people who work in zoos*.)

> **PPT**
> **Give extra support** using **PPT 2.7a**, which highlights the features that might prove difficult for a 5- or 6-year-old. Explore the complexities of these words and consider alternatives (for example, *first appearance* instead of *debut*).

Building skills

> **PPT**
> Demonstrate tailoring text to suit audience using **PPT 2.7b.** Change the complexity of the content, the type of sentences used and the language. Use **PPT 2.7c** to support students in completing **Q2**. You can show **PPT2.7d** as a possible set of sentences.

> **Give extra challenge** by asking students for further ideas for making the text for **Q2** more accessible for 5- to 6-year-olds. Ask them to think how the height or weight of the baby could be conveyed by a further sentence or an image, *or* how questions might be used to engage the interest of a child (consider the elephant's name).
>
> **PPT 2.7e** shows some possibilities. Once students have some ideas, they could sketch out a double-page spread from the book incorporating the text and images.

Developing skills

Tell students that this section focuses on adapting the same content to suit a different audience. This requires clear understanding of the reader's needs and capabilities. Students will need to weigh up what needs to be changed and what remains the same.

Ask pairs to read the instructions for **Q3**. Ensure they are clear that the letter will have a different purpose and audience from the original report and so requires a different style. Elicit what 'No reference to first person' and 'Lots of facts and stats' in column 2 of the table mean. Then use **Worksheet 2.7b** to offer further help for pairs on how to complete **Q3**. Feed back after 3-4 minutes. Key ideas to draw out:

- The *audience* has changed – it is now a named person, David Field, not a general reading public, but you do not know him (refer to the **Top tip**).
- The letter has to have a *personal* voice – it's your own reaction to the article.
- It has a viewpoint about what the zoo needs to do, so the letter will be *persuasive*.

Ask students to attempt to improve the opening paragraph in **Q4** independently. Point out what has changed in the example, e.g. the insertion of a personal pronoun ('I') and the use of an emphatic adjective 'delighted' to convey personal feeling. Students could either rewrite the new version, using synonyms for 'delighted' (e.g. 'overjoyed', 'extremely happy', 'very glad') or simply complete the sentence given. Deal with the further implications before students tackle **Q5**. Ask them as a class:

- Will you include any information from the original article in the letter? (Bear in mind that David Field is an 'expert' at the zoo, so repeating information such as '3-foot high calf' is probably unnecessary.)
- What new or different content will you need to invent or source from elsewhere?

Now ask students to draft the next two paragraphs on their own.

> **Give extra support** for **Q5** by providing a menu of words and phrases that could be used in the two subsequent paragraphs of the letter such as adjectival phrases like:
>
> - I was... *devastated, heartbroken, extremely sad, incredibly concerned about...*
> - Pronouns to show personal voice: *I, we, you/your*, etc.
> - Verbs related to persuasive action: *I implore, beg, ask, believe strongly that, feel passionately, would like to stress, need to say that...*

Applying skills

For **Q6**, display the **Sound progress** and **Excellent progress** criteria for the task on the whiteboard using **PPT 2.7f–g**. Encourage pairs to discuss the different language and content choices they made and to decide which is the most appropriate and why.

Towards A/A*	Writing at A* level meets audience needs fluently. Encourage students to practise regularly recasting information from one context to another to master this skill of writing to suit audience. For example, imagine you needed to cancel an appointment. For a friend, you might send an email: *'I'm sorry I'm not going to be able to make it tonight – something has cropped up.'* But how might this change if it was to cancel a job interview? Or a presentation at a charity ball? Or a first meeting with an elderly relative?

8 Voice and role

Assessment objectives

AO2 Writing

W4 Use register appropriate to audience and context

IGCSE examination

- **Paper 3** both sections, or **Component 4** Coursework Portfolio
- **Papers 1** and **2** will also award some marks for the quality of writing, including creating a voice or writing in role

Differentiated learning outcomes

- **All students must** attempt to use appropriate content bearing in mind the character and context they are writing about (Grade E/D).
- **Most students should** adapt text to create a convincing role using information provided to infer character traits (Grade D/C).
- **Some students could** change voice and role effortlessly in writing, manipulating language, structure and content appropriately and convincingly (Grade B/A).

Resources

- **Student Book**: pp. 56–60
- **Worksheet**: 2.8 Voice and role
- **PPT**: 2.8a–g

Other Student Book pages

- Choosing the right style for your audience, pp. 54–5
- Writing to review, pp. 96–7

Exploring skills

Read through the opening section on Student Book p. 56 with the whole class, using this opportunity to introduce/recap on prior knowledge about voice and role. Draw out examples of statements that 'chatty' or 'anxious' people might make to confirm students' understanding of *voice* and ask students to exemplify what a child of 10, a schoolteacher or an angry neighbour might say.

It might be helpful to discuss the concept of stereotyping, which can be patronising, insulting or inappropriate here. To achieve a Grade C, students need to make a clear attempt to write with a sense of audience. So stress that a clichéd or inappropriately humorous 'voice' would make a bad impression. On the other hand, voice used accurately and with a sensitive awareness and understanding will score highly.

Ask students to work in pairs on **Q1** to match the each speech bubble to one of the roles. Spend some time with the pairs, drawing out the specific language features being used by each character to give them their voice and relating this to *what is being said, how it is being said, the conventions being used.*

Give extra support with **Worksheet 2.8,** which takes students through **Q1** and allows them to record their evidence for and to reflect on why they have matched each speech bubble to each role.

Building skills

Use **PPT 2.8a–c** to focus students on picking out the context for and the character and background behind the voice they will need to capture. Discuss the context of the tournament and how Poppy might be feeling a bit vulnerable in strange company and a bit anxious with the test looming. Then briefly discuss Poppy's expressions in her diary entry '– at least I thought I had', 'This made me laugh', 'I couldn't eat anyway,' 'Am I going mad?' Ask: *What kind of person is she from these statements? Would you find her good company? Why? Why not?* Then ask students to work in pairs to answer **Q2**.

Ask students to read through **Q3** and discuss the other characters mentioned in the activity – Sonja, Raj and Jed. Ask: *What might they have thought of Poppy and why?* Take some initial feedback then set up the role play in groups of three or four. Ask students to take on the roles of Poppy, Sonja, Jed and/or Raj and complete the role play.

PPT **Give extra support** by using **PPT 2.8d** to start the role play conversation.

Give extra challenge after the role play by asking students to evaluate their choices of content and language – *on reflection, was anything inappropriate or out of character? Was anything clichéd or stereotypical? How could this have been avoided?*

Developing skills

Ask students to read through the text on Student Book p. 59 and see if they agree with the brief description of Poppy. Ask: *What else could be added to the list? Is there anything negative we can draw out from her previous entry?* Make sure students are able to pinpoint the section of text that has inspired each comment and steer students to sensitivity rather than caricature. It might be that Poppy is a little bit arrogant in not believing in last-minute preparation or it might be bravado as she realises that her peers are taking this more seriously than she is. Talk about the layers of meaning they could infer, such as *Poppy is quite vulnerable underneath her carefree image* and the multi-dimensional characters that people generally are.

PPT Direct students to the **Top tip** on Student Book p. 59, but advise them to be tentative when inferring character traits, particularly when only a small amount of stimulus text is provided. As a class, add a few more descriptive words to the list on **PPT 2.8e**.

PPT Read through **Q4** and the example of the next diary entry carefully with students before setting the diary writing task. Use **PPT 2.8f** to discuss the example together, modelling how students should question their own choices carefully.

Give extra support for **Q4** by using **Worksheet 2.8**, which shows how Poppy uses a combination of past and present tense narrative in her first diary entry.

Once students have written Poppy's next diary entry, introduce the concept of a change of context. Ask pairs to consider how their language changes when they are in different contexts (for example, the classroom, in the park, in the theatre, at a wedding, at a funeral.) Ask: *how do we change our language in different situations? How might different people infer different things about us from meeting us in different contexts?*

Ask students to work with partners through the bullet points in **Q5**. Students need to recognise that the purpose of the speech is *persuasive* rather than *informative or reflective*; the speech is *formal* whilst the diary is *informal*; the conventions of a speech are different to those of a diary, and the style is *objective* rather than *personal*.

Applying skills

PPT Ask students to work independently to assess the work of the two students for **Q6** on Student Book p. 60. Use the success criteria on **PPT 2.8g** to discuss how the student responses should be graded.

Then ask students to complete **Q7**, which requires a lot of inference about the character of Sonja. It will be helpful for students to return to Poppy's original diary first to extract information, then to look at the new information within **Q7** on Student Book p. 60. Remind students, via the **Excellent progress** criteria, to create three-dimensional characters through a sensitive portrayal rather than clichéd stereotypes.

Towards A/A* | To achieve the highest grades, students vary their style with assurance to suit audience and context. Using appropriate voice for role requires an understanding of how character can be inferred from very small amounts of information. There is a clear transfer of skills from reading to writing here that students will benefit from practising. For example, how does the following information help us to ascertain a voice for Leon? *Distracted, as ever, Leon wandered into the room without noticing the shock and disappointment oozing from his mother's face.*

1 Conventions of speeches

Assessment objectives
AO2 **Writing**
W2 Sequence facts, ideas and opinions
W4 Use register appropriate to audience and context

IGCSE examination
- **Paper 1** Question 2
- **Paper 2** Question 1
- **Component 4** Coursework Portfolio

Differentiated learning outcomes
- **All students must** understand and use the basic conventions of speech writing: attention-grabbing opening, lists and pairs (Grade E/D).
- **Most students should** appreciate and use writing in speeches that is fit for purpose, audience and form, making good use of the conventions of speech writing: first-person and second-person pronouns, present tense (Grade D/C).
- **Some students could** create powerful voices in speech writing that use tone, content, structure and language appropriately (Grade B/A).

Resources
- **Student Book**: pp. 62–5
- **Worksheet**:
  3.1 Analysing Hillary Clinton's speech
- **PPT**: 3.1a–f

Other Student Book pages
- Writing to persuade, pp. 88–9
- Writing to argue, pp. 90–93

Exploring skills

Explain to the whole class that speeches are written to be spoken and to have an immediate impact on listeners. For example, speeches are likely to make greater use of shorter sentences, repetition and signposting than many texts designed to be read. Being aware of the effect of what you say on your audience is essential, and being able to manipulate this form is a key skill in many aspects of life. As a warm up, ask students to give examples of powerful speeches they have heard or heard of. Then ask students to work in pairs to think about what makes these speeches memorable.

Read the short speech on Student Book p. 62 and use **PPT 3.1a** to annotate the features. Demonstrate use of first-person and second-person pronouns, lists, reasons, persuasive devices such as rhetorical questions, and emotive language.

Then ask students to work in pairs from **PPT 3.1b**, which shows the questions from **Q2**. Take some feedback to ensure that students' understanding of purpose, audience, direct address, informal language and personal references and voice is secure.

Come back together as a class to decide whether the speech is *friendly and informal* or is *hard-hitting and serious?* Emphasise that the speech is 'conventional' in that it uses many of the features you would expect to find in a speech written for that purpose and that audience.

Explore the concept of 'effective' here. Ask small groups to evaluate the choices made by the writer using the sentence starter, *'I think the writer's choice of language is effective here because...'* Support groups in commenting on appropriateness for audience and purpose.

Building skills

Draw attention to the topic sentence *'I'm here ... to ask you to vote for me'* in the speech on Student Book p. 62. Explain how this topic sentence sets the agenda that is followed in all the following sentences.

This extension activity will prepare students for pair work later in this section and will ensure a thorough reading of the speech for **Q3**. Organise students into groups of six. Using a large-print version of **Worksheet 3.1**, divide Hillary Clinton's speech into six parts and distribute one to each of the six groups.

> **Give extra support** by allocating the shorter paragraphs to students who find analysing formal language difficult.

Ask students to discuss in their groups what information is shared in this speech and what impact it might have on the intended listeners. Take feedback on the parts of the speech in the correct order so that all students get a gist of the whole speech. Invite students to read the whole text at this point.

Next, regroup the students by numbering each student in the original groups from 1 to 6, then asking all the 1s, 2s, 3s, etc., to join together. This should mean that there is an 'expert' on each section in each new group. Ask students to work as pairs within the new groups to answer each bullet point question in **Q4**. These questions can also be displayed using **PPT 3.1c**. Encourage group members to share their ideas about the techniques in each section.

Take feedback using the **Q4** bullet points and try to come to an agreement about how to judge the speech. Is it *hard-hitting, inspiring, emotional, funny*? Recap on the earlier point about what 'effective' means. Then discuss how the two speeches are different and which is the most effective for its purpose and audience, and why.

Developing skills

Ask students to read through the Clinton speech again and to tackle **Q5**. If they are confident about discussing Purpose–Audience–Form (PAF), ask them to work individually on the speech.

> **Give extra support** using **PPT 3.1d–f**, which shows the speech and highlights the purpose in red (to celebrate achievements), the audience in green (all women across the world) and the features of speeches in blue (for example, knocking down the opposing arguments). Ask students if they can see any familiar features of persuasive writing in the text, e.g. alliteration, emotive language and rule of three.

Take feedback as a class, drawing out the use of present tense, repetition, lists and short, simple *sentences ('We share a common future.')*. *Share* ideas about the use of tenses, grammar and different sentence types. Discuss the overall impact of the speech and the contribution made by each of the conventions chosen.

Applying skills

Ask students to read through the explanation of speech structure and answer any questions on structural features, the opening, middle, or ending of speeches. You could allow students to discuss their preferences from the speech extracts provided. Then introduce the speech-writing task in **Q6**. Encourage students to make full use of Hillary Clinton's speech, reminding them of some of its best features. Ensure that students provide details and use the **Sound progress** and **Excellent progress** criteria when evaluating their own speeches.

> **Give extra challenge** by setting a more unfamiliar task for high-attaining students. You could use: *Write a speech for your head teacher to give to a local electricity company, persuading them to do more to cut down on pollution, waste and general disregard for the local landscape.*
>
> Encourage students to find the appropriate voice and tone, and then create the content, rather than dwell on the details of the electricity company.

Towards A/A*	Although the terminal examination will probably be based in a familiar context or scenario, it is helpful for potential A* candidates to work with more unknown scenarios such as the one suggested in the 'extra challenge' task above. This will help them to develop high levels of flexibility and creativity in their writing.

2 Conventions of dialogue and interviews

Assessment objectives

AO2 Writing

- **W1** Articulate experience and express what is thought, felt and imagined
- **W2** Sequence facts, ideas and opinions
- **W3** Use a range of appropriate vocabulary
- **W4** Use register appropriate to audience and context
- **W5** Make accurate use of spelling, punctuation and grammar

IGCSE examination

- **Paper 1** Question 2
- **Paper 2** Question 1
- **Component 4** Coursework Portfolio

Differentiated learning outcomes

- **All students must** understand and use the basic conventions of dialogues – speakers take on roles addressing each other with some direction on performance (Grade E/D).
- **Most students should** appreciate and use writing in dialogues that is fit for purpose, audience and form, making good use of the conventions of dialogues: conflict, tension, turn-taking, overlapping speech (Grade D/C).
- **Some students could** create powerful characters in dialogue writing that use tone, content, structure and language appropriately (Grade B/A).

Resources

- **Student Book**: pp. 66–69
- **Worksheets**:
  3.2a Analysing dialogue
  3.2b Continuing the dialogue
- **PPT**: 3.2a–h

Other Student Book pages

- Conventions of speeches, pp. 62–5

Exploring skills

As a warm up for **Q1**, ask students to work in groups of three, with two in role as a teenager (Sandra) and her mum, and a third in role as a TV director.

Students should read the dialogue script, which is available as **Worksheet 3.2a,** and take advice from the director about their reading and behaviour. The worksheet offers some advice on performance, but most of it should come through the discussion.

Encourage the groups to discuss the questions in **Q1** and to explore how well they have understood the characters by carrying on the dialogue for another few lines.

Building skills

Read through the text on Student Book p. 67 drawing attention to the two headings: *Content and structure* and *Style*. Ask students what they know about these terms already and how they think each one will apply to the writing of dialogues. Then ask them to tackle **Q2**.

You could use **PPT 3.2a**, which shows the earlier text without punctuation, line breaks or direction, and ask students to name the features that will turn it into dialogue format. Incorporate the answer to the question, *Which earlier line does it carry on from?*, by showing the links between Sandra's first and second statements and pointing out how both speakers are, in effect, using monologue rather than dialogue here.

Elicit the element of *conflict* as characters respond differently to a shared situation. Explain how a dramatic dialogue manipulates structure to create tension and to explore relationships.

Give extra challenge by asking students to consider further director's notes for the dialogue, which shows the reader that the characters are not listening to each other at all. They can use **Worksheet 3.2a** to make additions to the director's notes.

Ask students to reread the dialogue before they tackle **Q3** in pairs.

Give extra support using **PPT 3.2b,** which shows the same scenario written using conventions of a novel. Help students to compare the two texts (novel and playscript) in order to define the key features of dialogue. Support the completion of a table comparing how dialogue is presented in novels and in playscript.

Developing skills

Ask students to read the text on Student Book p. 67, which explains **Q4**. Ensure that students are familiar with the instructions for continuing the dialogue by using **PPT 3.2c**. Spend some time working with the task using **Worksheet 3.2b**. Leave the instructions on the whiteboard and revisit as appropriate. Encourage students to develop the arguments Sandra and her mother begin in the opening lines. Display these lines on **PPT 3.2d**, if necessary.

If students revert to 'ping-pong' dialogue or are unsure of what it is, use **PPT 3.2e–f**. These slides show an example of what bad practice might look like along with an improved version. Invite students to explain what is lost in the example of 'ping pong' dialogue, i.e. no sense of depth of character or real feeling is established.

Give extra support with getting started by using **PPT 3.2d**. Draw out what we know about the characters first – *Sandra is insensitive and dismissive of other people; Mother is over-protective, anxious and nervous.*

Give extra challenge by introducing a new character – Sandra's teacher, Miss Featherstone, who is meticulously organised. Ask students to use this information to draft the dialogue at the airport when Sandra, Mum, Dad, the teacher meet.

Applying skills

Ask students to read through **Q5** on Student Book p. 68. You could use **PPT 3.2g** to run through the information provided about Siberian tigers and **PPT 3.2h** to look at the dialogue between the reporter and the conservationist.

You could advise students to use the bullets as on **PPT 3.2g** then use the numbers to trace evidence of use of this information in the interview. For example, 'with just under 500 tigers in the world' is linked to bullet 1.

Ask students to complete the four bulleted questions in **Q5** independently, ensuring first that their understanding of the terms *synonym* and *paraphrase* are secure.

Use **PPT 3.2h** to annotate feedback from the students on the task.

Then read through the text on p. 69 before asking students to write the interview dialogue for **Q6**. Encourage students to use the information from the website convincingly while maintaining a sense of 'voice' for the reporter and charity manager. Prompt them to think about both characters' purposes (to promote the charity's work and draw attention to what needs to be done to save the tiger population; to interrogate these suggestions).

Share a few examples of students' responses to **Q6** and discuss how their analyses demonstrate understanding of the dialogue conventions.

Towards A/A*	High-attaining students working at this level need to describe and reflect on dialogue conventions – how they are used effectively and how they can be subverted to achieve original and creative pieces of text. Provide opportunities for students to work with satirical pieces so they can send up conventions as appropriate. Examples can be found in Sunday supplements to broadsheet newspapers whereby, for example, young people might be satirised for taking their mobile phones too seriously. You could ask students to work with this scenario to create a satirical two-person dialogue called either 'The Youth of Today'.

3 Conventions of diaries and journals

Assessment objectives

AO2 Writing

W1 Articulate experience and express what is thought, felt and imagined
W2 Sequence facts, ideas and opinions
W3 Use a range of appropriate vocabulary
W4 Use register appropriate to audience and context
W5 Make accurate use of spelling, punctuation and grammar

IGCSE examination
- **Paper 1** Question 2
- **Paper 2** Question 1
- **Component 4** Coursework Portfolio

Differentiated learning outcomes
- **All students must** understand and use the basic conventions of diary writing – using time to structure their writing, and using personal emotions and feelings as content (Grade E/D).
- **Most students should** appreciate and use writing in diaries that is fit for purpose, audience and form, making good use of the conventions of diaries – first person, time-based sequence, personal reflection (Grade D/C).
- **Some students could** use the conventions of diary writing with flair, appropriately using a range of tenses, voices and content to explore feelings and engage the reader (Grade B/A).

Resources
- **Student Book**: pp. 70–1
- **Worksheets**: 3.3 Diary writing
- **PPT**: 3.3a–d

Other Student Book pages
- Writing to describe: structure, pp. 100–3

Exploring skills

As a starter, ask groups of four to discuss what they know about diaries already. Who writes them? Why are books and films made about them? Why are people interested in them? Do you know anyone who has written one?

Introduce or recap on examples of some famous diaries and diarists (real and fictional): Samuel Pepys, Anne Frank, Alan Bennett, Bridget Jones, Adrian Mole.

Then read the text on Student Book p. 70 and show the example diary using **PPT 3.3a**. Ask students to name the features (they could also obtain this information from the annotated version in the Student Book). Draw out what makes it instantly recognisable as a diary.

For **Q1**, elicit who is writing the diary and ask students whether they find the style of writing compelling or uninteresting as it is so personal to one particular person. Ask students whether they think that time would be well spent keeping a diary and what effect it would have on the writer. Introduce the idea of diary writing offering a means of organising and reflecting on one's thoughts and troubles. Discuss the fact that this can lead to diaries being very frank and emotional.

Building skills

Return to the central concepts of content, structure and style (CSS is a useful acronym to introduce here as it also features in later lessons), recapping on how these headings supported learning about dialogue and speech writing. Ask students to tackle **Q2** in pairs with one student looking at content and the other looking at structure and style. Give students five minutes to answer the question on Student Book p. 70 related to their heading, and then ask students to share their findings with another pair.

Give extra support using **Worksheet 3.3**, which explains the three headings further and could be used alongside **Q2** for targeted pupils.

Take feedback on what students have found in the diary extract and use the **Checklist for success** to revisit the main features we would expect to see in a diary entry.

Developing skills

Read the longer diary extract on Student Book p. 71, covering over **Q3**, and taking brief feedback on the CSS of this piece in comparison with the previous one. **Worksheet 3.3** could support the first bullet of **Q4** as it displays both texts together and gives explanations of content, structure and style.

As part of **Q4**, you could highlight features of the Kenyan diary that are immediately significant, using **PPT 3.3b** and **3.3c**. The red highlighted text shows the different content; the green shows similar structure; the blue shows different style (long, complex sentences). Also draw attention to the more developed ideas and style of the Kenyan diary.

Then ask students to work in pairs to answer the remaining bullets in **Q4**. Display these on **PPT 3.3d** to help confirm students' understanding of the questions. You might also need to recap on use of past and present tense, ellipsis, colons and lists, and the poetic devices of simile, personification and metaphor.

Applying skills

Ask students to work in pairs on **Q5** to discuss the picture they have formed of the diarist from Kenya. Encourage students to write a summary of no more than three bullet points about the writer and her interests.

Then ask students to complete **Q6** independently to demonstrate their secure skills in diary writing. You could use the **Checklist for success** on Student Book p. 70 to recap on what the success criteria for the task are.

> **Give extra challenge** by asking students to write a diary in the same style as the description of the garden in Kenya but instead describing their own garden. This could be a slightly tongue-in-cheek piece of writing, describing an urban setting:
>
> *Yesterday it was cloudy and rainy all day, the local youths starved of any fresh air and barely any daylight...*
>
> Ask students completing this to describe how they tailored content, structure and style in their writing to suit the task.

After students have finished their diary entry for **Q6**, invite them to work in pairs to peer-assess each other's writing, using the **Sound progress** and **Excellent progress** criteria on Student Book p. 71.

Towards A/A*	Diary writing can seem straightforward to potential A* students, and ensuring that they use the full repertoire of writing skills on these tasks can be difficult. Encourage students to read models of high-quality diaries on a regular basis and to try to imitate or subvert their style. Remind students that diary entries should be full and extended, and that in the exam they should include a maximum of two or three entries.

4 Conventions of reports

Assessment objectives

AO2 Writing

- **W1** Articulate experience and express what is thought, felt and imagined
- **W2** Sequence facts, ideas and opinions
- **W3** Use a range of appropriate vocabulary
- **W4** Use register appropriate to audience and context

IGCSE examination

- **Paper 1** Question 2
- **Paper 2** Question 1
- **Component 4** Coursework Portfolio

Differentiated learning outcomes

- **All students must** understand and use the basic conventions of report writing: using facts and details set out in paragraphs (Grade E/D).
- **Most students should** appreciate and use report writing that is fit for purpose, audience and form, making good use of the conventions of report writing: clear structure, use of first person when appropriate (Grade D/C).
- **Some students could** use the conventions of report writing fluently, moving from formal to informal style easily and maintaining a suitable voice matched to purpose, audience and form (Grade B/A).

Resources

- **Student Book**: pp. 72–3
- **Worksheets**:
  3.4a Features of report writing
  3.4b Content, structure and style of report writing
- **PPT**: 3.4a–i

Other Student Book pages

- Conventions of news reports and feature articles, pp. 74–77

Exploring skills

As preparation for this lesson, ask students to bring in examples of reports from magazines or websites. Reinforce the point that a report is a very familiar document in modern society in the media and other contexts.

As a starter, use **PPT 3.4a–d** to show types of reports on a slide show (A = *a police crime report*, B = *a school report*, C = *a weather report*, D = *a news report*). Then ask pairs to discuss the different reports from the PPT together with the reports they have brought to the lesson and to decide on the features these share.

Now read the text on Student Book p. 72 with the whole class and work through **Q1**. The report extract is written in the first person using the past tense; it is written chronologically and the tone is fairly informal. Ask students to consider why it has been written in this way.

As an extension, ask students to contrast the features of this report with the one on **PPT 3.4e**. The bullets on **PPT 3.4f** could be used during their discussion to draw out the different audiences, the different purposes and the different styles of the two reports.

Give extra support by providing alternative ways the texts could have been written using **Worksheet 3.4a**. Use the alternative texts to draw out the use of different tenses (present/past) and different orders (chronological/significant incident).

Building skills

Recap on how you may have used purpose–audience–form (PAF) and content–structure–style (CSS) to guide writing of diaries and dialogues in previous sections. Then ask students to consider how this might be useful when writing reports, to check that students are starting to understand the conventions of report writing. What advice would they give to a friend who needed to write a report about vandalism of a community centre?

Ask small student groups to read the report on Student Book p. 72 again and work through **Q2**. **Worksheet 3.4b** provides a table for groups to work with.

> **Give extra support** by explaining how to structure a report into five paragraphs. If writing a report on an incident which happened on a school museum trip, you might:
> - write an introduction (Paragraph 1)
> - then describe the coach journey (Paragraph 2)
> - describe what happened when you arrived at the museum (Paragraph 3)
> - then describe the incident when the valuable work of art was nearly damaged (Paragraph 4)
> - and finally, describe the journey home and reflect on the trip as a whole (Paragraph 5.)
>
> Ask students to make brief notes about this report thinking about the CSS and PAF. Students could write the five paragraphs on separate pieces of paper and evaluate the advantages and disadvantages of using a chronological structure. Ask: *Is it better to put the incident first to grab attention to what happened or to keep it 'forensic' by sticking to time order?*

Developing skills

Invite four students to each read a paragraph of the longer report on Student Book p. 73 to the whole class. Then ask groups of three to discuss the bullets in **Q3**. Use **PPT 3.4g–h** to display the text and the bullets. Before the groups start it might be useful to pick out the facts, the number of paragraphs, and examples of formal and informal language using the whiteboard.

Also draw attention to the second **Top tip** on Student Book p. 73, which reminds students that even if the report is for a student audience they should still largely use standard English.

> **Give extra challenge** by asking students: *What changes might need to be made if the report's target audience was parents of pupils at the school or ex-pupils?*
>
> You could also consider changing the purpose: *What would need to be changed if the purpose was to make people feel guilty about not getting involved?*

Applying skills

Recap on the skills that students need to demonstrate when answering **Q4**: for example, *an understanding of purpose–audience–form and how these are matched by choice of content–structure–style*. Explain the importance of choosing the right *language* to set an appropriate tone and of using the right *structure* to make the information clear for the audience. Highlight the importance of openings, paragraphing and closing text.

Ask students to work through **Q4** independently. Use the success criteria on **PPT 3.4i** to remind students of the features of effective report writing they have seen in this section and to encourage use of detail and development of appropriate voice. After students have finished their reports, invite them to work in pairs to peer-assess each other's writing, using the **Sound progress** and **Excellent progress** criteria on p. 73.

Towards A/A*	Students working at this level need to be able to adopt a mature stance quickly, establishing a clear viewpoint that is sustained throughout. They need to demonstrate their knowledge and understanding of content regardless of where their own sympathies or allegiances lie. Encourage students to work in role as reporters, drafting fictitious and real reports regularly from the local community.

5 Conventions of news reports and feature articles

Assessment objectives

AO2 Writing

W2 Sequence facts, ideas and opinions

W4 Use register appropriate to audience and context

IGCSE examination
- **Paper 1** Question 2
- **Paper 2** Question 1
- **Paper 3** Section 1 (Directed writing) or **Component 4** Coursework Portfolio

Differentiated learning outcomes

- **All students must** understand and use the basic conventions of writing in newspapers and magazines, using facts to explain a recent incident or asking questions to interrogate something (Grade E/D).
- **Most students should** appreciate and use information that is fit for purpose, audience and form when writing news reports or feature articles: personal or factual, chronology, expert view, scientific approach (Grade D/C).
- **Some students could** use the conventions of writing for newspapers and magazines in a highly original way by representing information from various sources creatively and matched appropriately to the needs of a new audience (Grade B/A).

Resources
- **Student Book**: pp. 74–7
- **Worksheets**:
  3.5a News report or feature article?
  3.5b Material for feature writing
- **PPT**: 3.5a–e

Other Student Book pages
- Conventions of reports, pp. 72–3

Exploring skills

Explain the difference between news reports and feature articles using the text on Student Book p. 74. Then ask pairs to decide which is which from the five headings in **Q1**. **Worksheet 3.5a** has the headings presented as cards that can be printed and cut up in order to make this an interactive starter activity.

Take feedback from students about the features that led them to place the headings in each category. *Is there a link between declarative sentences and news reports and interrogative sentences and feature articles here?* Discuss how news reports try to put across the facts and the details quickly and clearly whereas features interrogate an issue or the stories behind headlines. Discuss how news reports draw on social impact stories to some extent whereas features take a more scientific approach.

Building skills

As a lead in to **Q2**, ask five students to each read a paragraph of the news report on Student Book p. 75 or display **PPT 3.5a** and **3.5b**. Invite students to discuss the highlighted features of the text as evidence of whether it is a news report or feature article. Then ask:

- How many facts are presented?
- Is this a social impact story, or does it take a scientific approach?
- How many questions are asked?

Give extra challenge by asking students to recast the text into a feature article, changing the facts to a scientific interrogation with the title: *Why would a goat kill a man?*

For **Q2**, return to the content–structure–style (CSS) approach to analysing writing for different purposes and audiences. Ask groups of three to discuss the article *Mountain Goat Kills Hiker*, with one student in each group to taking responsibility for feeding back to the class on content, structure or style, using the annotated report text to help.

The questions are presented on **PPT 3.5c** and the annotated text is on **PPT 3.5d** for use as support or during feedback. (Content is annotated in red, structure in green and style in blue.) Draw attention to the use of third person; the combination of complex and simple sentences; the use of facts; the sense of drama created by using 'but', 'when', 'if' and 'apparently'.

Developing skills

Prior to reading the dangerous dogs article in **Q3**, use the **Checklist for success** on Student Book p. 76 to recap and extend understanding of feature articles. Organise students into groups of five and allocate one student to each of the features in the checklist. Explain that the appropriate students should raise their hands while you are reading if there is evidence that their feature is being used. For example, at the start of the second paragraph, the writer refers to *his* meeting with Lee Randall, *'whom I met'*. This shows the first feature in the checklist (use of personal references).

Then ask the same groups to work together to discuss the CSS for **Q3**. Groups should work through the questions on Student Book p. 77, making notes for feeding back later.

> **Give extra support** to targeted students by breaking down the questions:
> - When looking at the content, ask the students to look for the *who, what, where, when, why?*
> - When considering structure, ask how the mountain goat article tells us the information about the event. Are there any references to time? Are there connectives such as 'next' or 'later'?
> - When looking at the viewpoint question, ask why the writer has chosen to describe his subjects as *'a sweet guy with a sweet dog'*.

Applying skills

Ask students to read **Q4** individually. Recap on the **Checklist for success** for feature articles on Student Book p. 76. Invite students to come up with three features that they will *not* be using in this piece of writing.

Then distribute unannotated versions of the two articles on **Worksheet 3.5b.** Encourage students to spend ten minutes planning their writing by reviewing which facts or ideas from the two articles that they are going to use. Invite one or two suggestions using the model opening provided. This is also on **PPT 3.5e**, onto which students can draft their suggestions.

Towards A/A*	Highest attainers will benefit from opportunities to represent information in increasingly challenging ways. For example, they could take a flyer advertising painting and decorating services and recast it as a report warning about bogus workmen posing as tradesmen in order to steal from your house. They could write a report with the title '*Handyman proves to be charlatan*' demonstrating their skills in using the past tense, simple sentences for clarity and appropriate choice of material.

6 Conventions of letters

Assessment objectives
AO2 Writing
- **W1** Articulate experience and express what is thought, felt and imagined
- **W2** Sequence facts, ideas and opinions
- **W3** Use a range of appropriate vocabulary
- **W4** Use register appropriate to audience and context
- **W5** Make accurate use of spelling, punctuation and grammar

IGCSE examination
- **Paper 1** Question 2
- **Paper 2** Question 1
- **Paper 3** Section 1 (Directed writing) or **Component 4** Coursework Portfolio

Differentiated learning outcomes
- **All students must** understand and use the basic conventions of writing letters, making some attempt to use appropriate layout and style (Grade E/D).
- **Most students should** appreciate and use information that is fit for purpose, audience and form when writing letters, adopting a formal or informal style appropriately (Grade D/C).
- **Some students could** use the conventions of writing for letters in a highly original way by adapting style and structure to meet the needs of audience and purpose sensitively (Grade B/A).

Resources
- **Student Book**: pp. 78–9
- **Worksheets**:
  3.6a Comparing formal and informal letters
  3.6b Comparing the different styles
- **PPT**: 3.6a–d

Other Student Book pages
- Choosing the right style for your audience, pp. 54–5

Exploring skills

As a starter, ask pairs to discuss the features of an informal and a formal letter. If students have any examples of when they have written or received letters, ask them to describe them to their partner. Ask the pairs to imagine the importance of letters 20 years ago (before the internet and mobile phones) and then 40 years ago (with telephones only in some homes). Explore: *What are the differences between then and now? How have our expectations about communication changed?*

Then turn to **Q1** on Student Book p. 78 and look at the two examples of letters that might be written today. You could use **PPT 3.6a–b** to annotate them with students on a whiteboard. The features have been annotated in Student Book.

Distribute **Worksheet 3.6a** to support comparison of the features of a formal and an informal letter.

During class feedback, draw out the different layout, forms of address, tone and use of objective vs personal language. Highlight the similarities in structure and purpose.

Building skills

Support students with a more detailed scrutiny of the letters in this section, drawing attention to the use of vocabulary, sentences, punctuation and opening/closing. You could continue to use **Worksheet 3.6a** and **Worksheet 3.6b** to do this. Take this opportunity to recap on the conventions for opening and closing letters:

Dear Sir/Madam with *Yours faithfully*
Dear Mrs Someone with *Yours sincerely.*

Recap on the **Checklist for success** in letter writing on p. 78, which can also be displayed on **PPT 3.6c**. Discuss the similarities with other forms of writing – again, PAF (purpose-audience-form) and CSS (content-structure-style) are useful acronyms to use here.

Developing skills

For **Q3**, students consider a letter with a different purpose. The letter opening on Student Book p. 79 is a letter of complaint that continues shop assistant Davina's story. Run through the annotations on the letter to show that letters can be a vehicle for developing ideas as well as for relating events and expressing feelings. Ensure that students grasp how the ideas are developed and how paragraph cohesion is established. Also draw out students' thoughts on the level of formality and what language creates this.

> **Give extra challenge** by asking students to look in more detail at the language that creates the level of formality in the letter opening. They should identify the use of *expect* and *expectations* which balance the second paragraph nicely, as does *high levels of courtesy and advice*. They should also recognise the authority in *As you are aware* and *did not meet my expectations in either regard*. Compare this last example with the more informal and less precise *did not give me either*.

Applying skills

Introduce **Q4** by explaining that students will be writing a continuation of the letter of complaint to Mrs Sharp on Student Book p. 79. As a starting point, ask pairs to discuss the bullet points and come up with their own ideas for completing the letter. They should consider:

- the specific problem that Davina causes
- the way she is then unable/unwilling to help the customer
- the action the customer would like Mrs Sharp to take.

Students should use this as a chance to develop their own ideas for writing and could even role-play the events in the shop.

Before setting the task for students to complete individually, remind them to continue the same level of formality as the letter opening, to sustain the voice established for the customer and to decide how to end the letter in a way that makes an impact (but without overdoing it).

When they have completed their letters, ask pairs to peer-assess each other's using the **Checklist for success** on Student Book p. 78, and the **Sound progress** and **Excellent progress** criteria on p. 79.

Display the letter opening on **PPT 3.6d** as a reminder of the style and formality students should match.

Towards A/A*	Letter writing often allows students to show shades of meaning in their writing because it invites the writer to create a distinct personality and voice. A sympathetic understanding of audience and purpose together with an original perspective about the context will be awarded high marks.
	Support students in writing letters that convey personality despite considerable constraints. Letters from soldiers serving in the World Wars and Vietnam, which are readily available on the internet, demonstrate the way that personality can withstand unimaginable pressures.

7 Writing to analyse

Assessment objectives

AO2 Writing

- W2 Sequence facts, ideas and opinions
- W3 Use a range of appropriate vocabulary
- W4 Use register appropriate to audience and context
- W5 Make accurate use of spelling, punctuation and grammar

IGCSE examination

- **Paper 1** Question 2
- **Paper 2** Question 1
- **Paper 3** Section 1 (Directed writing) or **Component 4** Coursework Portfolio

Differentiated learning outcomes

- **All students must** understand some key techniques in analytical writing such as use of relevant evidence (Grade E/D).
- **Most students should** appreciate specific details and use analytical techniques such as making evidence-based judgements from clear points (Grade D/C).
- **Some students could** use the conventions of analytical writing proficiently, presenting clear analysis of complex issues and using a variety of techniques including subtle changes of tone to develop their line of thought (Grade B/A).

Resources

- **Student Book**: pp. 80–3
- **Worksheets**: 3.7 Stages in the analysis
- **PPT**: 3.7a–i

Other Student Book pages

- Writing to review, pp. 96–7
- Writing to inform, pp. 94–5

Exploring skills

As a warm up, invite students to come up with a working definition of *analysis* in two minutes. Ask them to consider how other school subjects such as history, geography and science might use the word. Then, as a lead in to **Q1**, ask students to read the text on Student Book p. 80 including the **Checklist for success** and to consider any changes to their initial perceptions that might be needed.

PPT Use **PPT 3.7a** to put the definition to the test. Show the text and ask students to work in pairs to consider an answer to the question and then to evaluate each of the bulleted options. Take feedback about each option as it is discussed and reinforce the meaning of *to synthesise* from the checklist. Explain why options 1 and 2 are wrong. (They are picking out facts rather than summarising a set of ideas or points and explaining what they mean.) Option 3 is correct because the text is an evidence-based judgment.

PPT Display the two key words *analysis* and *evidence* using **PPT 3.7b**. Recap what each word means then look at the two statements from **Q2** that also appear on **PPT 3.7c**. For the first statement, the *analysis* is the judgment that the rise in fares has put travellers off, and the *evidence* is the sharp decline in numbers. In the second statement, the *analysis* is that young people want more portable devices, and the *evidence* is the increase in sales.

Building skills

PPT Show students **PPT 3.7d**, which continues the story of the student's work experience. Organise students into groups of three to discuss how the text has been structured. The flow chart in the student book on Student Book p. 81 will guide their discussion.

Give extra support using **Worksheet 3.7** which can be cut up and used as a card sort activity to explain the structure very clearly.

PPT Then show students **PPT 3.7e** and ask the groups to fill in the gaps in the **Q3** text. If you have access to laptops, it would be useful for the groups to fill in the gaps themselves from the PPT.

PPT Remind students of the **Top tip** on Student Book p. 81 and spend some time reinforcing the cause-and-effect connectives that can ensure that writing becomes analytical. Then set **Q4**. Students have to create an analytical voice with which to examine the classroom. You could reinforce this by using **PPT 3.7f**, which gives a further example of how an analytical voice might view a classroom.

Developing skills

Explain to students that analysis could be described as being 'definitive' or 'tentative'. Use the examples of student work to demonstrate this, showing that use of data in A contrasts with use of modal verbs in B. However, stress that both A and B have a sense of authority that is convincing. These subtle differences in approach influence the tone of writing. Explore the ways this authority is achieved with the class and draw out the use of impersonal language, which both texts demonstrate.

Ask pairs to discuss the questions in **Q5**. Take feedback and revisit the concept of writing being successful when it is fit for purpose and audience.

PPT As an extension, ask students to change the tone of the extract on **PPT 3.7g** by altering the verbs. These are highlighted on the PPT to make it easy to work with either the whole class or a small group. There is an example of a changed text on **PPT 3.7h**.

> **Give extra challenge** by asking students to change the tone in a range of texts. They could look at other extracts from the Student Book, decide if they were 'definitive' or 'tentative' and then change them.

Applying skills

As a class, look at the text about mobile phone usage on Student Book p. 83. Then ask students to link the skills of summarising, using their own words and drawing conclusions together as part of an analytical process to answer **Q6**. Draw attention to the second **Top tip** on p. 83, which describes the importance of synthesis. Specific, relevant details are needed rather than repeated chunks of the original text.

PPT Set **Q7** as an independent task once the students' understanding is secure about the success criteria for analytical writing on **PPT 3.7i**.

Towards A/A*	An analytical voice is essential for students working towards this level. Subtlety in change of tone is crucial, so practice in using the modal verbs or removing them is essential – for example, *The village needs a by-pass to stop the traffic* compared to *It might be possible to reduce the congestion in the village by the building of a bypass.* You could set this type of task regularly as a starter activity. Also emphasise the use of impersonal voice and its impact as often as possible.

© HarperCollins Publishers 2013   Lesson 7 • 53

8 Writing to explore and discuss

Assessment objectives

AO2 Writing

W1 Articulate experience and express what is thought, felt and imagined

W2 Sequence facts, ideas and opinions

W4 Use register appropriate to audience and context

IGCSE examination
- **Paper 1** Question 2
- **Paper 2** Question 1
- **Paper 3** Section 1 (Directed writing) or **Component 4** Coursework Portfolio

Differentiated learning outcomes
- **All students must** relevant contributions when exploring or discussing a key topic or issue (Grade E/D).
- **Most students should** use detail, explanation and exemplification as part of a series of relevant points when exploring or discussing a key topic or issue (Grade D/C).
- **Some students could** discuss or explore relevant points in depth showing mature thought (Grade B/A).

Resources
- **Student Book**: pp. 84–7
- **Worksheet**: 3.8 Using well-chosen evidence
- **PPT**: 3.8a–b

Exploring skills

As a warm up, ask students to work in pairs to discuss a local issue. Guide students to a 'proposal' that local residents could be for or against. This could be an extension of a train line, the construction of a new hospital or the election of a new mayor. Once they have decided what their issue is, ask students to make a list of at least two points for and two points against the proposal. Then ask students to use these points to work in role as two people directly affected by the proposal; one could be for and one against. Allocate four students as 'listeners' who eavesdrop on discussions and then report back to the whole class on:

- the issues raised
- the points for and against
- the personal experiences they overheard.

As feedback, draw out the importance of facts about the issues, different points of view and personal anecdotes.

As a whole class confirm the importance of these three features for the success of a piece of writing to explore and discuss, using **Q1** and **Q2** on Student Book p. 84. You could use **PPT 3.8a** to display the text from p. 84.

Give extra support by explaining the strangeness of *yarrow flower shortbread* and *nettle soup*. Then describe the meaning of *foraging* in detail and explore the connotations of collecting food from woodland.

Building skills

Use **Worksheet 3.8** to make cards and distribute these to students as an interactive way of completing **Q3** on p. 85 of the Student Book (follow the instructions at the top of the worksheet). Set a time limit of two minutes and ask students to find a matching pair for their card so that the expert comment matches Dr Miles Better, the personal comment matches 'I bought a large bar of chocolate…', and the factual information matches the *British Medical Journal* research.

Then ask students to work as a group of six with the three different comments and to put them in the order they think will work best when writing an article. This might work best if students arrange their comments in a vertical list, dividing each section with 'However, ...' or 'In addition, ...'.

Discuss students' choices as whole-class feedback. Reinforce the **Top tip** on Student Book p. 85 about the importance of using a variety of techniques and then ask students to complete **Q4**. You could use **PPT 3.8b** to explore the conclusion provided as a whole class. The red and blue text shows the two sides, the green text suggests that the author is sceptical about any danger in chocolate and the highlighted 'not yet' at the end suggests ambiguity in the writer's viewpoint.

Developing skills

Ask students to explore their choice of anecdote by reading each one aloud to each other and then putting them in order – first choice, second choice, third choice. Discuss students' choices and reasoning as a whole class, keeping the focus on how the text suits audience, purpose and subject matter.

> **Give extra support** by asking students to make notes in a table such as this to support the activity in **Q5** on Student Book p. 86
>
> | Quotation | How does this draw readers of the school magazine into the article? | How does this tell us about the health benefits and risks of eating chocolate? | How does this entertain the reader or inform the reader about chocolate? |
> |---|---|---|---|
> | Every break-time ... | | | |
> | On the way to school ... | | | |
> | I love chocolate ... | | | |
>
> **Give extra challenge** by asking students to rewrite the quotations they did not choose to start their article with, ensuring that their improved versions meet the needs of the audience, purpose and subject matter.

Applying skills

Introduce the **Q6** task by explaining the range of information students have available from their work so far in this lesson, together with their own ideas for creating personal anecdotes, factual evidence and different viewpoints. Explain that the success of students' articles will depend on careful selection of a variety of pieces of relevant evidence. Use the **Sound progress** and **Excellent progress** success criteria on Student Book p. 87 to explain how they can improve the standard of their writing.

Towards A/A*	Convincing detail conveyed in a cogent manner is typical of writing at Grade A/A*. Encourage students to provide layers of detail, linking their personal anecdotes with expert opinion and facts. For example:
	'*I have not visited a doctor in 40 years despite a routine breakfast of* pain au chocolat *washed down with a great big mug of hot chocolate,*' *claims a healthy octogenarian from Paris. But, should we be asking what might have been if he had opted for fruit and cereal instead? Research just published in the* British Medical Journal *suggests that life expectancy rates increase when diet is restricted to non-dairy foods. Could the cycling-loving 85-year-old have competed in the* Tour de France *without his morning indulgence, we may ask? Or has the energy boosting wake-up call provided the extra a.m. power he thrives on?*

9 Writing to persuade

Assessment objectives
AO2 Writing
- **W1** Articulate experience and express what is thought, felt and imagined
- **W2** Sequence facts, ideas and opinions
- **W3** Use a range of appropriate vocabulary
- **W4** Use register appropriate to audience and context
- **W5** Make accurate use of spelling, punctuation and grammar

IGCSE examination
- **Paper 3** Section 1 (Directed writing) or **Component 4** Coursework Portfolio
- **Papers 1 and 2** will also award some marks for the quality of writing

Differentiated learning outcomes
- **All students must** understand some key techniques in persuasive writing, such as use of direct appeal (Grade E/D).
- **Most students should** appreciate and use persuasive techniques, appropriate content and clear evidence to support a viewpoint (Grade D/C).
- **Some students could** use a variety of techniques for emphasis, including imagery, as well as evidence to persuade (Grade B/A).

Resources
- **Student Book**: pp. 88–9
- **Worksheet**: 3.9 Using facts, statistics, expert opinion and anecdote to persuade
- **PPT**: 3.9a–e

Other Student Book pages
- How to approach assignments engaging with ideas and arguments from other texts pp. 232–5

Exploring skills

To begin with, ask students to discuss media texts that have persuaded them, or someone they know, to change their behaviour. For example:

- They might have bought a certain product, such as whitening toothpaste or a low-calorie drink, as the result of an advertisement.
- A poster warning about road fatalities might have convinced them of the need to use the footbridge instead of crossing a road.

Once students have decided on an example, ask them to come up with a list of three features that worked to persuade them to change. Was it statistics, or possibly real-life examples, or was it emotive vocabulary?

Look at the example of a persuasive text on Student Book p. 88 and compare the techniques it uses with the students' examples. Then ask students to work in pairs to discuss the bullet points in **Q1**.

PPT You could use **PPT 3.9a** to support whole-class discussion of the features used in the text. Show the annotations first, before revealing the lines connecting them to the appropriate feature.

PPT **Give extra challenge** by using **PPT 3.9a** to challenge high-attaining students to find examples of the techniques listed around the text before showing the arrows on the slide.

Building skills

Read through the introduction to this section and exemplify the difference between direct appeal and a rude or aggressive tone:

- *Do you want children to get hurt?* (rude, aggressive)
- *What could be more important than the safety and well-being of our precious children?* (direct appeal)

Ask students to explain the difference between:

- *Give us some money to help homeless people – you can afford it.*
- *Could you spare £2 to give a homeless person a hot meal?*

Then ask students to choose between the three sentences to close the parent's plea in **Q2** on Student Book p. 88. Then ask them to create two more rhetorical questions of their own for **Q3**.

Developing skills

Ask students to complete the task on **Worksheet 3.9** to recap on the difference between facts, statistics, expert opinion and personal anecdote, and their effects. Then use **PPT 3.9b** to emphasise the first **Top tip** from Student Book p. 89 and **PPT 3.9c** to demonstrate how to develop key points. The first two pieces of evidence have been developed; you could ask students to develop the other two examples in small groups before sharing their ideas with the class by typing them into the PPT slide in the space provided.

Use **PPT 3.9d** to explain the 'call to action' feature and reinforce the effect of the personal pronouns and intensifiers. Draw out the build-up of layers of persuasion in this text through whole-class discussion. Then ask students to work in pairs to discuss the bullet points in **Q4**.

> **Give extra support** by introducing a persuasion 'recipe':
>
> 1 *Take a fact and mix it with some explanation and maybe a statistic if you have one.*
> 2 *Then add a personal anecdote and a bit more explanation.*
> 3 *Next put in an expert opinion, combining it carefully with some detailed explanation of how this all links to the original fact.*
> 4 *And, finally, appeal to your reader with a strong, direct call to action.*
>
> Encourage students to make up recipes for themselves and try them out.

Applying skills

Recap the **Checklist for success** on Student Book p. 89 and then ask students to work individually to complete **Q5**. You could use **PPT 3.9e** to display the checklist and the **Sound progress** and **Excellent progress** success criteria on Student Book p. 89 while students are working.

Towards A/A*	Students working at this level need to use persuasive techniques with discernment, choosing the one(s) that will have the appropriate effect on the specific audience. Subtle persuasion is sometimes the most powerful approach – for example, for some readers, rather than focusing on facts and figures, it might be more effective to suggest that, instead of driving, parents combine the walk to school with a walk for the dog.

10 Writing to argue

Assessment objectives

AO2 Writing

W1 Articulate experience and express what is thought, felt and imagined
W2 Sequence facts, ideas and opinions
W3 Use a range of appropriate vocabulary
W4 Use register appropriate to audience and context
W5 Make accurate use of spelling, punctuation and grammar

IGCSE examination

- **Paper 3**, Section 1 (Directed writing) or **Component 4**, Coursework portfolio (Assignment 3)
- **Papers 1 and 2** require students to give an extended response, which could be to argue what is thought, felt or imagined in response to the unseen texts given.

Differentiated learning outcomes

- **All students must** understand key techniques in putting forward an argument, such as a clear opening (Grade E/D).
- **Most students should** use a clear structure presenting both sides when writing an argument text (Grade D/C).
- **Some students could** use the conventions of argumentative writing proficiently, presenting clear arguments in coherent ways (Grade B/A).

Resources

- **Student Book**: pp. 90–3
- **Worksheet**:
  3.10a Structuring an argument
  3.10b 'For' and 'against' an argument
- **PPT**: 3.10a–f

Other Student Book pages

- Paragraph cohesion, pp. 46–7
- Writing to analyse, p. 82

Exploring skills

Demonstrate to students how an argument might be presented by asking two students to argue about listening to music when doing homework. One is prompted to say *I think we should be allowed to listen to music* and the other to say *I don't think we should be allowed to listen to music*. Example arguments might include:

I think we should be allowed to listen to music because…	I don't think we should be allowed to listen to music because…
…it blocks out distractions in the room such as other students talking.	…it blurs your focus so you lose track of the question you are answering
…it really helps me concentrate on details in my thinking and planning.	…it makes students work in isolation instead of collaborating.

Ask students to feed back about how the arguments might be improved. Make a note of any recommendations. Explain that this lesson will be about these developing skills. Use the **Checklist for success** on Student Book p. 90 to cross-reference students' feedback with the skills required. Then ask pairs to complete **Q1**.

PPT You could use **PPT 3.10a** to display the argument text. Ask students to identify which of the features in the blue boxes are demonstrated by this text.

> **Give extra challenge** by asking specific students to improve the text using one of the features not used so far.

Ask students to revisit the argument about listening to music when doing homework and consider different ways the argument could be presented using these techniques.

Building skills

Use the simple structure at the top of Student Book p. 91 to explain how an argument could be presented and then ask two students to demonstrate this by carrying out the task on **Worksheet 3.10a**. This would be particularly effective if you position students on either side of the classroom. Ask the class to give feedback about the success of the argument. Were they persuaded by the argument in favour of the bike rental scheme?

Explain the alternative for presenting an argument: the counter-argument/rebuttal approach. Ask students to complete to **Q2–Q4** on p. 91. Use **PPT 3.10b** to point out the counter argument/rebuttal features in red before revealing the arrows.

Ask students to evaluate the two approaches they have looked at so far. For example, ask students how they would argue against the need to expand a leisure-centre car park – elicit the advantages of listing all the arguments against the plan first (so they remain in the minds of the audience). Or students might explore ways to present an argument about the closure of a children's ward in a local hospital. In this case, listing each point for and then each point against may give a clearer, more objective approach to this emotive issue. Then revisit the argument about listening to music when doing homework and select two students to try a counter-argument/rebuttal approach.

Remind students of the **Checklist for success** point: 'Add evidence or examples to support the points made'. Ask students to complete **Q5** and **Q6** on Student Book p. 92 individually. Use **PPT 3.10c** to show use of two types of evidence and the longer, complex sentence in the extract from Student Book p. 91. Then introduce the challenging **Q7** to the whole class. Use **PPT 3.10d** to emphasise the three bullet points and draft examples together.

> **Give extra support** by stressing the **Checklist for success** on p.92. Recap how this works on paragraph 1 and 2 before asking students to complete paragraph 3.

Developing skills

To prepare students for **Q8**, revisit connectives to structure an argument (see Student Book pp. 46–7 and 82) and show the two functions of connectives here:

- to *agree with* or *extend* the point
- to *dispute* the point.

Ask students to divide the eight connectives into two columns to make sure that the correct function is used when drafting. **PPT 3.10e** could be used to support the whole class in completing this task before students try **Q8**. There are five connectives to agree with the point and three to dispute it. Use **Worksheet 3.10b** to make a card sort in preparation for **Q9** and **Q10** on Student Book pp. 92–3.

Applying skills

Recap the features of writing to argue successfully using the **Checklist for success** on p. 90 of the Student Book. Then ask students to work in pairs to carry out the card sort on **Worksheet 3.10b**, putting the points for or against in a logical order.

Before they tackle **Q11**, encourage students to link similar points together to provide development of key points. Offer an example on the screen by showing **PPT 3.10f** for a short time. Withdraw the example once students are clear about the success criteria of the task given in the **Sound progress** and **Excellent progress** descriptions on Student Book p. 93. Recap the features that will set their writing apart from others':

- using counter-argument/rebuttals
- using a range of connectives accurately
- using a rhetorical question as a summary rather than as a marketing tool
- varying sentence types for effect.

> **Towards A/A*** Students aspiring to the top band mark in writing to argue should not just present a clear view from the start, but also weave a complex argument incorporating all sides and evidence. Discerning judgement about which features are appropriate to purpose and audience will be an advantage.

11 Writing to inform

Assessment objectives

AO2 Writing
- W2 Sequence facts, ideas and opinions
- W3 Use a range of appropriate vocabulary
- W4 Use register appropriate to audience and context

IGCSE examination
- **Paper 1** Question 2
- **Paper 2** Question 1
- **Paper 3** Section 1 (Directed writing) or **Component 4** Coursework Portfolio

Differentiated learning outcomes

- **All students must** be able to understand the key features and purposes of writing to inform (Grade E/D).
- **Most students should** include relevant information and present it clearly when writing to inform (Grade D/C).
- **Some students could** use and develop the conventions of writing to inform in a sophisticated way, using concision and objective clarity within an appropriate structure (Grade B/A).

Resources

- **Student Book**: pp. 94–5
- **Worksheet**: 3.11 Comparing two information texts
- **PPT**: 3.11a–g

Other Student Book pages
- Writing to review, pp. 96–7
- Conventions of letters, pp. 78–9
- Conventions of news reports and feature articles, pp. 74–7

Exploring skills

Introduce writing to inform as a way of communicating information – a vital life skill. Read through the opening section on Student Book p. 94 and the **Checklist for success** (which can also be displayed on **PPT 3.11a**). Clarify the differences between this and other types of writing (for example writing to analyse or promote, where any information provided is linked to offering evidence or to an intention to sell).

Show students the example information text on Student Book p. 94 or on **PPT 3.11b** and ask them to work individually to answer **Q1**. Ensure that students interpret 'main information' and 'clear sentences' correctly from the question. Take feedback, eliciting examples of information that is clear and presented in an accessible way.

Building skills

Recap on what an 'impersonal' and a 'formal' tone is in writing and refer to the first text as both of these. Then look at the second text, on Student Book p. 95 or display it on **PPT 3.11c**. Ask students to spot the features that are neither formal nor impersonal. The PPT will allow you to annotate the text with students' ideas. Then ask them to complete **Q2** producing their own rewritten more formal version of the text. A purely informative version of the text is provided on **PPT 3.11d**.

> **Give extra support** to students by spending more time comparing the two informative texts using the table provided in **Worksheet 3.11**. Focus on the third-person verbs used in the first text, then the second-person verbs in the second. Consider the use of slang and unusual sentences in the second text, as opposed to the complex sentence followed by a string of simple sentences in the first.

Developing skills

In this section, students need to differentiate between facts and opinions. Explain that sometimes writing to inform is combined with other purposes, so knowing how to identify and use fact and opinion is important.

PPT Ask students to consider the letter from Shahena on Student Book p. 95, which is also featured on **PPT 3.11e–f**. Examples of fact appear on **PPT 3.11e** and an example of opinion appears on **PPT 3.11f** (view in slideshow).

Encourage pairs to identify further facts and opinions to complete **Q3**, and then take feedback. Refer to the **Top tip** on p. 95 to remind students of the need to be clear and logical when writing to inform and of the usefulness of topic sentences in structuring their texts.

> **Give extra challenge** by asking students to write a brief information text about Shahena's town. They can use details from her letter and invent a few more. One feature that will support students in achieving higher grades for writing to inform is the use of concision. To encourage this, support students in using complex sentences, which contain a lot of information, rather than a series of simple sentences.

PPT **PPT 3.11g** provides a model of concise writing to inform. You could ask students to rewrite the red, blue and green paragraphs as a series of simple sentences instead of the complex sentences. Ask them to evaluate the difference that makes.

Applying skills

Recap on the success criteria for informative writing using the checklist on Student Book p. 94. Focus on the importance of clarity and giving accurate, unbiased information. You might also provide some reminders about the features of formal letter writing. Ask students to complete **Q4** independently.

When they have finished, spend some time reflecting on how the letter has been approached by different students. Talk together about the length of the two paragraphs they have written, stressing that quality rather than quantity is required in this type of writing, and study the **Sound progress** and **Excellent progress** criteria with this in mind.

Towards A/A*	Informative writing at the highest level has a logical order and sense of clarity throughout. Encourage students not to waffle unnecessarily when writing, by setting strict word limits in practice assignments and by regularly modelling concision. You could ask students to write an information text about their school in three paragraphs containing three sentences (one simple, one compound, one complex).

12 Writing to review

Assessment objectives

AO2 Writing

- W2 Sequence facts, ideas and opinions
- W3 Use a range of appropriate vocabulary
- W4 Use register appropriate to audience and context
- W5 Make accurate use of sentences, punctuation and grammar

IGCSE examination

- **Paper 3** Section 1 (Directed writing) or **Component 4** Coursework Portfolio (Assignment 1)
- **Paper 1** Question 2
- **Paper 2** Question 1

Differentiated learning outcomes

- **All students must** be able to understand the key features and purposes of writing to review (Grade E/D).
- **Most students should** include factual information and opinion in their review writing (Grade D/C).
- **Some students could** use fact, opinion and engaging description to entertain the reader when review writing (Grade B/A).

Resources

- **Student Book**: pp. 96–7
- **PPT**: 3.12a–d

Other Student Book pages

- Writing to inform, pp. 94–95

Exploring skills

Explain to the class that writing to review combines writing to inform with opinion and analysis. Striking the right balance between these elements is essential though, so warn students against giving too much opinion.

[PPT] Look at the example review on Student Book p. 96 and draw out the use of opinion and information. If preferred, you could display the unannotated text on **PPT 3.12a** and highlight examples of information and opinion.

Quickly recap the use of noun phrases when writing to engage readers by working through the **Key terms** panel with the class. Ask students to come up with their own examples of noun phrases.

For **Q1**, ask pairs to discuss a film, story or television programme they know well or have seen or read recently. Remind them to keep the ending to themselves in their spoken review.

[PPT] **Give extra support** by providing a frame for the review talk. You can display the one on **PPT 3.12b**.

Building skills

Explain to students the importance of adding punchy detail to the information being provided in a review. Emphasise that not only this will make a review text more engaging for an interested reader, but it might also engage people who might not otherwise have read the text/viewed the film. The review writer's key tools are well-chosen adjectives and adverbs, and well-punctuated complex sentences.

Read through this section on Student Book pp. 96–7 with the class and then ask them to complete **Q2**. Here is one possible model answer:

> This <u>hilarious</u> comedy stars Matt Le Blond as an <u>awkward</u> school-teacher who <u>unpredictably</u> falls in love with <u>newly-qualified</u>, <u>problem-solving</u> nurse, Jemma Jones.

62 • Lesson 12

Give extra support by providing targeted students with the example on **PPT 3.12c** and asking them to change the position of the adjectives to make a more interesting sentence. The adjectives and adverbs are highlighted.

Spend some time recapping the use of a 'subordinate clause', which can be dropped into a sentence to give more information, by reading the **Top tip** on Student Book p. 97. Revisit the way commas or dashes should be used to separate these clauses.

Developing skills

Read the review of *The Tempest* on Student Book p. 97 with the class. Then ask students to work in groups of three, with one looking at each of the bullet points in **Q3**. Invite students to share their notes with another group then ask them to assess their notes against the **Checklist for success**. Give students time to extend or change their notes. Then take feedback from the whole class.

Give extra challenge by asking students to find a recent review of a Shakespeare play online (ideally *The Tempest*). Encourage students to compare the example on Student Book p. 97 with a current play review. Advise them to look at the use of noun-phrases, complex sentences, factual information and opinion or analysis.

Applying skills

Remind students of plays, books, television programmes that they have watched recently in class or at home. Suggest they choose something to review that they know well and about which they have a clear opinion that they can support with evidence. Read through **Q4** and refer to the **Checklist for success**, which can also be displayed on **PPT 3.12d**. Ask students to complete the piece of review writing independently, and then to peer-assess with a partner, using both the Checklist and the **Sound progress** and **Excellent progress** criteria on Student Book p. 97.

Give extra support by putting key information from a class novel, play or film on the board for students to utilise within their review. This could take the form of a few sentences. For example, if students have just seen a film version of Steinbeck's *Of Mice and Men* or Fitzgerald's *The Great Gatsby*, you could remind students of the main characters, the main themes, the narrator or the different settings used in the novel.

Towards A/A*	When reviewing, it is important to have a very good reason for criticising or applauding a piece of work. Support students in providing clear reasons for a negative or positive judgement by asking them to be subtle about where their opinion sits in the opening sentences or by ensuring there is a trail of factual evidence to support their opening judgement. For example: *This terrible play* could become *An interesting interpretation* at the start of a review but end with *ultimately a disappointing attempt to portray a classic piece*. This more subtle approach to criticism is likely to be well rewarded.

13 Writing to describe: atmosphere

Assessment objectives

AO2 Writing

- **W1** Articulate experience and express what is thought, felt and imagined
- **W3** Use a range of appropriate vocabulary

IGCSE examination

- **Paper 1** Question 2
- **Paper 3** Section 2 (Composition)
- **Component 4,** Coursework Portfolio (Assignment 2)

Differentiated learning outcomes

- **All students must** be able to articulate an experience and use descriptive techniques to engage a reader (Grade E/D).
- **Most students should** appreciate and use techniques suitable for creating a particular atmosphere such as imagery and sensory language (Grade D/C).
- **Some students could** use the conventions of writing to describe with originality, creating atmosphere that is memorable or evocative with vivid pictures for the reader (Grade B/A).

Resources

- **Student Book**: pp. 98–9
- **Worksheets**: 3.13 Creating atmosphere
- **PPT**: 3.13a–e

Other Student Book pages

- Vocabulary, pp. 48–9
- Writing to describe: structure, pp.100–3
- How to approach descriptive and narrative assignments, pp. 228–31

Exploring skills

Introduce creating atmosphere with the idea of transporting the reader to another time, place and experience. Model the process using a visit to a famous place or destination. An example focusing on Venice is given below and also on **PPT 3.13a**:

> *I arrived in Venice in the rain. The sky was grey but the buildings were a rainbow of terracotta, blue, pink and gold. The water was turquoise, with a blue/green hue I had only seen on films about the coral reef. It was quiet. Quiet in a way that shocked. Thousands of people were rushing around, but with no traffic all was a silent movie. I felt choked by the beauty staring at me. The floating city took my heart and kept it.*

Explore the features of the example text as a whole class – the sights, the sounds, the emotive language, the personification. Students could be asked to sketch the scene or make a collage using material from the internet. Explain that ensuring that descriptive writing is in an appropriate style will make their writing stand out from the crowd.

Turn to Student Book p. 98 and read the opening text, which you could display as **PPT 3.13b**. Give students two minutes to create a list of images that immediately spring to the reader's mind as they are transported to the seaside. Explain the key term 'connotations' by focusing on the ideas brought to mind by 'rotten hulks of decaying dinghies' – death, waste, discarded items left over from the past. Then ask pairs to complete **Q1** and **Q2**.

Building skills

Lead in to **Q3** on Student Book p. 99 by reading through with students the **Checklist for success** on the same page. Ensure that everyone understands what is meant by the key terms used there: imagery, similes, metaphors and sensory language (recap using the text explaining imagery on Student Book p. 49 if necessary).

Using **PPT 3.13c**, point out the use of imagery (red) and sensory language (blue). Then ask students to work in groups of three to create their own additions to either text for **Q3**.

> **Give extra support** to less confident students by providing a skeleton writing structure:
>
> * *The children on the beach were so far away they looked like...*
> * *The hotels were once grand I'm sure. They had seen better days but now looked like...*
>
> Try to steer students away from creating images that jar with the overall description such as *The children on the beach were so far away they looked like particles of dust in an old shed.* Explain that the simile should link to the beach scene (*...like tiny seashells perched on the rocks*) rather than bringing in the new setting of, for example, an old shed.

Developing skills

Ask students to work in groups of three on **Q4** evaluating the potential for each phrase in the bulleted list of writer's notes on Student Book p. 99. Give each phrase a mark out of 5 and use these marks to decide which elements are most important and could create a powerful overall atmosphere. Compare choices across the class. You could use **PPT 3.13d** to annotate the positive and negative features of the writer's notes.

Ask students to continue working in groups of three for **Q5** evaluating the success of the two extracts (A and B). One student should read the first phrase of text A, 'I gasped at the myriad colours of the spider...', and then the other two students give a mark out of 5 and a reason for the score. Ask students to complete the task **Worksheet 3.13** to keep notes.

Draw the class back together for feedback (you could display the extracts on **PPT 3.13e** on the whiteboard). Use the bullet points for **Q5** to question students about the effectiveness of each phrase they have awarded 5/5 to.

> **Give extra challenge** by asking students to use two more of the phrases from the writer's notes to inspire an eerie mood – for example: 'ancient, ruined temple' and 'heavy rain which begins to fall'.

Applying skills

Prepare students for the independent writing task in **Q6** by revisiting the **Checklist for success** and the success criteria for **Sound progress** and **Excellent progress** on Student Book p. 99. Share some ideas about how to create a remote setting and a threatening mood. Then allow plenty of time for thinking, planning and drafting.

Towards A/A*	Students can score highly in a task requiring descriptive writing if atmosphere is created by pertinent language choices. Writers demonstrate their control of atmosphere by choosing original and appropriate similes and metaphors embedded within a descriptive paragraph, and by extending or revisiting them. Encourage high-attainment students to take risks, but also to maintain and develop ideas throughout a piece of writing.

14 Writing to describe: structure

Assessment objectives

AO2 Writing

- W1 Articulate experience and express what is thought, felt and imagined
- W2 Sequence facts, ideas and opinions
- W3 Use a range of appropriate vocabulary
- W4 Use register appropriate to audience and context
- W5 Make accurate use of spelling, punctuation and grammar

IGCSE examination

- **Component 4** Coursework Portfolio (Assignment 2)

Differentiated learning outcomes

- **All students must** be able to describe an event or person imaginatively (Grade E/D).
- **Most students should** use imaginative skills and techniques to keep the reader's interest and create detailed pictures through crafted composition (Grade D/C).
- **Some students could** use a range of complex structures, sentences and vocabulary to create vivid descriptions with an impressive overall effect on the reader (Grade B/A).

Resources

- **Student Book**: pp. 100–3
- **Worksheets**: 3.14 Varying sentences in descriptive text
- **PPT**: 3.14a–g

Other Student Book pages

- Writing to describe: atmosphere, pp. 98–9

Exploring skills

As a warm up, ask students to work in pairs to decide what makes the best descriptive writing. Remind the students of books they have read over the past few years in school, of news reports about significant events – maybe natural disasters or national celebrations. Then share the most powerful piece of description that you have read recently with students and explain why it had such an effect.

Put quotations on the edge of the whiteboard such as 'I could picture what was being described just as if I was there' or 'it made me feel like I was there', or 'I couldn't get the image out of my head'. Then turn to Student Book p. 100 and as a whole class discuss ideas for the task 'Describe an exciting moment or special event'. Read through the bullet points and collect further additions on the whiteboard for **Q1**.

Read the example text as a class and revisit the quotations on the whiteboard from earlier. Ask students about the images that linger. Read the **Top tip** and together decide whether this text describes a setting or simply recounts events.

PPT Use **PPT 3.14a**, if appropriate, to reinforce the structure of the paragraph. Explain that the structure is simple sentence/long complex sentence/complex sentence. Discuss how the conjunctions 'which' and 'when' trigger layers of extra information; 'which' triggers the release of further details about the 'dusty' street, expanding the picture of Pineapple Gardens, and 'when' gives uncle Sarfraz's arrival extra drama.

PPT **Give extra support** by providing the same text but punctuated differently and slightly rewritten on **PPT 3.14b**. Ask students to consider the change in pace between the two texts and the way that drama is created in the original but not in the modified version. Then invite students to describe the different effects. Use **PPT 3.14c** for shared drafting of the long sentence opening paragraph 2 for **Q3**.

Building skills

Read the text on Student Book p. 101 with the class, down to **Q4**. Ask students to convert the paragraph to numbers representing words in each sentence. Paragraph = 8+6+7+7+31. Then ask students to explore the effect of this structure in pairs for **Q4**.

You could then use **PPT 3.14d** to explore the use of personal pronouns and the move from third-person pronouns (*he, his*) to first-person (*me, my*) in the last sentence.

For **Q5**, read the paragraph as a class and draw out the monotony of the sentence structure through discussion. You could ask students to convert the paragraph to numbers again to emphasise the repetitive structure. Then organise students into groups of five and ask them to read the task on **Worksheet 3.14** before giving out strips of paper cut from the worksheet. Ask students to improve their sentences and then recreate the paragraph by reading collaboratively. They will need to evaluate their changes before drafting their own paragraph individually for **Q6** on p. 102.

Developing skills

As a whole class, read the first part of this section up to the end of the four bullet-points. Discuss ways of answering the question: 'How can this be done?' Encourage students to focus on specific techniques. Take suggestions and recap techniques used in previous sections, such as short sentences, specific small details, imagery.

Then read the rest of the text on Student Book p. 102 and evaluate the writer's planning of the first four paragraphs. Make sure that students understand that the plan contains description of *what the writer is going to do* rather than the piece of writing itself. **PPT 3.14e** shows a continuation of the writer's plan and you could use this as a model to support students in completing **Q7**.

Ask students to work in pairs to complete **Q8**. They could use a table to make notes on examples of the writer's use of time and place. Highlight the **Top tip**, which discusses how the character's memory is activated to give further insight about his past.

Give extra challenge by asking students to use the senses that the writer has not used so far. How could sounds have been used to create the present image or that of the past? Or smell? Encourage students to be original but to maintain the style of the original text, for example: *the sounds of bells and slamming desk tops combines with the smell of chalk.* What comparisons could be drawn to fit the description with the one already used, i.e. the writer recalls that he used to *run like the wind.*

Ask students to complete **Q9** on Student Book p. 103 using the description of the abandoned school to prompt ideas for the contrasting description of a modern school. **PPT 3.14f** provides a structure to use in preparation.

Applying skills

Begin by running through the points for **Sound progress** and **Excellent progress** on Student Book p. 103. Then recap the techniques used successfully so far: use of the senses to create a detailed picture in the reader's mind, use of short sentences for contrast or emphasis, establishing a distinct time, place and character with deliberate use of adjectives, adverbs and imagery. Use some images (such as those on **PPT 3.14g**) or sounds to help create the atmosphere for writing about the four settings: the beach, a remote place, a special event or the old abandoned school. Then allow plenty of time for planning, drafting and editing.

Ask students to complete **Q10** independently and extend the time limit to suit individual needs. It might be useful to have a range of reading texts ready for those who finish early, in order to prolong the writing time for the others.

Towards A/A*	Originality is key to gaining high marks in composition. You could encourage students to write less instead of more, giving pithy detail rather than excessive description. For example: *The rain poured and the cricket match was cancelled, which was a disaster for all the people involved in the hours of preparation* could become: *A cricket catastrophe: immeasurable waste and profound disappointment. This special event was to be atypical right from the start.*

15 Narrative writing

Assessment objectives

AO2 Writing
W2 Sequence facts, ideas and opinions
W3 Use a range of appropriate vocabulary
W4 Use register appropriate to audience and context

IGCSE examination

- **Paper 3** Section 2 (Composition) or **Component 4** Coursework Portfolio (Assignment 2)

Differentiated learning outcomes

- **All students must** be able to understand and use some features of good story-telling (Grade E/D).
- **Most students should** be able to create narrative stories using varied sentences and characterisation with vivid language and description (Grade D/C).
- **Some students could** use effective openings and closings, precise sentence structures and powerful characterisation to keep the reader engaged (Grade B/A).

Resources

- **Student Book**: pp. 104–7
- **PPT**: 3.15a–g

Other Student Book pages

- Writing to describe: atmosphere, pp. 98–9
- Writing to describe: structure, pp. 100–3
- Conventions of diaries and journals, pp. 70–1

Exploring skills

Introduce narrative writing to students by running through the **Checklist for success** on Student Book p. 104, which can also be displayed on **PPT 3.15a**. Then ask pairs to quickly come up with any additional features for **Q1**.

In **Q2** show students the model plan for a short story on which is also on **PPT 3.15b**. Ask pairs to come up with any improvements as **Q3** and to present them in **Q4**. Flag up the **Top tip** here so students don't feel trapped by a narrative formula. Try to steer ideas towards originality and away from the obvious plot line and character creation. It might be helpful to have an example ready such as: *The story starts with the humiliating performance, then tracks back to the lack of rehearsal time because the lead singer decided to take his girlfriend out rather than rehearse.*

Give extra support by revisiting the structure of a story: introduction, development, complication, climax, resolution. Explain how a complication can be started on a small scale with hints being dropped that become increasingly more noticeable. Suggest to students the idea that a complication needs feeding like a fire.

Building skills

Ask students to work in fours to put the good story opening techniques listed on Student Book p. 105, into rank order. Take feedback on which feature most of the class prefer. Compare their suggestions to the way films open, especially films derived from books. Then ask students to look at the two examples of story openings (also on **PPT 3.15c**.) Use the PPT to annotate the examples before asking students to work in pairs to complete **Q5**, which requires a title for the two pieces. Suitable titles might be *The Secret, My Little Sister, An Unexpected Visitor, Something Went Bump in the Night*.

Then ask students to work through **Q6** to **Q8**. Support the pairs as necessary. Ideas to emerge may include: *The first example uses dialogue and the second example uses important background information to open the story. They have different approaches in that the first one is first person and the second is third. Both use the same technique of withholding information, which makes the reader want to read on.*

> **Give extra challenge** by selecting students to hold a class debate about which opening is better. You could divide the class into two groups and allocate a chair, speakers and second speakers to debate the issue formally or you could take an open vote then select students to explain the reason why they voted that way.

Recap on the techniques that have been used most effectively to engage the reader. You could finish this section with a statement: *This class believes that opening a story with dialogue (or whichever opening is chosen) is best.*

Developing skills

Explain how characterisation works in narrative by reading the text on on Student Book p. 106. Select some characters from books that the students have read recently and ask: *What did he do? What did he say? What did he look like? What did other people say about him?* You could use 'Pip' in *Great Expectations* or 'Felix' in *Once*, for example.

Now discuss dropping information into a narrative using examples A, B and C. Ask students what was happening? Who was it? What were they like? Explain how each of the three sentences handles the three sets of information at once.

> **Give extra support** by breaking the examples down further:
> A Raf waited for us. He was the leader of our gang. Raf was a large, muscular boy with bushy eyebrows.
> B Our mother scolded us for being late. She had a tongue as sharp as a razor.
> C Jed was unaware of Liu's withering glances. He was feverishly texting on his mobile as he walked along.

Explain how combining several pieces of information into single sentences adds pace and interest to a narrative. Read the **Top tip** about adding clauses with the class then ask students to expand the sentences for **Q9**.

> **Give extra support** by providing models for **Q9**. For the story about 'A disappointing night', pupils could start with: *Priya, the older sister by two years and eight months, looked at her sister with the usual disdain.* Then ask students to complete and compare their sentences embedding information about Lucia.

PPT Students need to write an extended description for **Q10**. It might be helpful to use **PPT 3.15d–f** for this – it shows an example of how to construct a three- or four-part sentence from a group of ideas.

Ask students to read 'The dare' and answer **Q11**. The convincing details are the *chipped front tooth* and the *angry scar*. The hints suggest that the problem will lie with the little sister getting into danger. Revisit the **Top tip** to warn against stereotyping.

> **Give extra challenge** by asking students to write an opening that challenges stereotypes such as frail old ladies or bossy school teachers.

Applying skills

PPT Spend some time recapping all the features of successful narrative writing discussed in this section including the **Checklist for success**. Remind students of the effective openings and closings they have read in this chapter. Then ask them to complete **Q12** independently. You could use **PPT 3.15g** to recap on features too, if appropriate.

Towards A/A*	Successful narrative writing maintains a tight structure. Students working towards A* need to demonstrate effective use of techniques such as flashbacks or multiple narration. Support students in honing these skills by asking them to tell a classic story with events ordered differently or from a different character's viewpoint.

1 Understanding summary questions

Assessment objectives

AO1 Reading

R1 Demonstrate understanding of explicit meanings

R2 Demonstrate understanding of implicit meanings and attitudes

IGCSE examination
- Paper 1 Question 3

Differentiated learning outcomes
- **All students must** understand what a summary is and select some relevant points from a text (Grade G/F).
- **Most students should** pick out the key points of a text and use their own words to write a summary (Grade E/D).
- **Some students could** use concise, precise language to write an effective summary (Grade C).

Resources
- Student Book: pp. 110–11
- Worksheet: 4.1 Summarising information
- PPT: 4.1

Other Student Book pages
- Preparing to answer summary questions (Core), pp. 112–13

Exploring skills

Introduce the idea of summaries, using the opening paragraph of Student Book p. 110. Perhaps, as a quick additional task, get students to summarise one aspect of their weekend (such as their morning routine or what they watched on television) in exactly 25 words.

As a class, read the travel writing extract on Student Book p. 110.

Complete the discussion task from **Q1** by allocating pairs one of the three bullet points. Give the students two or three minutes to summarise their bullet point, then ask them to move around the classroom in order to receive summaries of the other two bullet points from their classmates. Afterwards, discuss which pairs had noted the clearest key points and feed back anything they found difficult.

Building skills

Read through this section on the sample question and the four sample bullet points on p. 111 with the class. Ask the students if there is anything they would add, for example: going back to a man's house and sitting on his roof. Use this opportunity to differentiate between correct responses that describe what he *does* and any incorrect responses that focus instead on what he *thinks* or *feels*.

Afterwards, ask students to work in pairs to complete the **Q2** selection and ordering task and then to feed back. Below is a list of points that students might come up with.

- Relevant points (in a logical order):
    - Work in small group
    - Use boat
    - Sometimes fish using dynamite
    - Have to dive into water
    - Flat-roofed house in orange grove
    - Wives cook
    - Eat fish stew and local fruit
    - Men and women eat separately.

- Irrelevant points:
  - Friendly and hospitable
  - Bad for environment but fun
  - Writer and wife eat with the men
  - Writer and wife don't meet women much.

> **Give extra support** by helping students to put their relevant points into a logical order. Tell one student to read the passage aloud, while the other puts an ascending number by the point as it is read out.
>
> Alternatively, simply ask students to divide their relevant points into things about *work* and things about *home*.

As a class, discuss why some things are relevant to the task and other aren't. Discuss what a logical order for the facts would be and why; explain that this could be achieved by arranging the points chronologically or by grouping them into themes.

Developing skills

Read through **Key terms** on Student Book p. 111, followed by the first **Top tip**. Then read this section and complete the two concision tasks in **Q3** and **Q4** as a class. For **Q3**, the statement could be written on the board and students challenged to come to the front and write underneath as many more concise offerings as they can come up with.

Use the tasks on **Worksheet 4.1** to develop the skill of concise summaries. The texts to be summarised in the second task can also be displayed on **PPT 4.1**. Encourage students to share their ideas and agree who has written the best summary for each bullet point.

Applying skills

Reread the original passage and ask students to complete **Q5**, the selecting and ordering task about the local people and their customs.

Students should include some of the following information in their notes:

- The people are nice and welcoming.
- They fish using dynamite.
- They aren't very considerate of the environment.
- They eat well and healthily.
- Guests are served first.
- Women serve the food and eat last, out of sight.
- Women aren't seen out a lot.
- Women do a lot of domestic or agricultural work.

> **Give extra support** by reminding students to be methodical: in any given question, they should list the relevant phrases, and then put them into the correct order.

During feedback, while listening to their peers' summary lists, ask students to spot any irrelevancies or phrases that would be better placed in a different order. Ask students who identify the latter to come up with suitable alternatives.

Invite students to look back at their work in pairs and decide whether they have reached the **Sound progress** success criteria listed on Student Book p. 111.

2 Preparing to answer summary questions

Assessment objectives

AO1 Reading
- R1 Demonstrate understanding of explicit meanings
- R2 Demonstrate understanding of implicit meanings and attitudes
- R5 Select for specific purposes

IGCSE examination
- **Paper 1** Question 3

Differentiated learning outcomes
- **All students must** understand what a summary is and select some relevant points from a text (Grade G/F).
- **Most students should** pick out the key points of a text and use their own words to write a summary (Grade E/D).
- **Some students could** select only relevant information and write a concise but thorough summary (Grade C).

Resources
- **Student Book**: pp. 112–13
- **Worksheet**:
  4.2 Locating, selecting, ordering and summarising

Other Student Book pages
- Locating information: skimming, pp. 8–9
- Locating information: scanning, pp. 10–13
- Understanding summary questions (Core), pp. 110–11

Exploring skills

As a class, read the **Checklist for success** on Student Book p. 112. If necessary, recap on skills of skimming and scanning (using the Student Book pp. 8–13).

Read through what is expected in the exam. Point out to students that in the exam, the extract they have to summarise will be 300–350 words long. Then read the travel-writing extract about wrestling in Pakistan on Student Book p. 112. Ask students to complete the **Q1** and **Q2** scanning tasks, and then feed back to the class. The text on p. 112 is just under 100 words long, so they should pick out about three key points:

- *shalwar kameez* (compared to baggy trousers), pulled up and tucked into the waist
- turban on the head
- *sundhro* (long, green material) wrapped around the waist.

Students should then complete **Q3** individually, writing their findings up as a short summary, using no more than 50 words.

Building skills

As a class, read the continuation of the travel writing extract. Students should then complete the note-making task in **Q4**. Students' feedback should include:

- aims – get hand inside back of opponent's *sundhro*; throw opponent to the ground
- rules – arms cannot be used in a wrestling grip; legs should be used to trip or overbalance opponent.

Developing skills

Read the section on the importance of ordering information and, for **Q5**, discuss how the details on rules and aims could be ordered. Ensure that students understand the basic idea of covering all the features of one area (such as rules) before they move on to the next (such as aims). Get across to students why it is appropriate to put these things in a chronological order, in order to show how the match would progress. However, make it clear that sometimes different types of ordering (such as by theme, or by cause and effect) will be more appropriate than chronological order.

Applying skills

Ask students to complete **Q6**, making notes on what happens in a typical match, ordering their notes, and then writing them up in their own words, keeping to the word limit of 75 words. You could ask students to focus on the second extract or, to make it a little more challenging, make use of both extracts. (Remind students that the reading passage in the exam will be longer than the extract on p. 113, and their summary will be 100–150 words in length.) Refer students back to the **Checklist for success** on Student Book p. 112, if necessary.

Students might include some of the following information:

- at the start – players help each other wrap their *sundhros* around their waists
- the match – dart about grabbing at each other; try to use legs to overbalance opponent; fast and furious; players try to grab the opponent's *sundhro* and throw him on his back; quite violent; lots of matches going on simultaneously
- after the match – the loser is sometimes knocked out; the audience don't give much consideration to the loser; the victor might help to revive the opponent.

Give extra support by helping students to find and logically order the relevant information. They may also need support with putting their lists of phrases into their own words.

Give extra challenge by encouraging students to be detailed yet concise. Ask them to remove any irrelevant information and try to find places where they can use one or two words instead of several.

During feedback, whilst listening to their peers' summaries, ask students to spot any irrelevancies or phrases that could be more concise. Invite students who identify the latter to come up with a suitable alternative. Ask students to look back at their work and decide whether they have reached the **Sound progress** success criteria listed on Student Book p. 113.

Give extra challenge by asking students to write a paragraph about any subject, and then challenge their partner to summarise it. This could be made more difficult by challenging their partner to summarise a particular aspect of the paragraph.

As an extension, to develop this skill further, hand out **Worksheet 4.2**. Read through the travel brochure extract with the students. Ask them to carry out the task of summarising the different things that a visitor can do when visiting Tokyo, using up to 75 words. As with the previous task, they should list the things that can be done, order them appropriately, and then write their summary in their own words.

Students might include most or all of the following information:

In Tokyo:
- use the railway line for a city tour
- visit Tsukiji fish market and eat sushi
- walk through Ueno Park or the Imperial Gardens
- visit the National Museum or the Palace
- visit temples and shrines
- go shopping in traditional Asakusa or modern areas.

Near Tokyo:
- visit beauty spots, such as Mount Fuji
- visit a sculpture park
- go for walks
- see hot springs and more temples
- get a boat to the Izu islands and go to the beach.

Again, students could assess their work using the **Sound progress** criteria in the Student Book.

3 Understanding summary questions

Assessment objectives

AO1 Reading
R1 Demonstrate understanding of explicit meanings
R2 Demonstrate understanding of implicit meanings and attitudes
R5 Select for specific purposes

IGCSE examination
- Paper 2 Question 3

Differentiated learning outcomes

- **All students must** select some relevant points from a text and write them up as a summary (Grade E/D).
- **Most students should** use concise language to write an effective summary (Grade D/C).
- **Some students could** use varied, complex sentences to construct a thorough and effective summary (Grade B/A).

Resources
- **Student Book**: pp. 114–17
- **Worksheet**: 4.3 Selecting and summarising

Other Student Book pages
- Preparing to answer summary questions (Extended), pp. 118–21

Exploring skills

Use the opening section of Student Book p. 114 to introduce the idea of summaries. Then, as a quick additional task, ask students to summarise their weekend in exactly 30 words. As an extra challenge, ask them to reduce their summary to 20 words and then to 10 words.

As a class, read the **Checklist for success** and the first extract on Student Book p. 114. Ask students to discuss the two bullet points in **Q1** on p. 115 and then to carry out **Q2**. Feed back as a class; students' comments should include the following.

- How the writer intended to spend the night:
    - staying low in his canoe, tied to a tree
- What he did wrong:
    - should have untied the bowline
    - shouldn't have underestimated the current
- Problems experienced by the author:
    - drift logs hitting the canoe
    - too dark to see them coming
    - current fast and rocking the canoe
    - lost control of the canoe
    - couldn't reach to untie the bowline.

Read the second extract on Student Book p. 115 and, using the table at the top of **Worksheet 4.3**, complete the task of summarising information (table headings are based on **Q3**). Students should share their ideas in pairs and feed back as a class. Their comments may include:

- Trying to get out of danger
    - by cutting the rope
- What happened to him and his canoe
    - the canoe being caught/pulled around by the current
    - the canoe tipping and taking in water
    - the author hitting a crossbar/thwart
    - the canoe submerging – then levelling off.

Give extra support for Q3 by helping students to use the glossary to cope with the unusual language.

Building skills

As a class, read through the advice about the importance of being selective and concise during the note-making and writing up stages. Get students to complete **Q4** in pairs and then to do the task using the bottom half of **Worksheet 4.3** to complete the mindmap for **Q5**. Students might include:

4(a) The author had a basic meal (a picnic of beans, bread and a tomato).

4(b) The meal made him think of his brother.

5(a) The dangers of tidal canoeing are:
- driftwood
- unexpected strong currents
- the canoe tipping over and/or taking in water
- the possibility of drowning
- being injured by hitting things.

5(b) The author tries to cope with them by:
- tying up his equipment
- tightening the strap on his glasses
- trying to cut the bowline so the canoe can follow the flow of the river
- holding on to the sides of the canoe.

Read through the first section of Student Book p. 116, and discuss **Q6** in relation to the students' own responses to **Q5**. As a class, discuss which points they think are irrelevant (the picnic, his brother, Mitchinson having tied the canoe to a branch, and him really loving danger) and why.

Developing skills

Read through this section, making sure that students understand the difference between a complex sentence and a simple sentence. Ask students to work through **Q7** on p. 117, using the notes on Student Book p. 116 (or the second half of **Worksheet 4.3**) to write their summary. Remind student of the **Top tip** on Student Book p. 117 suggesting how to deal with vocabulary that they are not used to.

Ask students to swap their responses with a partner and, using the **Sound progress** and **Excellent progress** criteria at the end of the Student Book p. 117, assess whether they have made sound or excellent progress.

As a class, listen to a few examples of work that displays excellent progress; students should pay particular attention to examples of concision and the use of complex sentences.

Applying skills

For **Q8**, ask students to look back at their notes from **Q4** (on what kind of meal he had and what it made him think). In pairs, they should write their points up as two complex sentences.

As an extension, tell them to look back at **Q3** at the top of **Worksheet 4.3** on what the writer did in the second part of the passage to try to get out of danger and what happened to him and his canoe. In pairs, ask them to use a complex sentence to summarise these aspects.

Towards A/A*	To achieve the highest marks for Paper 2 Question 3, students need to select information accurately and thoroughly, then summarise it in a concise manner. They also need to consider their written expression and use varied, complex sentences.

4 Preparing to answer summary questions

Assessment objectives
AO1 Reading
- **R1** Demonstrate understanding of explicit meanings
- **R2** Demonstrate understanding of implicit meanings and attitudes
- **R5** Select for specific purposes

IGCSE examination
- **Paper 2** Question 3

Differentiated learning outcomes
- **All students must** select some relevant points from a text and write them up as a summary (Grade E/D).
- **Most students should** use concise language to write an effective summary in their own words (Grade D/C).
- **Some students could** use varied, complex sentences to construct a thorough and effective summary (Grade B/A).

Resources
- **Student Book**: pp. 118–21
- **Worksheets**:
  4.4a Rewriting in your own words
  4.4b Analysing summary responses

Other Student Book pages
- Locating information: skimming, pp. 8–9
- Locating information: scanning, pp. 10–13
- Understanding summary questions (Extended), pp. 114–17

Exploring skills

Read this section on p. 118 of the Student Book on answering summary questions, and the usefulness of skimming and scanning skills. If necessary, recap on skills of skimming and scanning (using the Student Book pp. 8–13).

As a class, read Passage A, part 1 on Student Book p. 118, followed by the **Top tip**. Ask students to complete **Q1**, making a list of phrases about what worries the writer regarding the bus journey. Point out to students that some key phrases are similar, so they should try to collate a variety. Phrases in the class feedback might include:

- 'get me killed'
- 'grisly mountain bus crashes'
- '40 people were killed' or 'eight people died'
- 'bus plunged into a tributary' or 'fell into a gorge' or 'plummeted to certain death'
- 'dangerous curves'
- 'valley 300 metres below'.

Building skills

As a class, read the continuation of Passage A on Student Book p. 119 and the advice in the **Top tip**. Hand out **Worksheet 4.4a**, which will help students to complete **Q2**. Remind them to write their notes in their own words. Chosen phrases may include:

- 'what had formerly been the road lying…20 metres down the mountain'
- 'screech to a halt'
- 'carve a makeshift dirt track'
- 'follow on foot at a safe distance'.

> **Give extra support** by helping students to come up with alternative words and to be aware of words that they don't need to try to change (specific nouns which do not have many synonyms, such as road, track or mountain).

Developing skills

As a class, read Passage B. Using the second half of **Worksheet 4.4a**, ask students to complete **Q3** by finding seven phrases that show the problems with road travel and rewriting them in their own words. Problems selected will include:

1. the bus was very crowded
2. she had a stomach upset and there was no toilet
3. merchants tried to sell her things at the bus stop
4. other passengers pulled and prodded her
5. there were animals on board
6. it was extremely hot
7. she felt conspicuous as the only white person.

During feedback, ask students to spot whether anyone is *not* using their own words (and encourage them to come up with alternative words).

Applying skills

For **Q4**, ask students to look back at **Worksheet 4.4a** and their notes on Passage B. Ask students to work in pairs, arranging the points that they have made about the problems with road travel into a spider diagram. Using the prompts from Student Book p. 121, they should link similar points together and then number them in a logical order.

> **Give extra support** by helping students to group similar ideas from the passage together to avoid repetition.
>
> **Give extra challenge** by pushing students to consider the effects of ordering their information in different ways.

Now ask students to work independently on the **Q5** task of summarising the different problems with road travel that are described in Passage B. Make sure that they use their spider diagrams to help them order their writing. Remind them to use their own words and not to exceed the word limit of 100–150 words. (Explain to students that in the exam, they will read a longer passage than this, which means they will find up to 15 key points and their summary will be 200–250 words in length.)

> **Give extra support** by helping students to begin sentences (such as, *One problem with bus travel is…* or *The writer also describes…*), and ensuring that they maintain relevance.
>
> **Give extra challenge** by encouraging students to use complex sentences in order to make their summary concise and gain marks for written variety.

Distribute **Worksheet 4.4b**. Ask students to carry out the task of reading through the sample answers and discussing why the first response is stronger than the second. Focus on how the second answer includes irrelevance, the student's own opinions, and comparison, as well as copying words directly from the original text. Explore how the first answer achieves a concise, controlled summary and uses a much wider variety of complex sentences.

Students should then review their work in pairs and, using the **Sound progress** and **Excellent progress** criteria on Student Book p. 121, assess how well they have done and how to improve.

Towards A/A*	To achieve the highest marks for Paper 2 Question 3, students need to select information accurately and thoroughly, and summarise it in a concise, controlled manner. They also need to consider their written expression and use varied, complex sentences, as these questions offer marks for a sophisticated writing style.

1 Understanding comprehension questions

Assessment objectives

AO1 Reading

R1 Demonstrate understanding of explicit meanings
R2 Demonstrate understanding of implicit meanings and attitudes
R5 Select for specific purposes

IGCSE examination
- Paper 1 Question 1

Differentiated learning outcomes
- **All students must** understand that there are three types of comprehension question and be able to recognise the wording of each type (Grade G/F).
- **Most students should** be able to select words required to answer a basic literal comprehension question (Grade E).
- **Some students could** use synonyms and inferences to answer all types of comprehension questions (Grade D/C).

Resources
- **Student Book**: pp. 132–3
- **Worksheet**: 5.1 How do we make inferences?

Other Student Book pages
- Selecting information, pp. 14–15
- Explicit meaning, pp. 16–19
- Implicit meaning, pp. 20–27

Exploring skills

Explain that understanding literal meaning is a skill that is required to tackle any form of assessment in the Cambridge IGCSE – indeed, it is tested explicitly in some parts of the formal examination paper. (You could show students past papers and identify the question where these skills are examined.)

Read the two sample questions on Student Book p. 132 and ask students to identify the key words: 'State' and 'What'. Unpick the meaning of the word 'state' – link it to the word 'statement' and explore the contexts in which this is used (for example, a statement is often taken in a situation where legal proceedings may ensue). Discuss that both words require a specific, fact-based answer, not an opinion or interpretation. Ask students to write down their definitions of these key words.

> **Give extra support** by encouraging some students to revisit the skills of selection covered in Section 1. They could work through Student Book pp. 8–27 and more specifically pp.14–15.
>
> **Give extra challenge** by setting a quick internet-based task, whereby students have to create a fact-file explaining (a) what a hurricane is and (b) five effects of a recent hurricane such as Hurricane Irma on Florida. This will consolidate their ability to select fact from opinion or analysis.

Read the extract in **Q1** aloud and ask students to consider what question **(a)** is asking them to find. Draw attention to the wording 'Florida in the hurricane season'. This suggests that they are looking for general things, not specific damage or things that happened in 1984. They may focus on 'we were nervous', but this is about the people not Florida. They may then focus in on 'the storm approaching'. This would be a correct point to note down, as it suggests that during hurricane season there are storms or it is stormy.

They may ponder the significance of the word 'wild', which would require inference and so is not the correct answer, but in fact later the ideas intimated by 'wild' are made explicit by the phrase 'a huge gust of wind'.

Ask students to tackle question **(b)** without help. They should find two things: the house roof removed and the golf clubs displaced. Take answers from students and discourage them from making generalisations, such as 'buildings damaged' or 'objects moved/blown away'. When the question is closed like this, it is best to use the specific example given.

Building skills

Ask students what a *synonym* is (referring them to the **Key terms** box). You may wish to consolidate this with a quick-fire quiz finding synonyms for five phrases from the passage: *board up, bring in, evacuate, pile in, take off*. Suggestions for each might include: 'cover over', 'gather in/lead in', 'leave/abandon', 'get in together/squeeze in', 'remove'.

Explain that there is a second type of comprehension question that tests this ability. Take them through the task outlined in **Q2** on Student Book p. 133 where they look for the key words that tell them they need to find synonyms (i.e. 'Using your own words'). They could add these key words to their notes about 'State' and 'What'.

Ask students to work in pairs and create a question that focuses on a specific word or phrase (as **(b)** does) to replace questions **(a)** and **(c)**. For example, for **(a)**, they could suggest: *'Using your own words, explain what the writer means by "evacuate our homes".'*

Developing skills

Introduce the idea that there is a third type of comprehension question that requires students to *interpret* what they have read and to draw new ideas from it. Ask them if they know what this skill is called (i.e. inference).

> **Give extra support** by directing students back to pp. 20–27, where they can review the skills of inference and deduction.
>
> **Give extra challenge** by asking students who are confident that they can define inference to create a poster explaining the 'clues' that can help us to draw conclusions about people and places in texts. (This recaps ideas covered in Chapter 1 of the Student Book, but the activity could also be completed by students who have not studied that chapter.) To complete this challenge, students can use the task on **Worksheet 5.1**.

Invite students individually to identify the wording that tells them that this is a question where inference is expected: 'suggest about'. Once again they can add this to their notes.

Students can then complete **Q3** on Student Book p. 133 individually.

Applying skills

Ask students to look at the notes they have made during the course of the lesson. They now have the clues that will help them to identify the three types of comprehension question. Ask them to write down a definition for each of the three question types and how to recognise them.

Before students complete **Q4** individually, it is worth reminding them that to achieve a high standard on Paper 1, they need to be able to recognise the kind of answer that is required and provide it. They also need to pay close attention to time management so as to gain a high mark out of the total of 20 across the sub-questions in Question 1 (the comprehension questions).

Once students have finished Q4, invite them to peer-assess their answers in pairs, using the **Sound progress** criteria on Student Book p. 133.

2 Preparing to answer comprehension questions

Assessment objectives

AO1 Reading

- **R1** Demonstrate understanding of explicit meanings
- **R2** Demonstrate understanding of implicit meanings and attitudes
- **R5** Select for specific purposes

IGCSE examination

- Paper 1 Question 1

Differentiated learning outcomes

- **All students must** be able to recognise the wording that tells them where to find answers and how many answers to select (Grade G/F).
- **Most students should** be able to select words required to answer a basic literal comprehension question (Grade E).
- **Some students could** use synonyms and inferences to answer all types of comprehension questions (Grade D/C).

Resources

- **Student Book**: pp. 134–5
- **Worksheet**: 5.2 Proms – comprehension questions
- **PPT**: 5.2a–h

Other Student Book pages

- Selecting information, pp. 14–15
- Explicit meaning, pp. 16–19
- Implicit meaning, pp. 20–27

Exploring skills

Explain that the purpose of this lesson is to make sure that students know how to locate, and then write up, the answers to comprehension questions.

Ask students if they know what a prom is. If they do not, explain that it is a formal leaving party for students finishing school or college and that it often involves quite extensive preparations and activities, such as hiring/making evening dresses and attending formal dinners. Proms are often much enjoyed by family members and younger students, who sometimes line up to await the arrival of the prom guests at their venue. There is plenty of footage of proms on the internet.

Show slides **PPT 5.2a** and **5.2c**, which contain the two sample questions from Student Book p. 134 and ask students which words tell them where they can find the answers. Then show answers using slides **PPT 5.2b** and **5.2d**. Ask students to discuss **Q1** either as a whole class or in small groups.

> **Give extra support** by asking students to work through Student Book pp.10 and 11 in Chapter 1, which teach the ways in which key words can be used to help the reader to find information.
>
> **Give extra challenge** by asking students to write the answers to **Q1** parts **(a)**, **(b)** and **(c)**.

Building skills

Remind students that some questions will require them to explain what words mean by using their own words. Ask them what the term is for when they replace a word with another with a similar meaning. (They should remember the word *synonym* from Lesson 1.) Explain that there are sometimes no synonyms for a word, or the synonym would be so clumsy and wordy that it would be a waste of effort to create it.

Look at the examples given in **Q2** on Student Book p. 135 and explain that the brackets mean that those words do not have to be reworded. They are not the focus of the question. You could use sequins, nails and hair as examples of where a synonym would not be appropriate, as these are nouns that are hard to replace succinctly.

Ask students to complete **Q2**, using the top part of **Worksheet 5.2** to write their answers.

> **Give extra support** by suggesting that students consider other words similar to those they have to give synonyms for. For instance, 'slicked back' could be worked on by using the word 'slick'. Students may have heard of the term 'oil slick', which would help them understand a slick as a wet, smooth area – hence, 'slicked' means made smooth and shiny by being wetted.
>
> **Give extra challenge** by asking students to each create a collage of images to help weaker students to visualise one of the key words that need to be explained.

Developing skills

Read on and remind students that in Lesson 1 they came across some of this third type of comprehension question, i.e. one that involves inference.

Read the extract aloud. Ask students whose viewpoint the text is written from. Ensure that they understand the term 'paparazzi' and why both prom-goers and teachers would be keen to have photographs.

Ask students to complete the table for **Q3** in pairs, using the bottom half of **Worksheet 5.2** to note down their answers. If they have difficulty with the first quotation, 'like paparazzi', use the following prompt questions:

- Why might it be important for the prom goers to have photographs of the event?
- Can they take pictures of themselves?
- Would members of the public be allowed to get near them if they were just getting out of cars?
- Would members of the public be allowed in the prom venue?
- How would the teachers be feeling about their students on this occasion?
- Why might it be important for younger students/the general public to see photographs of this event?

If students have problems with the second phrase, 'formed a human shield', then use the image on **PPT 5.2e**.

Applying skills

Ask students to complete **Q4** independently using what they have learnt from exploring the word 'paparazzi' and the image of a 'human shield'.

More confident students may wish to also consider the effect of 'bossily' and 'like bouncers'. Explain that knowing how long to make an answer will depend upon the number of marks available for it. Generally, a question worth one mark would demand a simple one-part answer. In this case, there are two main things that the teachers do, so a minimum of two marks would probably be given. For three or four marks, other aspects of the explanation could be explored.

Use **PPT 5.2f–h** to model an extended answer. Explain to students that both answers show an understanding of what the teachers were doing, but the first gives far more explanation and a range of possible answers and would, therefore, gain more marks if they were available.

Then invite pairs to peer-assess their answers using the advice above and the **Sound progress** criteria on Student Book p. 135.

You may wish to remind the class that higher-achieving students will locate the words needed to answer a question quickly and with relative ease. They will write their answer up confidently, knowing where to look for words and deciding whether their own words or inferences are needed. They will also be able to phrase answers comfortably.

3 Understanding writer's effects questions: explaining meanings

Assessment objectives

AO1 Reading

R1 Demonstrate understanding of explicit meanings

R2 Demonstrate understanding of implicit meanings and attitudes

IGCSE examination
- Paper 1 Question 1

Differentiated learning outcomes

- **All students must** explain the meaning of basic words that they encounter (Grade G/F).
- **Most students should** infer and explain the meaning of words and phrases, usually putting them into their own words (Grade E/D).
- **Some students could** infer and explain the meaning of challenging words and phrases, putting them into their own words (Grade C).

Resources
- **Student Book**: pp. 136–7
- **Worksheet**: 5.3 Understanding writer's effects questions
- **PPT**: 5.3a–g

Other Student Book pages
- Preparing to answer writer's effects questions (Core), pp. 138–9

Exploring skills

Remind students of the two skills they will need to answer the questions on a writer's effects in Paper 1:

- locate the section of the passage that the question refers to
- explain the meaning and analyse the effect of these choices using your own words.

Read through the **Exploring skills** section on Student Book p. 136, including the extract, and use the **Key terms** box to ensure that students understand the importance of context and the usefulness of synonyms.

Using **PPT 5.3a–d**, work through the bullet points for **Q1** in order to explore the possible meaning of the word 'expectant'. Student answers could either be written on the whiteboard in the spaces provided, or possible answers can be made to appear automatically (in blue text) after each mini-discussion by clicking the PPT.

Building skills

Explain to the students that when explaining what a word means, the best answers do not use the words from the text but offer concise summary that shows understanding of the meaning. Answers that rely on lifting words or phrases from the text, and show little or no understanding, may not be awarded any marks.

Using **PPT 5.3e–f**, explore the three answers given in **Q2** on Student Book p. 137. Begin by deciding how many of the three answers are correct, and then discuss which of the remaining two answers is the best and why. (The correct answers can be displayed by clicking on the PPT slides.)

> **Give extra support**, when showing **PPT 5.3f**, by ensuring that students understand that, while the first explanation is as correct as the second explanation, its use of the word 'expecting' is too close to 'expectant' – this could suggest to the examiner that the word has not been fully understood.

Developing skills

Ask students to complete **Q3** in their pairs.

Use **PPT 5.3g** to remind students of the process they should follow in order to explore the word 'enlightened':

- What is the context or situation?
- Who are 'waiting to be enlightened'?
- What other similar words come to mind?

As a final check, ask students:

- Have you written your explanation in your own words?

> **Give extra support** by handing out **Worksheet 5.3**. Read through the example given (deconstructing the word 'wide-eyed'), then help students to fill in the table for 'enlightened' and to come up with a possible definition.

After five minutes, ask the students to move around the classroom comparing answers. During feedback, they should suggest which was the best answer that they heard and why. Focus the students on the two success criteria:

1. explaining the meaning of the word accurately
2. using their own words.

Applying skills

Read through this section of the Student Book on p. 137, including the extract and the **Top tip**. Ask students to complete the **Q4** tasks, using the system that they have been practising this lesson.

- What is the context or situation?
- What other similar words come to mind?
- What other clues can you use – for example, how do the people described as being 'grateful' and 'accusing' feel, or how does a snake move?
- Have you written your explanation in your own words?

During feedback, possible responses might be:

- 'snaked' suggests they moved in a line, following the twists and turns of the street
- 'grateful' suggests he was thankful to the man for helping him
- 'accusing' suggests the boy felt the teacher had done something wrong or had let them down.

> **Give extra support** by helping the students to work out what is happening in the text and what people are thinking or feeling. With the first bullet point, ask them to think of how a snake moves and how this might link to a group of students walking through a city centre.
>
> **Give extra challenge** by asking students to think about what other phrases in the texts suggest to us. For example, they could consider why the teacher only gives a 'nod of the head', or how the use of two questions links to Billy being 'accusing'.

Invite the students to move around the classroom comparing answers. During feedback, get them to identify who had come up with the best responses and why. Focus them again on the two success criteria: explaining the meaning of the word accurately and using their own words.

Finally, ask pairs to look at the **Sound progress** criteria on Student Book p. 137 and self-assess how well they have done.

4 Preparing to answer writer's effects questions

Assessment objectives
AO1 Reading
- R2 Demonstrate understanding of implicit meanings and attitudes
- R4 Demonstrate understanding of how writers achieve effects

IGCSE examination
- Paper 1 Question 1

Differentiated learning outcomes
- **All students must** be able to explain what words might mean, and whether they suggest something positive or negative (Grade G/F).
- **Most students should** explain how words are used by authors to convey meaning (Grade E/D).
- **Some students could** use technical language to analyse how a range of words convey explicit and some implicit meanings (Grade C).

Resources
- **Student Book**: pp. 138–9
- **Worksheets**:
  5.4a How words and phrases suggest ideas and emotions
  5.4b Exploring parts of a sentence and word classes

Other Student Book pages
- Understanding writer's effects questions: explaining meanings, pp. 136–7

Exploring skills

As a class, use the opening paragraph on Student Book p. 138 to discuss the meaning of the phrase 'implicit meanings' from the Assessment objective R2. As an example, you could ask students what a 'house' is, and then ask them how the word 'home' is different. What extra implied meaning is there (such as warmth, family, identity)?

Afterwards, read through the **Q1** extract, bullet points, **Top tip**, table and commentary, ensuring that students understand how the effect of the word 'plucked' has been analysed.

> **Give extra support** by talking about synonyms for 'plucked' so students understand how it sounds more aggressive. Ask them which of these words sounds worst and why: *take, remove, pluck*.
>
> **Give extra challenge**, if doing the above as a class, by asking students to think of synonyms that could sound more aggressive (for example: *wrench, rip, grab, haul*).

Building skills

For **Q2**, re-read the extract on Student Book p. 138, then hand out **Worksheet 5.4a**. Ask them to fill in the table in pairs, and then feed back as a class. Ideas might include the following:

- The verb 'dumped' suggests he was dropped or thrown into the house by something stronger than him, as if he was worthless. This contrasting image of weakness and power suggests how helpless he was.
- The verb 'forced' means being made to do something. It implies strength and power being used against the boy. Again, it suggests he was helpless because he didn't have a choice in what was happening and he couldn't stop it.

> **Give extra challenge** by getting students to also consider the effects of other powerful words in the quotations (such as 'beautiful', 'crumbling' and 'crowded').

Developing skills

Read through this section on Student Book p. 139. Then ask students to complete Task 1 on **Worksheet 5.4b**, to make sure that they understand the idea of subject, verb and object as parts of a sentence, as well as the idea of word classes.

As a class, discuss **Q3** on Student Book p. 139. Then ask students to look over their work from **Q2** and check that they have mentioned that 'dumped' and 'forced' are verbs; if they haven't, work together as a class to rephrase their sentences to include information about word classes. This will provide the answers to **Q4**.

> **Give extra support** by doing additional work on word classes. Put a random list of words on the board (verbs, nouns, adjectives). Ask students to come up and circle a verb, or an adjective, etc.
>
> **Give extra challenge**, if doing the additional word class task above, by asking students how they could turn some of the adjectives into adverbs (often just by adding –ly at the end).

Applying skills

Read the extract about the Juvenile Home on Student Book p. 139, and ask students to complete **Q5**. Before they begin working, read through the **Checklist for success** as a class. To help them with this task, students could work in pairs completing Task 2 on **Worksheet 5.4b**.

> **Give extra support** by helping students to work out the meaning of each of the words in bold. With the word 'ramshackle', ask them to consider whether it sounds positive or negative, and get them to imagine what a desk in a really old classroom might look like.
>
> **Give extra challenge** by encouraging students to include references to word classes and to consider how each word links to details in the rest of the extract on Student Book 139.

Feed back as a class. Responses might include:

- 'cramped' suggests the Home is uncomfortable and not big enough to cope with the number of children. This might also tell us that students wouldn't be able to concentrate and wouldn't get enough help or attention.
- 'ramshackle' suggests that, like the rest of the Home, the classroom is old and has fallen into disrepair. This might imply that the people running the Home don't care about the children's education and don't have suitable resources for learning.
- 'cracked' also shows the state of disrepair; the blackboard would be difficult to read and this again shows their lack of commitment to educating the children.

As you discuss students' ideas, ask them to look back at the **Checklist for success** and the **Sound progress** criteria on Student Book p. 139 to assess how well they have done.

5 Understanding writer's effects questions

Assessment objectives
AO1 Reading
R4 Demonstrate understanding of how writers achieve effects

IGCSE examination
- Paper 2 Question 2

Differentiated learning outcomes
- **All students must** select appropriate quotations and be able to describe what they suggest (Grade E/D).
- **Most students should** select a number of relevant quotations and begin to explain their effect (Grade D/C).
- **Some students could** select a range of brief quotations and analyse different effects on the reader (Grade B/A).

Resources
- **Student Book**: pp. 140–1
- **Worksheet**:
  5.5 Exploring a writer's effects further

Other Student Book pages
- Vocabulary, pp. 48–9
- Preparing to answer writer's effects questions (Extended), pp. 142–5

Exploring skills

Read through the advice about language questions in the first paragraph on Student Book p. 140, along with the sample question. Emphasise the point that writers choose words in order to create effects very deliberately, and then read the extract. Ask students, in pairs, to read the **Q1** speech bubbles and decide which of these offers comments on the language effects achieved by the writer.

During feedback, explore why the second speech bubble is the best; discuss what is wrong with the first speech bubble (there's some commentary on effect, but it doesn't comment on specific language and focuses more on an irrelevant opinion from the reader) and the third speech bubble (it offers a good selection of language, and shows clear understanding of meaning, but there is no exploration of the effect it is meant to have on the reader).

> **Give extra challenge** by encouraging students to comment specifically on the effect of the word 'raged' and seeing if they can identify that the phrase as a whole is a simile (the clue being in the word 'like' – see Student Book p. 49).

Building skills

Read through this section on Student Book p. 141 and, as a class, explore the different effects achieved in the bullet-pointed quotations. Comments could include:

- The words 'plucked' and 'dumped' suggest a sudden and horrible event, while 'beautiful' and 'crumbling' create a good contrast.
- The simile implies that even nature is ill, as if there is no hope left; it is also an example of pathetic fallacy – nature reflecting the narrator's feelings.
- The long sentence builds up description and keeps the audience waiting; the two short sentences create excitement, revealing the beach and making us dwell on it. (You may like to explain to abler students that the short sentence, 'The beach.' is termed a 'minor sentence' – although it does not have a main verb, it can be understood as a complete unit of meaning. As well as being of use in their own writing, they could use the term in their responses to writer's effects questions.)

For **Q2**, ask students to discuss other techniques that authors use to create effects. Responses might include: first-person or third-person narrative, dual narratives, the use of different senses, cliffhangers, creation of mood, different styles of writing such as dialogue or diary form.

Developing skills

Show students how the example in italics on Student Book p. 141 links to the second bullet point in **Building skills**. Ask them to choose either the first or the third point to complete **Q3**. Share suggestions from their sentences. These might include:

- In the first example: *the narrator was shocked by the sudden move*, or *is bitter about where he currently lives.*
- In the third example: *the narrator seems to sense danger*, or *thinks that he/she has failed*, or *is excited/relieved by the sight of the beach.*

Give extra support by asking students to focus on the last two sentences of the third bullet-point example ('sentence variety').

Give extra challenge by encouraging students to pick out the range of feelings that the narrator has in the third bullet-point example, group them into separate sentences, and relate them to specific words or phrases.

Extend skills in identifying language and its effects through getting students to work in pairs on the task on **Worksheet 5.5**. As a class, discuss how effective the text about the abandoned house is at creating a creepy atmosphere. Consider the effect of specific vocabulary, images, sentence structures and grammar.

Applying skills

Read through the extract and ask students to write their paragraph for **Q4**, offering as much detail as they can.

Give extra challenge by encouraging students to complete part **(b)** of the **Q4** task as well. Ask them to focus on how language, sentence structure and grammatical features convey what the Juvenile Home is like, what the teachers are like, and how the young people are made to feel. The **Applying skills** section in the previous lesson plan also contains some ideas that may be helpful to start them off.

Share paragraphs as a class. Responses might include:

- Vocabulary – the pronoun 'they' sounds mysterious and threatening; the 'van' and the 'wire-meshed windows' create a sense of being trapped.
- Imagery – the simile shows he is being treated like an animal; his lack of value is emphasised by the repetition of 'stray' and the fact that he is not put 'up for sale'.
- Sentence variety – the shortness of the first four sentences makes the image stand out, emphasising the feeling/sense of disgust at how he is treated.

Ask pairs to review their paragraphs together and then focus them on the **Sound progress** and **Excellent progress** criteria at the bottom of the Student Book p. 141. Draw their attention to the difference in skills for making 'sound progress' and making 'excellent progress':

- selecting suitable words, compared to selecting the most powerful words
- explaining meaning, compared to exploring the effect of specific words and techniques.

Invite students to consider how well they have done and what they need to remember next time in order to improve.

Towards A/A*	To gain the highest marks for reading, students need to carefully select the 'best' phases from the text. These will allow them to explain *how* the author is achieving an effect, rather than just showing *what* the author is writing about. Students need to refer to a range of specific literary techniques, sentence structures and grammatical features (such as simile, metaphor, lists, short sentences, adverbs, pronouns and tense), and consider how they affect and imply meaning.

6 Preparing to answer writer's effects questions

Assessment objectives

AO1 Reading
- R2 Demonstrate understanding of implicit meanings and attitudes
- R4 Demonstrate understanding of how writers achieve effects

IGCSE examination
- Paper 2 Question 2

Differentiated learning outcomes

- **All students must** be able to identify relevant words or phrases and explain their meaning (Grade E/D).
- **Most students should** identify a range of relevant phrases and explain what they suggest (Grade D/C).
- **Some students could** select and analyse the effects of a text's most powerful, interesting descriptions (Grade B/A).

Resources
- **Student Book**: pp. 142–5
- **Worksheets**:
  5.6a Analysing a writer's effects
  5.6b Using the language of analysis
- **PPT**: 5.6a–f

Other Student Book pages
- Understanding writer's effects questions (Extended), pp. 140–1

Exploring skills

As a class, read the **Checklist for success** on Student Book p. 142 (checking for understanding of terms like 'sensory or emotive appeals') and ensure students understand the idea of inference.

Complete the short extension task on inference, using **PPT 5.6a**, which includes a few lines from *A Christmas Carol* by Charles Dickens. Students might come up with the following inferences about the place:

- It's winter; the cold is quite painful but also makes people miserable.
- There isn't much light, partly because of the gloomy weather and partly because the city buildings block natural light.
- Inside the buildings it is really smoky, from people's fires to keep warm.
- The fog is damp and is everywhere; it seems unstoppable, like a person attacking.
- You can hardly see the other buildings because it is dark and the fog is so thick, and this makes the city look creepy.

Then, as a class, read through the first *Set in Stone* extract on Student Book p. 142 and ask students to complete the **Q1** synonyms task. Invite feedback as a class.

Give extra support by helping students to identify which words could be altered. For example: 'screech' (scream, call, howl), 'unseen' (hidden, veiled, invisible), 'creature' (animal, monster, beast), 'faintest' (slightest, quietest, barely perceptible).

Give extra challenge by inviting students to consider how different words can change the atmosphere of the writing by having different emotional or sensory associations. For example, if you change the word 'creature' to 'animal', it sounds less mysterious, but if you change it to 'monster', it sounds more frightening.

Building skills

Read through and complete **Q2, Q3** and **Q4** (selecting phrases, discussing why they create a sense of mystery, writing analysis) and the **Top tip** on Student Book p. 143. Use **PPT 5.6b–d** to structure these tasks and any feedback.

Read the second extract from *Set in Stone* on Student Book p. 143, as well as the two bullet points that follow.

88 • Lesson 6 © HarperCollins Publishers 2013

PPT

Read through **Q5** and show students how the text has been annotated; hand out **Worksheet 5.6a** and ask students to complete the task of highlighting and analysing words that create effects or feelings. Pairs should then share their ideas and, for **Q6**, do Task 2 on **Worksheet 5.6a**, and write a short response. Use **PPT 5.6e** to discuss the sample response provided. Then take oral feedback.

> **Give extra support** by providing students with prompts to start their comments. For example: *The phrase 'very isolated spot' is effective because…*, or *A sense of loneliness is created by the phrase…*
>
> **Give extra challenge** by encouraging students to consider the different feelings that the writer evokes in the reader.

As an extension, hand out **Worksheet 5.6b** to build up students' analytical vocabulary and show how analysis can be structured. Ask pairs to use the vocabulary bank to fill in the gaps. Not all phrases need to be used and some could be used more than once.

Developing skills

As a class, read the extract on Student Book p. 144 and then the **Top tip**. Ask students to use the bullet points in **Q7** to make notes on the extract. They might begin with:

- *In this passage a man is searching for grouse. He climbs up…*
- *The weather is wintry ('cold… frosted'). We are also told that…*
- *The setting is a forest which seems dark and endless ('grey monotony of beech and maple'). The setting also seems…*
- *The man cannot find any grouse, which is emphasised by the repeated short sentence, 'No birds'. He also imagines that the birds are…*

Applying skills

Read through the example question, the suggestions on how to approach the question, the sample response, and the annotations. Then set **Q8**, asking students to write up their answer to part **(b)** of the question.

> **Give extra support** by providing students with prompts to start their comments. For example: *In the narrator's fantasy, being able to fly makes him feel…*

Feed back as a class. Emphasise the importance of selecting techniques and use 'particularly powerful' words to exemplify this. Comments might include:

- The repetition of 'could' shows imagining the impossible.
- The verb 'glide' is used to suggest a feeling of power, grace or majesty.
- The adjectives 'smug, feathery' suggest that grouse frustrate him.
- Comparing himself to an 'old ogre' and the birds to 'darling princesses' shows he likes killing them, regardless of how nice they are or how it makes him seem.
- The list of three negative words ('impenetrable, confusing, secretive') contrasts with words like 'smile' and 'glide' to show the difficulty of hunting in reality.
- The description of the sky suggests a lack of hope, which is emphasised by the final short, blunt sentence.

PPT These bullet points can be shown to the class on **PPT 5.6f**.

Ask individuals to use the **Sound progress** and **Excellent progress** criteria on Student Book p. 145 to consider how well they have done and how they could improve.

> **Towards A/A*** To achieve the highest marks for reading, students need to select the text's most original or evocative words and phrases, alongside literary techniques, sentence structures and grammatical features. This range of devices needs to be grouped logically to offer considered analysis of how feelings and ideas are conveyed.

1 Understanding extended response questions

Assessment objectives

AO1 Reading

- **R1** Demonstrate understanding of explicit meanings
- **R2** Demonstrate understanding of implicit meanings and attitudes
- **R5** Select for specific purposes

AO2 Writing

- **W1** Articulate experience and express what is thought, felt and imagined
- **W2** Sequence facts, ideas and opinions
- **W3** Use a range of appropriate vocabulary
- **W4** Use register appropriate to audience and context
- **W5** Make accurate use of spelling, punctuation and grammar

Differentiated learning outcomes

- **All students must** highlight words from the text that influence their response (Grade E/D).
- **Most students should** explain how certain responses match or don't match the highlighted words in the task (Grade D/C).
- **Some students could** explain the full potential and requirements of a task based on highlighting key elements of a question (Grade C).

IGCSE examination

- Paper 1 Question 2

Resources

- **Student Book**: pp. 158–9
- **PPT**: 6.1a–e
- **Worksheet**: 6.1 What voice and tone?

Other Student Book pages

- Developing an extended response (Core), pp. 160–1

Exploring skills

Display the sample question from **Exploring Skills** on Student Book p. 158, using **PPT 6.1a**. Modelling the first bullet for them using **PPT 6.1b**. Give students 5 minutes to highlight the key words from the question, using the PPT to annotate the extract if appropriate. Remind students that their annotations must address form, purpose, audience and voice for **Q1**.

After they have compared their answers with a partner, take brief feedback focusing on how these selected words will inform their responses. Discuss the point that there are perhaps *two purposes*:

- to ask for time off
- to reassure the head teacher about safety.

These will both need to be dealt with in the answer.

> **Give extra support** by making sure all students are clear about the requirements of the sample question as detailed on Student Book p. 158. For example, do not assume all will have realised that they are *not* writing from the point of the view of the ranger. Do this by getting students to read the requirements, shut the book and then 'test' them as a class or individuals on questions such as:
>
> - What role are you asked to take in this question?
> - Are you told how to start your response?
>
> **Give extra challenge** by asking students to consider the appropriate voice and tone for particular tasks by using **Worksheet 6.1**. Answers for Task 1 are 1 = B; 2 = A; 3 = D; 4 = C. For Task 2, students may choose one or two paragraphs to write if four is too many for the time available.

Building skills

Look at the grid in **Q2** on Student Book p. 159 and ask the class to suggest how the second column should be completed. Then, organise students in pairs and give them 15 minutes to complete column three after you have talked them through the first two rows. Remind them that 'voice' is key here – this is a student writing, not the expert guide from the radio, so something of the student's personality should come through in the letter.

PPT The suggested responses for columns two and three are given on **PPT 6.1c–e**. Show this slide after students have suggested their own versions, as a backup for their ideas.

Developing skills

Read the sample response in **Q3** out loud to the class to emphasise the unsuitability of the response, and then give students 5 minutes to discuss in pairs whether it has addressed all the necessary requirements of the task. Use the grid from **Q2** to guide the discussion.

Possible responses from pairs may include:

- bad: informality/slang; uses first name for head teacher; does not fulfil purpose to reassure; abbreviated, short sentences, use of capitals, overuse of exclamation marks
- good: does mention that some preparations have been made.

Give extra challenge by asking students what the effect of beginning with a question like 'You cool with us going?' is. (Is it a real question, with different answers, or does it assume something? If so, what? It assumes the head teacher will say 'yes'.) Elicit what effect the question is likely to have.

Applying skills

Before students rewrite the opening to the letter in **Q4**, ask volunteers to change the opening address ('Hi Carl!') and first line ('You cool with us going?') as a piece of shared writing to stress what needs to be done. Focus on the first short question – point out that it is chatty and abbreviated.

> *Dear Mr [name]*
>
> *I am writing to you to request your permission for...*

Give students 15 minutes to write their paragraphs. When completed, they can exchange paragraphs with a partner and evaluate these against the **Sound progress** criteria on Student Book p. 159. Each student then has 5 minutes to highlight:

- how any key elements of the task have been met
- where appropriately formal but not unfriendly language has been used.

Students should then redraft or rewrite as necessary.

Complete the lesson by pointing out that there are many different ways to begin the letter. It may be the case, in fact, that you would not mention your enthusiasm, preparations or ask for permission all in the first paragraph, but would instead sequence your ideas more carefully.

2 Developing an extended response

Assessment objectives

AO1 Reading
- **R2** Demonstrate understanding of implicit meanings and attitudes
- **R5** Select for specific purposes

AO2 Writing
- **W4** Use register appropriate to audience and context

IGCSE examination
- **Paper 1** Question 2

Differentiated learning outcomes

- **All students must** write a basic draft in answer to an extended response task (Grade E/D).
- **Most students should** write a draft which covers the required content from the task set and shows understanding of voice and role (Grade D/C).
- **Some students could** write a draft which covers the requirements of the task, and includes their own ideas alongside content from the passage (Grade C).

Resources
- **Student Book**: pp. 160–1
- **PPT**: 6.2a–b
- **Worksheet**: 6.2 Understanding the passage

Other Student Book pages
- Exploring responses: Paper 1, pp. 170–4

Exploring skills

As a lead in to **Q1**, ask pairs to discuss for a few minutes how they would feel if an elderly relative, who was very close to them, decided to set off on a very dangerous journey or trip. How would they react? Would they attempt to stop them? How?

Then, read aloud the passage on Student Book p. 160 about Anthony Smith, stopping to check understanding of any difficult vocabulary or sentence constructions. This time students should imagine they are Anthony's grandson and think about what he would be feeling about his trip.

Give extra support by supplying or explaining difficult or idiomatic vocabulary: for example, 'racking his brain' = thinking very hard; 'beg to differ' = politely disagree; 'gammy' = damaged or not working properly.

Building skills

Once this is done, check understanding of the extended response task by giving out **Worksheet 6.2**. Give students 15 to 20 minutes to complete the questions, and then to highlight the key words in the task for **Q2**. Suggested answers for the three bullets are:

- 'sail 3000 miles across the Atlantic' on a raft
- he's 84 – and has a 'gammy' leg
- 'it's safe and it's easy'; 'interesting'; 'having an older crew should prevent any unnecessary risk-taking'.

The key words are highlighted in **PPT 6.2a**.

Display the task with the highlighted key words by purpose, audience, form and voice using **PPT 6.2b**.

Developing skills

Recap on how the highlighted words will assist with the writing of the task. For **Q3**, give students 5 minutes to note down the grandson's objections, and then compile a list on the board that could be used.

> **Give extra challenge** by asking students to list some extra ideas around the character of Anthony Smith and the grandfather: for example, suggesting other adventurous things he might have done which could be included in the interview. Ask *What else can you infer about Anthony, other than him being optimistic and adventurous?* Answers might include: *reckless, restless, fit for his age, young at heart.* Remind students to make sure their inferences are rooted in detail from the passage.

Model how the first question in the sample conversation on Student Book p. 161 could be developed as follows by writing up on the board:

Interviewer:	So, can you tell viewers about your grandfather's incredible plans?
You:	Well, he's aiming to travel 3000 miles across the Atlantic on a rickety old raft. He tells me it's made of pipes – metal ones, I think, but I thought they rusted!
Interviewer:	And what do you feel about his wish to venture across the Atlantic?
You:	I guess it's good that he still feels able to have a go at something so tough…
Interviewer:	But, how do you feel personally? You must be worried about…

Ask students how the last question above could be developed to make inferences from the text to match bullet 2 in the task on p. 160 (about 'concerns'). For example:

- the **point** is: he's travelling across the Atlantic
- the **detail** is: the boat is made of gas pipes
- the **inference** could be: Anthony is a bit of a hoarder of recycled items.

So the question could be: *But, how do you feel personally? You must be worried about the materials your grandfather has used to construct his raft?*

Now, ask them to come up with a further question to match the final bullet in the task on p. 160, the one that refers to 'reassurances'. For example:

- the **point** could be: he's looked at the possible dangers
- the **detail** could be: the statistics about fatalities/the buoyancy of the craft…
- the **inference** could be: he is well-informed and knowledgeable.

So, a possible question might be: *Interviewer: Has your grandfather tried to boost your confidence about his trip?*

Applying skills

For **Q4**, students should work individually to draft a response to the sample question on p. 160. They can either choose to use (and develop, as above) the frame for the interview as provided on Student Book p. 161, or write their own script from scratch.

Draw their attention to the **Top tip** and the **Checklist for success**, so that they ensure the conversation is more than just 'ping-pong' dialogue, developing and expanding some of the lines for each speaker – and perhaps going in new, but related directions.

Encourage students to develop a convincing voice for both the grandson and the interviewer, and to balance the information from the text with their own ideas that build on what is there. As part of this task, students could follow this web link to: **http://gasballoon.com/antiki** (the official site for the raft trip), and how it went.

Ask individuals to review their work and, using the **Sound progress** criteria from Student Book p. 161, to consider how well they have done and what they need to do to improve.

3 Developing an extended response E

Assessment objectives

AO1 Reading
- R1 Demonstrate understanding of explicit meanings
- R2 Demonstrate understanding of implicit meanings and attitudes
- R5 Select for specific purposes

AO2 Writing
- W4 Use register appropriate to audience and context

IGCSE examination
- **Paper 2** Question 1

Differentiated learning outcomes
- **All students must** complete a draft extended response in journal form written from Alfredo's point of view (Grade D).
- **Most students should** include both information from the passage and their own ideas to show creativity in their journal entry (Grade C/B).
- **Some students could** write a journal entry with a distinct, original voice in a way that addresses all the content and style requirements (Grade A).

Resources
- **Student Book**: pp. 162–5
- **PPT**: 6.3a
- **Worksheets**:
  6.3a What's implied?
  6.3b Journal or diary writing plan

Other Student Book pages
- Exploring responses: extended response tasks/Paper 1, pp. 174–9

Exploring skills

Organise students into groups of three or four to read the passage in **Q1**. If four per group, divide the text into four roughly equal chunks to read it; or, if three per group, read it as a dramatized narrative – one person (the most skilled reader) reads the narration, while the remaining two read the spoken words of the writer and Alfredo.

Before they start **Q2**, ensure that students understand the distinction between 'explicit meaning' and 'implicit meaning'. Students can then work on their own for 5 minutes to jot down the explicit information from the passage. You may also need to support students by explaining vocabulary such as 'per capita income' (how much each person earns) or 'just perceptible' (difficult to see or make out).

Explicit information for this passage means what happens in terms of events. Example responses from class feedback could include:

- Alfredo makes the writer remove his watch.
- They discuss how to buy tickets and what sort/type.
- Alfredo forces his way to the front of the queue, and comes back with tickets.
- They go into the stadium having been searched at the entrance.
- They sit on the concrete steps.
- The author observes the different sections of the ground and crowd.

Give extra challenge by asking students to think about all the other potential stories that could have been told here. Who else could have narrated these events? How would it have been different? (Ask students, for example, how this story would have been told by one of the 'Balcony' people, or one of the players or managers.)

Building skills

Students can return to work in threes or fours for **Q3**. As a way of guiding the discussion, they can use **Worksheet 6.3a**, which provides some possible inferences for each point. The most likely inferences are:

94 • Lesson 3 © HarperCollins Publishers 2013

1 = C This applies to all groups, whereas it is not true that all Salvadorean society is 'passionate about football' – are the Balcony people? Also, not all the crowd are 'like animals'.

2 = D The writer is clearly 'fascinated', as much of his description is taken up by observing their behaviour. He is possibly also 'frightened' as his description of the plateau suggests it is a 'sight more terrifying than the Suns'.

3 = A Alfredo is streetwise; he tells the author to hide his watch, acquires tickets with ease and looks out for the author in general.

Encourage students to back up their interpretations with reference to the language from the text, as shown above.

For **Q3**, groups can decide on their inferences and then suggest them through a spokesperson who feeds back to the class as a whole via a short plenary.

Developing skills

Display the task in **Q4** on **PPT 6.3a** and ask for suggestions from the class for the key words and what they tell us about:

- the role/voice ('Alfredo')
- the form, audience and purpose ('journal entry' – so for himself, reflecting on the day)
- what to include ('about the day', and as set out by the bullets in the task itself).

Q5 acts as preparation for the writing response in **Q7**, so it is important that pairs work carefully on the set questions. It also links back to the **Extra challenge** earlier in this lesson, in which students consider different narrative perspectives. Possible responses include:

- Alfredo knows his way around – through showing how to get tickets quickly, which tickets to buy, what Paul should look out for (i.e. touts).
- He says that 'most of the people' are 'thieves', but he might only be referring to the touts and those outside the stadium, not Salvadoreans as a whole.
- He's very excited as he could not 'hope' to see this game in Santa Ana.
- Alfredo's voice is clear and confident, but wary, too, seeing potential problems. He uses short, imperative sentences, 'Take your watch off', but there is also pathos – and personal excitement – in his reflection 'I could never see such a game…'.

Give extra support by reminding students that they have already made inferences about Alfredo when completing the worksheet. These can feed into this task here.

Feed back by asking students to sum up their overall ideas about Alfredo, and how they might show this in their answer, as exemplified in the Band 1 example on Student Book p. 164.

Applying skills

Students should work independently to plan their response in **Q6** and then draft it for **Q7** (which can be completed as homework).

Give extra support by giving out **Worksheet 6.3b** to assist some students as they tackle **Q7**. This contains a journal/diary writing frame based on the plan on Student Book p. 165.

| Towards A/A* | To ensure a top mark, focus on the 'voice' of the character, perhaps using a greater range of punctuation and variety of sentence lengths to demonstrate excitability. |

4 Developing a directed writing response C E

Assessment objectives

AO1 Reading
- R3 Analyse, evaluate and develop facts, ideas and opinions
- R5 Select for specific purposes

AO2 Writing
- W2 Sequence facts, ideas and opinions
- W4 Use register appropriate to audience and context

IGCSE examination
- Paper 3 Section 1

Differentiated learning outcomes
- **All students must** write two paragraphs of the article, with some reference to the stimulus texts (Grade D).
- **Most students should** write the two paragraphs, add an appropriate title, use the stimulus texts, and make some inferences to make the response fit the voice/role (Grade C).
- **Some students could** write the whole article, drawing on all elements of the texts provided, and demonstrate a convincing voice, style and persuasive tone (Grade A).

Resources
- **Student Book**: pp. 166–9
- **PPT**: 6.4a–c
- **Worksheet**: 6.4 The four elements of the task

Other Student Book pages
- Exploring responses: Paper 3, pp. 180–7

Exploring skills

Begin by drawing students' attention to the particular focus of Paper 3's approach to directed writing – for example, the fact that they will have to make use of more than one text, and also transfer ideas and content from the stimulus texts into a different form of writing.

Read through with the class the **two stimulus texts** provided (the 'Interview Notes on p. 166 and the parent's letter on p. 167). As the **Top tip** on p. 166 indicates, students can begin to make inferences even *before* they have read the task. Give them 10 minutes to discuss in pairs and copy and complete a grid such as this one to help them consider what they can already infer:

Text extract	Inference?
'Five boys...' 'Boys are volunteers...'	That no girls volunteered? Girls did volunteer but weren't made welcome...? That it's an all boys' school?
'3-4 calls a day'	Scheme not open at right time? Not well advertised? Not seen as very useful to students?
'Only one student complained...'	Unhappy callers didn't think it was worth complaining? Callers felt intimidated about complaining?

Building skills

Read the task aloud to the class. Make sure they are clear that for the response they will have to use both texts provided.

To assist with this, split the class into pairs for the **Q2** role-play. They should spend 10 minutes researching their role, so they are clear about *what* they will say and the points they will make. Once they have done this, run the role-play.

> **Give extra challenge** by running the role-play as 'forum theatre'. In this, one pair begins the role-play, but if either Paolo or the interviewer runs out of things to say, they can ask the audience (the forum) to provide a line/question. Or the audience member who suggests the idea can take the place of the role-player, so the dialogue continues.

Developing skills

Now, it's time to deal with **Q3** – getting to grips with what the task requires. Ask pairs to spend 5 minutes discussing the bulleted points in **Q3**. Feed back as a class. Students should recognize that:

- 'you'/the writer are a 'fellow student'
- the purpose is to argue
- the form is a newspaper article
- the audience is anyone at your school.

Then, as a whole class, read over the sample plan provided under 'Content and structure', pointing out the inferences made – some of which will match with what was mentioned earlier in the lesson. For **Q4**, ask the class as a whole to suggest further points to add to the plan: for example, should there be something on the need for training for volunteers? Or is the issue of bullying at the school worth addressing?

Now, point out to students that having a plan of what to include is one thing, but getting the appropriate **style and tone** is another. For this, students will need to draw on what they know already about how to write newspaper articles.

Organise the class into groups of four. Hand out **Worksheet 6.4** and explain that each member of the group is responsible for filling in one of the four elements. Allow students 15 minutes to discuss and complete this table. Each student should keep their own copy of the table to assist with the writing task later in the lesson.

> **Give extra support** by suggesting students reread Chapter 2, Lesson 6: Audience (pp. 50–3) and Chapter 3, Lesson 5: Conventions of news reports and feature articles (pp. 74–7), Lesson 9: Writing to persuade (pp. 88–9) and Lesson 10: Writing to argue (pp. 90–3).

For **Q5** ask pairs to look at the two responses. Display **PPT 6.4a–c** to demonstrate what else might be considered effective about Response B. You could ask for suggestions from students first before revealing the PPT annotations.

The key point here is that it is not possible to respond at a high level without drawing inferences from the texts of the kind dealt with earlier in the chapter.

Applying skills

Students should now write the first two paragraphs of the article, as instructed in **Q6**. Point out to them that the original task did not indicate whether the scheme is good or bad, and so this is something they will need to decide upon before they plan and write their answer.

Ask pairs to compare their completed paragraphs quickly, using the **Sound progress** and **Excellent progress** criteria on Student Book p. 169, to ensure they have managed to get the content and style right.

You may then wish to allow some students to complete the whole article for homework, if they feel confident.

Towards A/A*	Students will gain higher marks by making use of appropriate conventions from writing to argue/persuade, but must ensure they also show evidence of using inference based on the given material to shape their own response.

1 Understanding composition tasks Ⓒ Ⓔ

Assessment objectives

AO2 Writing

- W1 Articulate experience and express what is thought, felt and imagined
- W2 Sequence facts, ideas and opinions
- W3 Use a range of appropriate vocabulary
- W4 Use register appropriate to audience and context
- W5 Make accurate use of spelling, punctuation and grammar

IGCSE examination

- **Paper 3** Section 2 (Composition)

Differentiated learning outcomes

- **All students must** highlight key words from a specified task (Grade E/D).
- **Most students should** explain differences and what this means for their writing, between the key forms in each task (Grade C/B).
- **Some students could** choose tasks creatively, having evaluated their own skills and linked them to the best option for a high grade (Grade A).

Resources

- **Student Book**: pp. 190–1
- **PPT**: 7.1a–b
- **Worksheet**: 7.1 Features of narratives and descriptions

Other Student Book pages

- Writing to describe, pp. 98–103
- Narrative writing, pp. 104–7

Exploring skills

Run through the opening paragraphs on Student Book p. 190 carefully with the class, making sure everyone is clear what the requirements of the composition task are. In particular, ensure they understand that they have only to write in response to **one** task from the total of four tasks on offer (two writing forms, descriptive and narrative, with two choices in each).

As a starter activity, put the class into pairs. Each member of each pair is then given either 'descriptive' or 'narrative' and has to write down a sentence to explain their given writing form. For example:

- for 'descriptive': *writing that provides a vivid and detailed picture of a place, situation or person*
- for 'narrative': *writing that tells a story or recounts an engaging series of events.*

Ask each pair to join with another pair, to make a group of four, and share definitions. Then, working with their original partners, ask them to tackle **Q1** on Student Book p. 190, linking the given tasks to the two forms of writing. Take feedback as a class:

(a) descriptive: comes from the same root as the word 'describe'; also, the task is limited to a specific sensory situation at one moment

(b) narrative: 'story', another word for 'narrative', is mentioned in the task; also, the word 'start' hints at a series of events – a plot.

Building skills

Students can continue to work with their partner to complete the grid for **Q2**. A handout version they can write onto is provided on **Worksheet 7.1**.

> **Give extra support** by guiding some students on how to fill in the grid for the two writing forms: narratives and descriptive texts. **Worksheet 7.1** provides some suggestions which they can place into the grid.

Developing skills

Ask students to read the panel of advice above **Q3** carefully to themselves. Elicit from them that the key thing is to choose the task which will best allow them to express their ideas and 'show off' their language skills. This doesn't mean picking the 'easiest' task – they may come unstuck if it is one for which they have no ideas.

If you wish, you can tell students to close their books and display the sample question (see **PPT 7.1a–b**). Take them through the process in **PPT 7.1a** first and then ask for suggestions from the class via **PPT 7.1b**, before showing them the model highlighting and annotations on Student Book p. 191, if you wish.

Point out that the information given presents opportunities. Ask students to work on their own for 5 minutes to make notes on the following questions that you can write on the board.

- Why is 'almost midnight' a good thing to see in the task for story-telling? Is it better or worse than, say, breakfast time? What opportunities for creativity does 'midnight' offer? (For example: *it is atmospheric and possibly spooky and mysterious*.)
- Who are the two main characters in the story likely to be – given this title? What other possibilities might there be? (For example: *probably will be the narrator and the person coming to the door – unless the person coming to the door is a messenger, who doesn't appear again*.)

Applying skills

Ask students to work on **Q4** on their own highlighting or listing the key words from the suggested task. Ask them to share their highlighted words with a partner and check to see they selected the same ones.

At this point, you may wish to ask students what the implications are for their response (for the style conventions for descriptive writing covered in Chapter 3, Student book pp. 98–103), but detailed work on this follows in the next lesson.

Towards A/A*	To ensure a top mark, students need to think creatively about the opportunities that titles give to include original ideas, language and thinking, and not just look for what appears the most straightforward. For example, writing a narrative entitled 'The worst day of my life' might tempt them to write about a disastrous day at school when writing in role as a gladiator or some form of animal might prove more fruitful. They should also consider whether a title offers the opportunity to use an unusual structural device or set of specific narrative conventions that they can show mastery of, such as time-shifts.

2 Planning and developing a composition

Assessment objectives
AO2 Writing
- **W1** Articulate experience and express what is thought, felt and imagined
- **W3** Use a range of appropriate vocabulary

IGCSE examination
- **Paper 3** Section 2 (Composition)

Differentiated learning outcomes
- **All students must** generate basic ideas for the descriptive task (Grade E/D).
- **Most students should** add their own focused detail to their plans for a descriptive piece (Grade C/B).
- **Some students could** propose or plan for unusual or original responses to the descriptive task using lateral or imaginative thinking (Grade A).

Resources
- **Student Book**: pp. 192–3
- **PPT**: 7.2a–d
- **Worksheet**: 7.2 Developing a narrative response

Other Student Book pages
- Understanding composition tasks, pp. 190–1

Exploring skills

Warm up by reminding students that the composition tasks given provide a series of signposts or indicators that will help them develop their response. Check understanding of the process by questioning them about the sample task on Student Book p. 192. For example, ask:

- How would the descriptive response be different if the customer was 'happy'?
- What would the difference be if the customer were not *in* a shop but *outside* it – for example, protesting on the pavement about the poor services with a sign held up for all to see?

Allow students two minutes to highlight the key words in the descriptive writing task in **Q1**. Then give a further five minutes to jot down the implications – what each of these key words means for their answer.

Briefly ask for feedback, and draw out the point that the task automatically requires certain vocabulary. For example, synonyms for 'relaxed' which they may need in their response ('comfortable', 'calm', 'contented', etc.).

Building skills

When it comes to **Q2**, students should ideally work on their own when generating ideas for the shop task, but you may wish to prompt them by displaying an image of a busy shop, perhaps downloaded from the internet or using the image shown on **PPT 7.2a**.

> **Give extra support** by showing targeted students a visual prompt: for example, an image of a busy shop. Get them to work in pairs to label anything they notice in the image of the shop and customers. For example, the type of shop/goods it sells; possible sights and sounds (canned music, noisy children, traffic going past, other customers, tills or phones, etc.); gestures, looks and clothing of staff and customers.

Developing skills

Organise students into groups of three, and ask two students to quickly role-play a situation in which a customer complains about a digital camera that has broken. The customer has already had to have it replaced once. However, it is out of warranty and the assistant won't replace it!

The role of the third member of the group is to make notes about the body language of the customer and the shop manager that could be used in a piece of descriptive writing. Their task will be to observe closely (hands, face, position of body and tone of voice).

For the role play to work and to help students focus on details, the 'performers' will need to use:

- variety of tone, pitch, and speed when speaking
- gesture and movement that fits the situation and their role.

PPT Display **PPT 7.2b** to remind performers of how to get the most out of a role play. Then model the highlighted elements in the scripted role play in turn on **PPT 7.2c**, pointing out that they show actions (chewing gum, slamming camera down, etc.), vocal sounds (coughing), and gestures/movements (shifting from foot to foot) and tone of voice ('grumpily', 'bored'). You could then ask volunteers to read the lines and act out the modelled example.

After the role play is complete, using both the notes made in the previous lesson and their imagination, ask students to complete **Q3** individually. Give them a target of covering at least half a page of A4 solely on the customer's description.

> **Give extra challenge** by running through the **Top tip** on Student Book p. 193, which suggests taking an original view of the situation. Then elicit five alternative or unusual ways of dealing with this situation (the item being returned could be very unusual or perhaps the shop is full of precious breakable items).

Applying skills

PPT Read aloud the sample task to be developed in **Q4**, and then give out **Worksheet 7.2**. This provides the task and space for planning/developing a response, with explanations of what each bullet means. To further support learners, display **PPT 7.2d**, which provides a highlighted version of the task with key words shown.

The class could discuss the implication of each key word in turn, for example:

- narrative – uses key conventions of narrative texts (time sequence, exciting events a problem or complication, strong characterisation)
- content – uses the words in the title such as 'lost umbrella' and all its links and connotations: something mysterious happened to its owner, is the owner absent-minded, how it got there?

| Towards A/A* | To attain the highest marks, students must use the task's key words to plan a detailed response, but should also look for opportunities to follow unusual or original ideas: for example, how an item such as an umbrella might in its shape, colour and design reflect the person who left it – for example, slim, old, broken and dark – or what it might tell them about the owner's personal tastes or lifestyle. |

3 Descriptive writing: imagery and sensory detail

C E

Assessment objectives

AO2 Writing
- W1 Articulate experience and express what is thought, felt and imagined
- W3 Use a range of appropriate vocabulary

IGCSE examination
- **Paper 3** Section 2 (Composition)

Differentiated learning outcomes
- **All students must** be able to explain the difference between a simile and metaphor (Grade E/D).
- **Most students should** write at least three similes or metaphors of their own (Grade D/C).
- **Some students could** link a range of similes and metaphors together for an overall effect (Grade B/A).

Resources
- **Student Book**: pp. 194–5
- **Worksheets**:
  7.3a Overall effects
  7.3b Linking imagery
- **PPT**: 7.3a–b

Other Student Book pages
- Writing to describe, pp. 98–103
- Descriptive writing: structure and detail, pp. 196–9

Exploring skills

Read carefully with the class the definitions of 'similes' and 'metaphors' that come before **Exploring skills**, but also draw attention to the advice about not overloading a piece of writing with too much imagery.

For **Q1**, ask students to work in pairs for 2–3 minutes briefly discussing the two examples given. Then, take feedback, eliciting ideas such as:

- For the simile 'broken brick on sandpaper', the senses and effects are:
  sound (*harsh, grating*), colour/sight (*light brown/sandy*) and touch (*gritty, rough*).
- For the metaphor 'tiny splinters of ice':
  colour/sight (*very small, bright, thin, pointed*) and touch (*sharp, very cold*).

Give extra support by asking students to sketch what they see in the description – this can help visualise what is being described.

Give extra challenge by asking students to say how less obvious senses might link to a description – for example, what might sandpaper *taste* like? What *sound* might ice make if it 'splintered'? Explain that the best images work on multiple levels.

Building skills

Elicit responses for the bad example given ('honey' is smooth and soothing), and then ask students to work on **Q2** and **Q3**, before taking feedback. The best choices for **Q2** are 'sharp whip' and 'speeding missile'. For **Q3**, a range of choices is possible, but be sure *appropriateness* in the choice is rewarded. Use this chance to talk about the need for images always to be suitable for the topic concerned referring the **Top tip** on p.195.

Give extra support by displaying **PPT 7.3a–b**, which allows students to select appropriate images from a list provided. You could ask students to discuss the list of options in pairs and agree on their choices.

Give extra challenge by asking more confident students to think of suitable similes and metaphors to complete the sentences in an original way. Encourage them to be original and avoid clichéd imagery, e.g. 'as cold as ice'.

Developing skills

Distribute **Worksheet 7.3a,** which contains the text above **Q4** on Student Book p. 195. Ask students first to work on their own on the passage relating to **Q4** ('The midnight lake...') to underline the three similes and circle the two metaphors, before discussing the answers to the bullets in **Q4**. Then, ask them to highlight any imagery in the second passage ('There was a wild rush...') before working in pairs to answer **Q5**. Then, feed back responses to both **Q4** and **Q5**.

Q4: the three similes are: 'shone like a huge, silver brooch'; 'glittered like miniature diamonds'; 'like the richest prince on earth'.

The two metaphors are: 'the sky's dark neck'; 'the moon was...an enormous locket'. The sense these mostly appeal to is that of sight.

Q5: for the worksheet task, students should have highlighted: 'like bees racing towards their favourite lily'/'swarmed over barriers like soldier ants'/'tide of beetles'. The linking idea is huge numbers of moving insects.

For the second bullet point in **Q5** on Student Book p. 195, elicit from students that option **A** ('I was a tiny leaf... storm') and option **B** ('leader of an army') *both* work for different reasons. **A** captures the idea of the insect world swarming uncontrollably, but, as the writer is described as one of the creatures in the passage, **B** could be appropriate, if not quite as powerful in the way the idea is expressed.

Applying skills

Before completing **Q6,** quickly check that students fully understand the concepts of simile and metaphor by asking the whole class to respond to a series of images by raising their hand if it is a simile and keeping it down if it is a metaphor. In this way, you can visually check that everyone has understood. Examples to use are:

- *The old woman looked as fragile as a single moth in the path of a storm.*
- *The storm was a cloak of dust and hail enveloping the land.*
- *The snow field was like a perfect white handkerchief.*
- *The sand-dunes were a living, breathing animal shifting in its sleep.*

Now, give students 15 minutes to:

- choose one of the three ideas provided in **Q6**
- jot down some ideas, perhaps connecting a city with the given idea – for example: city like a jungle: *skyscrapers = enormous trees; roads = streams and rivers*
- then, draft the description, making sure they check they have used the full range of senses and that all their chosen images are appropriate to their subject.

> **Give extra support** by handing out **Worksheet 7.3b**, which provides some possible ideas for one of the given tasks. Weaker learners can use what they think are the best of these ideas and try to put them into sentences using connectives.

Finish the lesson by asking selected students to read out their descriptions. Stop to point out particularly appropriate or sophisticated use of imagery, and ask the class which senses are appealed to in each case. Reward writing that uses images that match across the whole piece and fit in well with the chosen topic. Encourage students to identify examples of writing that meet the criteria of **Excellent progress** on Student Book p. 195).

Towards A/A*	Encourage students to think of metaphoric usage of verbs. This is something that can be fluently embedded into writing. For example, the sentence 'The queue *splintered* in two when we neared the stage' gives a very visual sense of the type and shape of the queue as it moved.

4 Descriptive writing: structure and detail C E

Assessment objectives

AO2 Writing

W1 Articulate experience and express what is thought, felt and imagined
W3 Use a range of appropriate vocabulary
W4 Use register appropriate to audience and context
W5 Make accurate use of spelling, punctuation and grammar

IGCSE examination
- Paper 3 Section 2 (Composition)

Differentiated learning outcomes

- **All students must** build detail and write descriptive paragraphs from a given stimulus (Grade E/D).
- **Most students should** select particularly appropriate vocabulary to engage the reader's interest (Grade C/B).
- **Some students could** combine the full range of language and literary techniques to sustain the reader's interest (Grade A).

Resources
- Student Book: pp. 196–9
- PPT: 7.4a–d
- Worksheets:
  7.4a Making a spider diagram
  7.4b Focusing on movements

Other Student Book pages
- Writing to describe, pp. 98–103
- Descriptive writing: imagery and sensory detail, pp. 194–5

Exploring skills

Read aloud the **Checklist for success** on Student Book p. 196. Then, as a quick starter, pair students together and give them 5 minutes to jointly write a paragraph about a mysterious room. They should take it in turns to add parts of sentences, handing back to the other on linking words. For example:

Student 1: *The room had an old shabby carpet with...*

Student 2: *... a tiger's head at one end, which had...*

Student 1: *... one eye missing...* etc.

You could pin the resulting paragraphs to the wall and compare them with work the students produce by the end of this section.

Now ask students to work independently to copy and complete the spider diagram in **Q1**. Alternatively, weaker students can do the task on **Worksheet 7.4a**, which has some suggested 'legs' for them to develop. Praise those who have developed their diagram with lots of 'legs' and further detail, filling the page as much as they can. If students can achieve a level of detail that provides specifics, such as colours, clothing or objects in the room, all the better.

Building skills

For **Q2**, ask students to work alone to improve the Band 3 sample (the first extract) on p. 197. You could complete a shared version first, asking for class suggestions.

Give extra challenge by asking students to find any other opportunities within the sample sentences in the Band 3 sample to add detail: for example, adjectives for the door (*oak*) or adverbs for how the narrator looks in (*partly/dimly see*) or more specific alternatives (*see/just make out/glimpse/observe*).

Feed back ideas, complimenting those who add the most convincing and focused detail. Then, ask students to complete **Q3** on their own before evaluating their

104 • Lesson 4   © HarperCollins Publishers 2013

paragraphs together (**Q4**). The final task in this stage, **Q5**, requires them to describe the room out loud, linking back to the starter but on this occasion with their partner prompting them. Use the example on Student Book p. 197 to prompt them.

Developing skills

Once students have grasped the importance in descriptive writing of sometimes focusing on small detail rather than story-telling through events, they can work on their own to complete **Q6** and **Q7** on Student Book pp. 198–9.

> **Give extra support** by providing weaker students with prompts for each sentence of their paragraph – for example:
> 1 *I knelt down very slowly and carefully on the...*
> 2 *I began to...*
> 3 *At that moment...*

To help build towards **Q7**, you could distribute **Worksheet 7.4b**, which is intended to help students develop their use of sentence structure to convey movement or gesture. Refer to the **Top tip** on Student Book p. 198 as students are starting this task.

Next, ask students working on their own to complete the paragraph in **Q7**. Share paragraphs when they are complete, either within groups or as a whole class.

Applying skills

Draw attention to the importance of *character* and *voice* when writing descriptively. The *emotion* of the person describing a scene or event can add a great deal to the atmosphere or tone. (Demonstrating this skill in their work can also help students access the higher mark bands.) Read aloud the two given examples in **Q8**, and then ask what emotions are conveyed by the second, longer version? Sadness? Calm reflection? Angry passion? What key words convey this? ('I grew up in...'/'my heart sank'/'like my memories... crumbling away'.)

Now write or display the text in **Q9** on the board and explain to students that this is their chance to enjoy developing their own ideas. Students should work on their own. Give them 10–15 minutes to write a draft and then self-evaluate whether human emotions are portrayed through the details described or through the thoughts and actions of the narrator.

> **Give extra support** by displaying **PPT 7.4a–d**, which allows students to select appropriate adjectives to portray emotions, and then links the chosen emotion to what is found and how the narrator then behaves. You could then demonstrate how one choice would work in the final slide (**7.4d**), and ask for suggestions of how to build the character's voice further in the way shown. What might other photos show?
>
> **Give extra challenge** by asking more confident students to use phrases with present participles to give a different start to sentences, such as *'My head spinning, I...'* or *'My eyes brimming with tears, I...'*.

Once they have finished, pairs can share drafts and peer-assess them using the **Sound progress** and **Excellent progress** criteria from Student Book p. 199.

Towards A/A*	Students will need to combine all the descriptive skills explored here for the highest marks, ranging from rich vocabulary and vivid imagery, through to convincing voice and character, in order to create a sustained atmosphere that affects the reader. In addition, they will take care to structure their description, avoiding narrative yet creating an assured sense of progression.

5 Narrative writing: structure and detail

Assessment objectives

AO2 Writing
W1 Articulate experience and express what is thought, felt and imagined
W3 Use a range of appropriate vocabulary

IGCSE examination
- Paper 3 Section 2 (Composition)

Differentiated learning outcomes
- **All students must** develop a basic narrative from given information (Grade D).
- **Most students should** be able to include narrative techniques such as flashbacks and twists (Grade C/B).
- **Some students could** come up with original, yet believable narrative changes or surprises (Grade A).

Resources
- **Student Book**: pp. 200–3
- **PPT**: 7.5a–e
- **Worksheet**: 7.5 Elements of narrative writing

Other Student Book pages
- Planning and developing a composition, pp. 192–3
- Narrative writing: characterisation and dialogue, pp. 204–5

Exploring skills

As a warm up, ask students to talk to a partner about a favourite story:

- What made them want to read, watch or listen to it?
- What features of stories they have experienced could be used in this task?
- Which would be more difficult? (Perhaps the number of characters or locations.)

Quickly go over the **Checklist for success** on Student Book p. 200 to ensure the class is clear about effective stories, in the context of the exam. Then ask the pairs to work through the table in **Q1** to generate a range of further ideas, and in **Q2** to make decisions about their particular story – the more interesting, the better. Ask pairs to share their ideas, and then vote or discuss as a class which might be the best. Keep them focused on the fact that they won't have very long to write in the exam.

Building skills

Briefly read aloud the bullets at the top of Student Book p. 201 that that describe what make a good narrative. Then ask students to read the two openings in **Q3**, and to work independently to decide which techniques are used in each extract.

> **Give extra challenge** by introducing the 'cut-out' cards in **Worksheet 7.5**, which also contain some other features of the second extract. Display the extracts on the board using **PPT 7.5a–b**. and ask more confident students where the cards should be attached to the two extracts. Ask them to explain the reasons for their choices.

Ask students to work through their ideas for what happened to the brother (**Q4**) and to complete **Q5** before comparing their work to a partner's (**Q6**). They should then work on **Q7** on Student Book p. 202.

> **Give extra support** by setting up a guided group of weaker students to work with for **Q5–Q7**. Start by using shared writing techniques to build on the short example in **Q5** on Student Book p. 201 by completing the next sentence using the verb form 'had' to explain where and what had they been doing: for example,
>
> - *My brother had been sent to the shop to...*
> - *My brother had had a row with my father...*
>
> Subsequent sentences can provide more detail of the flashback situation.

Developing skills

Quickly go over the structure for a typical narrative outlined on Student Book p. 202, but point out to students that they have to be flexible with this. For example, a story might begin with a 'complication' (*I hung by my fingertips from the window-ledge. How did I get myself into this mess?*), but emphasise that even here, there is a 'back-story' of what must have led up to this moment.

> **Give extra support** by asking students to plan a story with four to five parts and then put the complication first. If they struggle, take an example such as *Little Red Riding Hood* and ask how that would begin if it started with the complication. (*The wolf stood in front of Red Riding Hood. 'Hello, my dear,' he said, in a deep voice.*)

Encourage students to work independently for **Q8**. They write a paragraph for each ending including their 'twist'. Tell them to think about the possibilities from the story. For example, if the brother was away so long, what things (other than being penniless) might have kept him away or brought him back? A good twist should surprise but should still be believable.

Applying skills

Ask students to work together to read and then analyse the two examples on Student Book p. 203, and then to answer the questions in the **Q9** bullets. They need to understand that the slight tweaks or changes in style and vocabulary choice will have an impact on meaning. For example:

- Example 1: The first long sentence fits the drawn out idea of a shadow waiting, but then the short, sharp sentences and questions create a nervy, jumpy feeling of tension and suspense.
- Example 2: the word 'loitered' suggests criminality; 'staring' is stronger, more direct and deliberate than 'looking'; 'evaporated' makes the shadow inhuman, more ghostly perhaps.

You could use **PPT 7.5c–e** to give students practice in manipulating the model text on **PPT 7.5d** to change the meanings. Display **PPT 7.5e** and annotate further changes, as suggested by the class. Use the terms from **PPT 7.5c** to guide choices.

Students should now have had plenty of practice at considering the structure, adjectives, verbs, etc., when asking for suggestions. The aim is to make this an engaging first paragraph via individual choices of language, style, vocabulary and the potential story ideas. They should now attempt to write their own response in **Q10**.

As part of this process, it will be helpful for students if you give them a copy of the mark scheme for composition (narrative writing) from the CIE website and encourage them to decide on the elements they are targeting (see **Worksheet 10.3c(3)** for more information).

After initial drafting, students should peer-assess against the mark scheme, jot down positive coverage of key elements in the margin of the draft, and add two areas for development at the end of the draft. Then they can rework the draft as a final copy and summatively assess each other's work against the same criteria (perhaps with a different partner's response).

> **Towards A/A*** Students can impress by having a clear idea of how they are guiding the reader's response through careful choice of plot, language and structure. By 'playing with the reader' (as long as this is done appropriately), they can show they are in control of their writing. They can also manipulate by using surprise in terms of what information they reveal and when, or in terms of who tells the story – perhaps through an unusual or original viewpoint.

6 Narrative writing: characterisation and dialogue

Assessment objectives

AO2 Writing
- W1 Articulate experience and express what is thought, felt and imagined
- W2 Sequence facts, ideas and opinions
- W3 Use a range of appropriate vocabulary

IGCSE examination
- Paper 3 Section 2 (Composition)

Differentiated learning outcomes

- **All students must** complete part of the story from the narrative outline provided (Grade E/D).
- **Most students should** write a narrative which demonstrates improved conversation with action, description, and reduced speech (Grade D/C).
- **Some students could** write their own narrative based on the given title which shows all the features explored (Grade B/A).

Resources
- **Student Book**: pp. 204–5
- **Worksheet**: 7.6 My narrative: 'The Escape!'
- **PPT**: 7.6a–f

Other Student Book pages
- Narrative writing, pp. 104–7
- Narrative writing: structure and detail, pp. 200–3

Exploring skills

Explain that 'balance' in a story means having an appropriate amount of conversation and action. A story that is just conversation would be very dull, and would lack detail and colour; on the other hand, a story without any dialogue at all could seem a little lacking in pace or immediacy.

Read the two examples on Student Book p. 204 aloud to the class, and then ask students to work in pairs on **Q1**, before taking brief feedback. Points to elicit during feedback:

- Mina is lying in bed, passing the time by looking at the walls and reading.
- Details that add to the feeling of Mina's boredom include:
  - 'already' indicates a repeated action
  - the 'dull, fading flowers', as if they've been looked at many times
  - 'three times' for the reading of the book
  - how she 'sighed'
  - the clock that 'ticked slowly' – it seems slow to her, because she is bored.

Give extra support by asking weaker students to draw any details they can 'see' from the second description – this will immediately give them a sense of the visual quality of the extract.

Give extra challenge by asking students to suggest how the weather might reflect Mina's mood (you could introduce or recap the term 'pathetic fallacy' – see **Key terms** on Student Book p. 25) and to write one or two sentences to add to the second description. This can form part of the extra writing they do for **Q2**.

Building skills

Before students complete **Q2**, you might want to display the grid showing the different elements of the story, using **PPT 7.6a**, so that students are clear about the relation of the section they are writing to the rest of the narrative.

Give extra support by displaying **PPT 7.6a** to show the different elements of the narrative structure, and then **PPT 7.6b** for the table shown on Student's Book p. 205. Then show **PPT 7.6c**, which provides elements for another story, and ask the class to identify the different elements (introduction, development, etc.) before displaying **PPT 7.6d**, which supplies the correct order.

Give extra challenge by revealing and discussing **PPT 7.6e** with any students who are interested in thinking even more deeply about structure. Prompt students to think about how a 'second reversal' could be added to the Mina story? Add their ideas to slide **PPT 7.6f**.

Developing skills

Explain that writing effective dialogue is key to good narratives. Read aloud to the class the **Checklist for success** on Student Book p. 205 aloud to the class, eliciting what is meant by each bullet, for example understanding that:

- 'reveal something about characters' – means information about something they have done or intend to do, or shows a side of their character, such as ambition, anger, etc.
- 'don't overuse "speaking verbs"' – means to avoid repeating use of words verbs and adverbs related to speech, e.g. 'he said', 'she added', 'she called'.
- 'broken up with action or description' – means putting in details about how characters move or appear, or details about the setting or atmosphere.

Then, invite pairs to work together first to each read aloud the two versions of the dialogue in **Q3** and then to discuss what has changed between the first and second versions, before they complete the improved version.

Give extra support by asking pairs to list what has been *cut* from the first version (e.g. 'Well...I have to say that...in you because you haven't done your homework, so I'm really, really cross') and what *new detail* about Mina's mother has been added to the second? ('angrily turning her back and starting to wash the plates').

Give extra challenge by asking how the writer has changed the way we are told about the homework in the two versions. (In the first, Mina's mother tells us it is the homework that is the problem; in the second, the writer makes us wait, and it is Mina who realises that homework is the problem – it is implied, not told to us directly.)

Applying skills

Explain to students that they can now either complete the Mina story based on the grid at the top of Student Book p. 205, together with any further ideas that have emerged from the lesson, or they can write their own response to the title 'The Escape'. If they choose the latter, they can use **Worksheet 7.6** to plan their response.

Once students have finished, pairs can share drafts and peer-assess them using the **Sound progress** and **Excellent progress** criteria from Student Book p. 205.

Towards A/A*	For the highest grade, students need to write a compelling, original narrative with believable characters and a well-judged balance between dialogue and action. They should include twists, flashbacks or other narrative features to keep the reader interested, and their vocabulary choices should be vivid and appropriate. Their spelling must be correct, the punctuation clear and useful, and their handwriting legible.

1 Understanding the form, purpose and style of different texts C E

Assessment objectives
AO1 Reading
R3 Analyse, evaluate and develop facts, ideas and opinions
R4 Demonstrate understanding of how writers achieve effects

IGCSE examination
- **Component 4** Coursework Portfolio (Assignment 3)

Differentiated learning outcomes
- **All students must** read and respond to the provided range of texts that use different conventions (Grade E/D).
- **Most students should** be able to discuss and write about basic comparisons and contrasts between texts on a similar theme or subject (Grade C/B).
- **Some students could** discuss and write about the full range of possibilities which the different texts represent, and link this to other reading or research (Grade A).

Resources
- **Student Book**: pp. 216–23
- **PPT**: 8.1a–c
- **Worksheets**:
  8.1a 'Snake' by D.H. Lawrence
  8.1b Dangerous ideas in the wild

Other Student Book pages
- Exploring responses: assignments engaging with ideas and arguments from other texts, pp. 249–54

Exploring skills

This chapter provides a range of engaging texts in different forms and genres, which we hope will stimulate your students' imaginations. You can use the texts and the activities with students to help them practise for the coursework assignments, and to encourage them come up with ideas and creative topics of their own.

To begin, explain to students that as a way of generating ideas and practising key writing skills needed for their assignments, they are going to work with a range of texts which are loosely linked by the theme, 'Danger in the wild'.

However, make sure you remind students that it is only in **Assignment 3** that they will need to respond directly to texts.

After students have read 'Alone in the Balloon' on Student Book p. 217, put them into groups of four to work through **Q1** and the three bullets that follow in **Q2**. They should be aware that the form and purpose of this text (as a personal prose account) is perhaps less important than it might be in a media text or poem, for example, so for now, spending time on the final bullet is perhaps most relevant.

> **Give extra challenge** by asking students to consider creative writing opportunities based around what they have read. Do they know of anyone who has faced danger in a similar way? Could they find out more about the incident, or about other balloon adventures perhaps and write about it in a similar way to Branson? A web search for 'Branson Balloon Crash 1987' will lead them to more detailed accounts.

Building skills

To reinforce the sense of adventure in the extract from *My Ántonia* by Willa Cather, students could read the text on Student Book p. 218 aloud in threes, with each person taking a different role (Jim as narrator, Ántonia's speech, Jim's speech).

Give extra support by offering targeted students help with the text, especially the direct speech and difficult vocabulary. Before the reading aloud, suggest to students that they read the text to themselves and underline any vocabulary they can't understand; they should then discuss these words briefly in their threes to work out meanings. They can use the glossary to help, too.

Once they have read the text aloud, groups can work together through the bullets in **Q3**, keeping their own notes. Then, on their own, they should begin work on the piece on both texts in **Q4**. Use **PPT 8.1a–c** to model how they can respond well to this short writing task. Display each slide in turn – showing responses at different levels, and link this to the writer's effects questions that students face in Papers 1 and 2.

Developing skills

Read through 'Snake' on Student Book p. 220 as a class. Once students have had a chance to ask about any difficult vocabulary, put them into pairs. First, ask them to discuss and answer **Q5** before distributing a large sheet of card to each pair. Down the middle ask students to draw a line, with 'The snake and Ántonia' on one side, and 'Snake' on the other. Taking one element (from form, style, voice, viewpoint), ask each pair to make a comment in both columns on this aspect in both texts. Then, pairs move onto the next card, and add a new comment on a new element, and so on till the cards are completed. These can be pinned up for display and reflection.

Once completed, students move back into their pairs and complete **Q6** and **Q7**. (The complete version of 'Snake' is supplied as **Worksheet 8.1a.** Once students have read it and completed the tasks, ask them to 'think, talk, share':

- *think* – what message does the poem have, if any?
- *talk* – with your partner about your idea
- then *share* your idea with another pair and report back to the class as a whole.

Q8 is an individual task. Before students select their task, ask them to share with you any ideas about how the voice/viewpoint might change in each of the three bulleted options in **Q7**.

Applying skills

Students should read the final text on Student Book p. 222 to themselves. After they have spent 10 minutes making notes on the bullets in **Q9**, ask them to work with a partner for **Q10**.

As an extension, give them a time limit and, as a class game, the pair that win are the ones who come up with the most alternative perspectives for telling the skyscraper story. (If they are struggling, prompt them to think of other animals or creatures and people who work or live in such a building.)

Q11 asks students to think about particular possibilities around the theme of 'Danger in the wild'. They could use **Worksheet 8.1b** to stimulate their ideas and record potential titles.

Towards A/A*	Make sure students have a clear command of the main conventions of different types of texts, but then challenge them to try out different ways of mixing those conventions – for example: • a story with a clear moral message persuading the reader not to do what the writer has done • a travelogue with personal emotions alongside a descriptive account and factual information about a place or event.

2 How to approach informative, analytical and argumentative assignments Ⓒ Ⓔ

Assessment objectives

AO2 Writing

W1 Articulate experience and express what is thought, felt and imagined
W2 Sequence facts, ideas and opinions

IGCSE examination
- **Component 4** Coursework Portfolio (Assignment 1)

Differentiated learning outcomes

- **All students must** generate ideas, write a plan for their assignment and attempt a first draft of it (Grade E/D).
- **Most students should** write a plan, add further detail and try out a different opening paragraph before completing their draft (Grade C/B).
- **Some students could** plan and draft a challenging and original assignment with complex ideas and developed details (Grade A).

Resources
- **Student Book**: pp. 224–7
- **PPT**: 8.2a–c
- **Worksheets**:
  8.2a Trying out structures
  8.2b Key assignment points

Other Student Book pages
- Exploring sample responses: informative, analytical and argumentative assignments, pp. 240–5

Exploring skills

Ask students to spend two to three minutes discussing the differences between the writing types in this assignment – for example, thinking about what sorts of texts inform but don't argue a point of view. They should also consider what is likely to interest an audience in this sort of writing. Points will include:

- interesting or unusual facts
- a personal connection to the information
- revealing insights into a place, person, animal or historical situation.

Then, ask students to think for 5 minutes about what interests them. They could look at the plan one student has created under 'My interests' and quickly list their own ideas. Then, with three other students they can share ideas – sometimes other people's interests can spark new ideas, so they might like to rewrite or add to their original list.

Next, ask them to look at the notepad in **Q1**. Ask the class: can they see links between it and the first set of 'interest' notes? How has the 'interest' been developed? (The student is now thinking about the form of writing he or she might use.) Ask students to copy and complete the notepad example, and think about what the student might have written about for Form 3, the diary entry, and Form 4, the leaflet. An example might be: 'Form 3: *how I heard a radio programme about Komodo dragons, and what my parents said when I told them I wanted to do something to help them.*'

Building skills

Read through the bullet list on p. 225 with the class, and point out that these examples are in some cases quite a development from the first ideas the student had. For example, how is an article on 'Lion taming' linked to the 'My interests' set of notes?

Students should come up with their own assignment ideas for **Q2** based on the initial 'My interests' notes they completed. In **Stage 1** they must select a title to work with. Then can use a spider diagram like the one in **Stage 2** to generate further ideas for **Stage 3** later. Emphasise that they will need a minimum of eight to nine points to create an interesting and well-developed assignment. Encourage students to consider whether the title they have selected will challenge them to produce their best work.

Developing skills

Before students begin **Stage 3**, in which they develop their points, ask them as a class: what would make for interesting reading? Is it just *more* information or further points of view? Elicit from them ideas such as:

- quirky or surprising details (*Did you know that...?*)
- 'colour' or information linked to the senses (sights, sounds, smells – about places, people, events)
- anecdotes (short accounts of interesting moments)
- surprising or revealing facts and statistics
- personal connections, where appropriate
- links to other ideas, texts, facts, situations.

Then move onto **Q3**. Read through the questions and then distribute **Worksheet 8.2a**. Ask students to write down their key points for their chosen assignment in the strips – this can be in any order. Once they have done this, they should order them logically.

> **Give extra support** by handing out or displaying **Worksheet 8.2b**. This shows an example list of points for the Komodo dragon article. Ask for suggestions as to how these points might best be ordered.

Now, in pairs, ask students to discuss the three beginnings under **Q4** and to decide which they think works best.

Use **PPT 8.2** to get students thinking about **Q4** in more detail. Students can read the three different beginnings to the lion taming task on Student Book p. 227, or you can display them in **PPT 8.2a–c**. As a class, talk about the different effects of each beginning. Elicit the different sort of audience that each would appeal to:

- Beginning 1 is clearly anecdotal, and based on personal memory. It starts with a vivid event and is dramatic, drawing the reader in. It also establishes the writer's interest. It is likely to appeal to readers who enjoy personal writing and reflections.
- Beginning 2 focuses on facts and the subject as a historical topic, using the example of Rose Flanders Bascom to interest the reader before linking her life to the student's. Readers might be girls or women drawn to the story of a woman facing challenges.
- Beginning 3 is less personal, explaining the idea of 'lion-taming' in a professional, factual manner. Likely readers will enjoy detailed, factual texts – perhaps ones that provide advice, guidance and information.

Applying skills

For **Q5**, students should write a first draft of their assignment, having written a full plan first. More confident students could look at their drafts and begin to move paragraphs around, or alter opening sentences to create new effects. They should have a clear sense of audience – are they looking to establish an intimate, personal tone with their reader or a more detached, factual style?

Encourage students to peer-assess their drafts. Each pair should review their partner's draft using the **Sound progress** and **Excellent progress** criteria on Student Book p. 227. From their partner's comments, each student should identify two to three points that could be improved in a subsequent draft.

Towards A/A*	High-attaining students make very specific and deliberate choices about the ways in which they structure their information and ideas to create a convincing voice or viewpoint in order to affect their audience's response. For example, consequences are emphasised, revealed or explained through connective words and phrases (*From that moment...; The truth is...; Because...*).

3 How to approach descriptive and narrative assignments

Assessment objectives

AO2 Writing
- **W1** Articulate experience and express what is thought, felt and imagined
- **W3** Use a range of appropriate vocabulary

IGCSE examination
- **Component 4** Coursework Portfolio (Assignment 2)

Differentiated learning outcomes
- **All students must** come up with a story idea of their own, and create a basic plan (Grade E/D).
- **Most students should** write a plan, add further detail and write a draft (Grade C/B).
- **Some students could** use the ideas provided as a springboard for writing several different drafts of stories or descriptions before evaluating what works and what doesn't (Grade A).

Resources
- **Student Book**: pp. 228–31
- **PPT**: 8.3a–i
- **Worksheet** 8.3 Evaluating my story idea

Other Student Book pages
- Exploring sample responses: descriptive and narrative assignments, pp. 247–9

Exploring skills

The tasks here build on the initial work done on Student Book pp. 216–23, where students responded to a whole range of texts provided. Here they begin by looking at how one theme – 'Danger in the wild' – can generate ideas and then a possible story.

Using **PPT 8.3a–e,** model how students could get ideas from the theme by first listing as many words as possible and then selecting from these, i.e. 'exploring', 'friendship/ friends', 'water'. Finally, show them how to connect ideas in order to come up with a key central narrative, as expressed in the final concept, *'Two school friends...'*.

Give students 10 minutes in **Q1** to come up with their own story idea around the given topic and to note down its key elements. Remind them that they in the actual assignment they can come up with whatever story idea or theme they want! Point them in the direction of the **Top tip** on Student Book p. 228.

Give extra support by suggesting that students use the questions in the speech bubbles on p. 228 in the Student Book to flesh out their ideas. It may be useful to support targeted students by asking them these questions directly and offering some answers, in places.

Building skills

Students should now work on their own and use the **Checklist for success** on Student Book p. 229 as provided on **Worksheet 8.3** to evaluate their own idea. Remind them about the five-part story structure modelled on Student Book p. 229, and go over it again, if necessary. Also draw students' attention to the need for their plot to 'go somewhere' via the **Top tip.**

Once students have drafted their idea, they should discuss it with a partner in **Q2**.

Now give them the chance to redraft and improve their idea, which should not just be 'in their heads' but noted down in writing.

Developing skills

Discuss as a class the two sets of requirements for 'descriptive' and 'narrative' writing to ensure they are clear about what is similar and different about them.

Read the story and description extracts on Student Book p. 230 aloud. Then ask pairs to spend 10 minutes on **Q3**, noting down the following:

- the information conveyed – what we find out about events, characters (if any), setting and so on
- how we find out about characters – through their words, thoughts and feelings as well as through description of them
- the style and detail – particular language used; tenses; imagery
- the viewpoint – who is narrating, or from whose viewpoint we see the events.

Then, use **PPT 8.3f–g** to display the texts one at a time and ask students for indicators of 'story' and 'description' under the headings given above. These can be marked on the slides. Elicit the features that are displayed in the final slides **PPT 8.3h–i**. Of course, you should point out that some stories might begin in the same way as the description and can be told in the present tense, too.

For **Q4**, ask students to work independently for 4–5 minutes to come up with original or interesting ideas. These could be shared with a partner, and then in groups of four, before selecting the best one to share with the class as a whole. Give credit for the most interesting ideas proposed.

Then, ask students to complete **Q5** as an independent activity.

> **Give extra support** by working with a selected group of less confident students to come up with shared ideas, focusing perhaps on the narrative story. Give them a starter sentence, then work together to develop the sentence into a 'dual narrative'. For example:
>
> *The moment I saw that lady in the market I recognised her. But my memories of her were not of the poor, dishevelled wretch who limped past me. Once, she'd been my mistress and...*

Applying skills

Before students undertake **Q6**, ask them to revisit the key conventions of narratives and descriptive pieces in the panels on Student Book p. 230. Direct them to the **Top tips** about these two forms on Student Book p. 231, which mention key ways of developing their ideas.

Q6 invites students to begin developing an idea for a potential story or descriptive piece. Students might take their inspiration from the world around them, things they have experienced and other texts they have read or pictures they have seen. The main thing is to focus on what will make their audience want to read their work.

Towards A/A*	To attain the highest marks, students should be ambitious in their approach to the task, generating original ideas that show imagination and an ability to engage the reader via their use of unusual structural and linguistic devices. This will lead to exciting and vivid descriptions or narratives with a strong sense of atmosphere and/or character and setting.

4 How to approach assignments engaging with ideas and arguments from other texts

Assessment objectives

AO1 Reading
R2 Demonstrate understanding of implicit meanings and attitudes
R3 Analyse, evaluate and develop facts, ideas and opinions
R4 Demonstrate understanding of how writers achieve effects

AO2 Writing
W2 Sequence facts, ideas and opinions

IGCSE examination
- **Component 4** Coursework Portfolio (Assignment 3)

Differentiated learning outcomes
- **All students must** express a personal viewpoint based on the text read (Grade E/D).
- **Most students should** draw out key arguments from a text, explain counter-arguments clearly and use some persuasive techniques in a planned response (Grade C/B).
- **Some students could** draw out key arguments, explain counter-arguments and use the full range of persuasive techniques when planning a response (Grade A).

Resources
- **Student Book**: pp. 232–5
- **Worksheets**:
  8.4a Pandas: annotated article
  8.4b Putting the counter-arguments
  8.4c Pandas: a counter-argument
- **PPT**: 8.4a–f

Other Student Book pages
- Emotive language, pp. 28–31
- Paragraph cohesion, pp. 46–7
- Writing to persuade, pp. 88–9
- Exploring sample responses: assignments engaging with ideas and arguments from other texts, pp. 249–254

Exploring skills

Explain to students that Assignment 3 differs from the other two written coursework assignments in that students must actively respond and refer to a non-fiction text they have read. For that reason, students are also assessed for Reading in this task.

As a whole group, read through the Chris Packham article on Student Book pp. 232-3 and give students 5-10 minutes to work on **Q1**.

Give extra support by using the annotated text on **Worksheet 8.4a** to suggest where students could look for their answers or to prompt them.

Building skills

Set up groups to the groups to compile their points for **Q2**. These will be the arguments Packham makes in his article. Then, ask groups to deal with **Q3**, which asks them to consider first of all whether they agree with Packham or not.

You could take brief feedback at this stage – perhaps a point or opinion from each group, or just a show of hands to get a sense of how students feel, but stress that in responding to the text they will need an informed response, based on carefully thought-out ideas. This will lead to the next part of **Q3**, where students are asked to list both arguments and counter-arguments in the given table. Some prompts assist in the latter, but it might be a good idea to display or distribute **Worksheet 8.4b** at this point – the worksheet reproduces the grid from **Q3** and shows how one of Packham's arguments from the article has been countered by one from the suggested bullet list.

Then, before taking feedback, move on to **Q4**, which learners can complete independently. They should end up with specific examples of the techniques that Packham uses, such as emotive language. At this point, take feedback on both the arguments Packham makes and the persuasive techniques he uses, such as chatty, direct phrases. Use the annotated text on **Worksheet 8.4a** to elicit further points.

> **Give extra challenge** by asking students if they can identify examples of Packham's use of imagery to create memorable ideas or pictures in the reader's mind (for example, the description of the river dolphin and the 'cherries on the cake' idea).

Before they move onto planning their letter in **Developing skills**, give groups a chance to feed back ideas as a whole class. You could, if you wish, set up a short class debate, with one half of the class proposing the motion – 'This house believes pandas should be allowed to die out' – and the other half opposing it.

For the debate, divide the class in two. Select two people on each side. Ask the first person on the pro-side to 'propose' the motion, giving a short speech setting out some of the key points. Then, the first person who opposes the motion will put forward his/her main points against.

Next, the supporting speaker on the pro-side can present some further points, before the second speaker on the opposing side rebuts them. At this point, the audience (the rest of the class) can ask each set of speakers particular questions. The debate should be controlled and managed by a 'Chair' who can be either the teacher or a student who has the authority to manage the debate.

Developing skills

Planning the letter is the next stage and this forms the main part of the task given here. First, read carefully through each step of the task on Student Book p. 234. Read aloud the advice under 'Content' on p. 235, including the final bullet about referring to other texts. You could at this point introduce an article that responded directly to Packham's (see **Worksheet 8.4c**), but you may prefer for students to develop their own ideas, without being influenced by that text.

Finally, for this stage, look at the table of beginnings and endings under **Q5**, and ask students to make a note – either mentally or literally – of the sort of start and end they would use for their letter. Which has most impact? Which sounds most professional?

Make it clear that, although some possible beginnings and endings for the letter are provided, students will need to come up with the sequence of points, as well as deciding the most effective order. Extra support for this is available in **PPT 8.4**. Model approaches using **PPT 8.4a–e** and then use **PPT 8.4f** to share ideas as a class.

Applying skills

Before students write their full plan in **Q6**, which will be quite close to an actual draft of the letter, make sure they are clear about the function of topic sentences. Use the **Top tip** to recap that these are the sentences in paragraphs, usually but not always the first sentence, that sum up or introduce the main idea or point of the paragraph is (see also Student Book pp. 46–7 for more about topic sentences). They are especially useful in argumentative or persuasive writing such as this.

Encourage pairs of students to peer-assess their plans, using the **Sound Progress** and **Excellent Progress** criteria on Student Book p. 235. From their partner's feedback, each student should identify two or three points to improve in their full draft.

| **Towards A/A*** | To gain the highest marks, students should try out different ways of opening and closing paragraphs, and using persuasive techniques within paragraphs to strengthen their points. They should also be able to identify the specific techniques used by Packham and write about how he uses them to affect the reader. |

5 Ways of developing your own views

Assessment objectives

AO1 Reading

R1 Demonstrate understanding of explicit meanings
R2 Demonstrate understanding of implicit meanings and attitudes
R3 Analyse, evaluate and develop facts, ideas and opinions
R5 Select for specific purposes.

IGCSE examination

- **Component 4** Coursework Portfolio (Assignment 3)

Differentiated learning outcomes

- **All students must** decide on an argument in response to the texts read, and explain some of their key points (Grade E/D).
- **Most students should** decide on and plan their argument and the form it will take, and plan how they will add their own ideas (Grade C/B).
- **Some students could** plan a response to the given text, arguing their own viewpoint in imaginative ways and synthesising key ideas and information (Grade A).

Resources

- **Student Book**: pp. 236–9
- **Worksheets**:
  8.5a Do you agree or disagree?
  8.5b Options for responding
- **PPT**: 8.5a–d

Other Student Book pages

- How to approach assignments engaging with ideas and arguments from other texts, pp. 232–5

Exploring skills

Explain to students that writing a response to a non-fiction text may mean drawing on alternative views on the same topic or additional information from other sources.

Display the 'Adopt a panda' web page on Student Book p. 237, and briefly read aloud the notes made just above **Q1** on p. 236. Then, in response to **Q1**, ask pairs to note down their ideas briefly, and then share these with the class as a whole. For example, mentioning the image on the web page in which the pandas appear to be 'hugging'. Ask the class to give some initial views on the different way pandas are presented here compared with Chris Packham's article.

Give extra challenge by adding a further question to the pair discussion: *Is it fair to judge this website on one screen? Is the presentation of pandas any different across the website as a whole?* (Allow students extra time for internet research.)

Building skills

Point out that, having noted down some of the key information from the website and having considered the visual representation of pandas, students are now in a better position to respond to Chris Packham's arguments, however they choose to do so. Remind them that they must not copy or make many direct references to this new information, but should attempt to use it to develop their ideas in their own words.

Ask students to work in pairs again to complete the table in **Q2**. Chris Packham's arguments are listed in column 1, and responses to it (which may be based on the WWF site) should be put in columns 2 and 3.

Give extra support by encouraging students to use **Worksheet 8.5a** to assist them. This provides some of the arguments that they could place into the columns.

For **Q3** on Student Book p. 238, allow pairs 2–3 minutes to look at how the writer has expressed his/her point. Ensure that students are clear about what *synonyms* are and how these help the writer express things in his/her own words.

Developing skills

Students should now work on their own to write their own paragraph as required by **Q4**. They will need to decide beforehand whether they agree or disagree with Packham's argument – they may need to refer back to their completed grid from Student Book p. 236 (see also **Worksheet 8.5a**). You can use **PPT 8.5a–b** to show students how to start with appropriate topic sentences for either a positive or negative response.

Next, allow time to build the rest of the paragraph, reminding them to use connectives, as in the sample in **Q3**, to link or signpost ideas. Then show them **PPT 8.5c–d**, which contain two worked examples of paragraphs for and against Packham's ideas. You can point out particular skills used in each, such as the use of personal anecdote in the first.

Applying skills

Students can work in groups of three for the next stage in the work. First, ask three students to read aloud the transcript on Student Book pp. 238–9, taking the roles of the presenter, Professor Ahmed and Steve Unwin, before discussing the bullets in **Q5**, and making their own notes about the topics covered and the views expressed.

Possible responses might be:

- The general theme is introduced in the presenter's opening question – 'Conservation – a force for good or a huge and expensive waste of time?'
- The 'montage' of wildlife images, and the presenter's opening words establish the subject matter.
- The different views and roles established by the language and register used:
    - the presenter's summative/provocative comments and rhetorical questions ('You have argued for many years…'; 'But species are disappearing, aren't they?')
    - Unwin's counter-points expressed forcefully ('That is very defeatist. Charities have shown, time and time again…')
    - the Professor's less assertive approach ('Er… I wouldn't put it quite like that').

Students now have a chance to think about how they can pick up these texts and 'run' with them. Emphasise that whatever piece they choose from the bulleted list in **Q6** on Student Book p. 239, they will need to refer to the points and arguments expressed and respond to them, develop their own ideas/opinions and write in an appropriate way for their chosen form.

Distribute **Worksheet 8.5b,** which gives students a chance to consider which (if any) of the three options in **Q6** they wish to choose. They can use the grid provided to make notes, or can write a new idea into the fourth column.

Once they have selected an idea, they should present it to you and be able to explain how they would use information and ideas from the texts to develop a suitable response. They should explain any ideas of their own that they plan to include.

Students can assess their plans against the **Sound progress** and **Excellent progress** criteria on Student's Book p. 239. Invite those who are ready to draft a response based on their plan, reminding them of the importance of producing full and fluent paragraphs.

Towards A/A*	High-attaining students will respond to ideas and arguments, and argue their own viewpoint, using the points from the chosen non-fiction text, but also drawing on their own knowledge or alternative sources to create an informed and original response.

1 Using the right language for your audience

Assessment objectives

AO3 Speaking and Listening

SL3 Communicate clearly, fluently and purposefully as an individual and in dialogue with other speakers

SL4 Use register appropriate to audience and context

IGCSE examination

- **Component 5** Speaking and Listening Test (Individual task and discussion)
- **Component 6** Speaking and Listening Coursework (Individual activity, pair-based activity and group activity)

Differentiated learning outcomes

- **All students must** use a spoken style that attempts to match the audience (Grade E/D).
- **Most students should** use varied spoken styles and registers to match the audience (Grade C/B).
- **Some students could** select and use appropriate spoken styles and registers to match the audience (Grade A/A*).

Resources

- Student Book: pp. 258–61
- PPT: 9.1a–j

Other Student Book pages

- Audience: formality and informality, pp. 50–3

Exploring skills

Begin with a short discussion of the following terms to establish students' understanding:

- 'audience': whoever is listening to the speaker
- 'appropriate language and tone': accurate standard English is normally expected.

It will be useful, here, to introduce the concept of tone. Allow 5 minutes for **PPT 9.1a–d**, to let students see and hear which factors contribute to tone. This can either be a class activity, or students can work in pairs, with a short feedback session to the class.

> **Give extra challenge** by encouraging students to identify and explain how the three aspects work in the example sentences on **PPT 9.1c**:
> 1. uses vocabulary that features 't', 'd', which helps emphasise annoyance/disgust
> 2. uses soft 's' sounds and long vowels to create a peaceful mood
> 3. uses straightforward vocabulary and grammar to avoid emotion, and concentrate on method in the instructions.

Explain that tone is created not just by how we use the voice itself, but by all features of speech – vocabulary, grammar, content – and should always suit the audience.

In **Q1**, persuasion is a major purpose of the talk, so vocabulary and grammar that create a conciliatory tone should be selected. Allow 2 minutes for each audience, plus 2 minutes for a brief plenary. **PPT 9.1e–j** contains suggested model responses with a brief explanation for each presentation scenario in **Q1**.

Start **Q2** as a class activity with a volunteer reading out the sample extract on Student Book p. 258. Elicit reasons why this talk is unsuccessful for the intended audience. Features that combine to make this sample talk inappropriate include:

- use of slang or vogue words and expressions: 'As if', 'like', 'man'
- non-standard grammar: 'They don't know nothing about stuff happening to us every day'; 'They ain't...'; 'We was...'
- no real consideration of the audience: this may be appropriate for the speaker's peers, but not for parents
- mostly opinion; only one fact!

Q3 can be done in pairs, taking the factors listed above into account, and with the partner deciding whether the incorrect features have been successfully corrected.

> **Give extra support** by modelling the reworking of the speech extract:
>
> *'Thing is, nobody likes any rules'* might become *'To begin, few people our age will admit to liking rules, even if they know they are necessary.'*
>
> The speaker wants the audience on his/her side, so this is less dogmatic and forceful, but still acknowledges the younger person's natural resistance to authority.

Building skills

Pairs should now read the passage on Student Book p. 259. They should recognise Sara's tone as suitable for her audience and understand how she has achieved Band 1.

Q4 can then be done in pairs or fours, with feedback to the whole group. Emphasise to students that they must both identify Sara's use of the features in the bulleted list and explain how these make her talk appropriate to her audience. Allow 15 minutes.

Developing skills

In **Q5**, give pairs 5 to 10 minutes to identify the factors that make Carlos a Band 1 speaker and the other two Band 4s. Then agree, line by line, how to improve each feature listed in **Q5**.

> **Give extra support** by offering a guide to improving Majid and Lennie's talk.
>
> Majid: 'Boring traffic jams.' This is an incomplete sentence, which adds nothing valuable to his first sentence. Both Majid and Lennie simply voice their anger. They show no awareness of who is listening and ignore Carlos's attempt to elicit useful information, which might help to turn this into a genuine discussion.
>
> Carlos actually asks Majid to be more specific, suggesting he has a better grasp of the way the conversation may go and can guide the direction of the discussion.

In **Q6**, direct students towards a clear understanding of how both speakers are manipulating their language to adopt an appropriate tone in a difficult circumstance. There is an implicit awareness from each speaker of the needs of his/her audience: the customer has an important engagement; the official is limited in what he/she can do to solve the problem. Both try to maintain a civil tone: correct standard English, no offensive vocabulary (though 'It's appalling' reveals the customer's growing anger).

For **Q7** students can engage in the analysis, either singly or in pairs for those with less confidence. Remind the students that they are assessing the suitability of the extract for a class similar to theirs. Again, it will be useful to read the sample opening aloud.

Applying skills

Q8 is probably best set as homework. Students will need some time to assimilate what they have learnt in the lesson. Stress to them that, despite the guidance offered in the Student Book, content is only one factor to consider when selecting the appropriate speaking style. A follow-up lesson can be allocated to give students the chance to peer-assess their work, using the **Sound progress** and **Excellent progress** criteria on Student Book p. 261.

Towards A/A*	High-attaining students will select appropriate vocabulary and varied sentence forms. Their vocabulary should be clearly right for the subject: for example, assuredly employing specialist terms in informative contexts or, in emotive contexts, using terms that elicit the response desired from the audience. Similarly, with sentence forms, there will be fluent crafting: in precision of expression in informative presentations and in subtle implications in persuasive ones.

2 Choosing and researching a presentation topic

Assessment objectives

AO3 Speaking and Listening

SL2 Present facts, ideas and opinions in a sustained, cohesive order

IGCSE examination

- **Component 5** Speaking and Listening Test (Individual task and discussion)
- **Component 6** Speaking and Listening Coursework (Individual activity)

Differentiated learning outcomes

- **All students must** use material that shows some knowledge of the topic (Grade E/D).
- **Most students should** be able to present well-researched and coherently organised material (Grade D/C).
- **Some students could** present thoroughly researched and carefully shaped material (Grade A/A*).

Resources

- **Student Book**: pp. 262–5
- **PPT**: 9.2a–f

Other Student Book pages

- Structuring your presentation, pp. 266–7

Exploring skills

Read through the opening section including the **Checklist for success** on Student Book p. 262. Point out that a student's first consideration is: what do I want my audience to take away from my presentation? Also ask students for possible purposes, such as informing or arguing.

Sum up by reinforcing that students need to link the topic to the listener's experience. The topic may be very personal (the birth of a sibling) or about a rather obscure topic (the hammered dulcimer). The student may be very enthusiastic about the subject; the audience may not be. They may even be hostile to a view being expressed.

Before students answer **Q1**, use **PPT 9.2a–f** to run through possible areas, and levels, of research, to put them in a better position to decide which they could talk about most successfully.

> **Give extra support** by listing a variety of sources for research purposes: for example, libraries, websites (caution that not all are reliable), news agencies (such as newspapers, television and radio), specialist magazines, other people.
>
> **Give extra challenge by** offering some less age-related topics; these may encourage some students to be more thorough in their research, or to look deeper into a subject they are interested in. Examples might include the following:
> - Argue that some sports stars are overpaid.
> - Persuade people that they should relax more.
> - Inform people of the greatest threats to our way of life.

Building skills

Regarding the difficulty of a chosen topic, point out that a mainly factual presentation may seem more straightforward than one involving persuasion; but to engage the audience successfully is not particularly easy – no one wants to listen to a list!

Allow 5 minutes for students to complete **Q2** in pairs. Then hold a 5-minute feedback session to share the findings.

> **Give extra challenge** by asking students to assess, and compare, the effect of each of the two presentations on the audience. Is the selection of material effective?

Point out to students that the sample Band 3 presentation extract gives mostly information while the sample Band 1 extract mentions almost nothing about the trip, but immediately begins to discuss wider issues regarding school trips in general. Here is a good example of how, usually, a Band 3 candidate will *present* a topic competently, to interest the audience, whereas a Band 1 candidate will *develop* a topic, to make the best impact on the audience.

Developing skills

Spend a few minutes discussing 'relevant' content. Obviously, this refers to important details, which are clearly connected to the main topic. Sometimes, however, a detail may not appear relevant immediately: it may, for example, offer a light moment in a serious topic. For example, mentioning that Lucy was probably still chewing her breakfast is a humorous touch, reinforcing the fact that many students struggle to get up early, even for something they will enjoy!

Tell students, that an audience may be deeply involved in the presentation, but will still need moments to assimilate or reflect on what they have heard. Including some less vital details (such as Lucy's breakfast) will give the audience the necessary listening space, enhancing their overall appreciation of the presentation.

Q3 could be done in pairs after reading the extract about Muhammad Ali on Student Book p. 264. Take feedback, eliciting the following from students:

- There are seven facts.
- They are used to demonstrate how he quickly established himself as a top-class boxer.
- The student's main point is that Ali is the greatest boxer, but that he is also well known for his political stances.
- Apart from the factual record, she says he was handsome and includes his own quotation of himself. Here is an example of a detail that, at first, could seem trivial, even irrelevant, but it suggests why he was 'loved' (for his character) as well as being regarded as a great boxer. She does not say that he was handsome, just because she thought him good looking!

Run through the bullets at the foot of Student Book p. 264 to summarise for students the strengths of the Muhammad Ali extract.

Applying skills

Whilst **Q4** is obviously an individual task, it could also be done in pairs, to encourage self- and peer-assessment. Remind students of the discussion and conclusions on the sample responses shown at the top of Student Book p. 263. Band 3 students present topics; they show good knowledge of the topic and are generally successful in suiting material to their audience. Band 1 students select and shape their material to manipulate the audience response.

Remind students to research more material than they think they will need. They may need to do some quick 'editing' as they speak, or someone in the audience may also be knowledgeable on the topic and require detailed answers to questions not covered by the presentation.

Towards A/A*	High-attaining students will research thoroughly. Their presentations will show clearly that they have considered all aspects of the topic, but have used only the most suitable for the purpose, with each detail assuredly matched to an appropriate point of view. They will appear to be completely in command of the material. This will be reinforced by the assured use of the most appropriate speaking style, as well as by expressing views that demonstrate a strong personal response to many aspects of the topic.

3 Structuring your presentation C E

Assessment objectives

AO3 Speaking and Listening

SL2 Present facts, ideas and opinions in a sustained, cohesive order

SL3 Communicate clearly, fluently and purposefully as an individual and in dialogue with other speakers

IGCSE examination

- **Component 5** Speaking and Listening Test (Individual task and discussion)
- **Component 6** Speaking and Listening Coursework (Individual activity)

Differentiated learning outcomes

- **All students must** use facts and ideas to give a straightforward presentation (Grade E/D).
- **Most students should** organise facts and ideas to present a topic clearly (Grade D/C).
- **Some students could** shape their material to convey the presentation as effectively as possible (Grade A/A*).

Resources

- Student Book: pp. 266–7
- PPT: 9.3a–i

Other Student Book pages

- Delivering your presentation and answering questions, pp. 270–1

Exploring skills

Emphasise to students the importance of an effective structure. This aspect alone can raise the grade of a presentation:

- It gives the speaker an air of confidence and authority.
- It gives the audience confidence that this is a presentation with direction, which is worth listening to.

In this respect the opening and ending are very important. Begin by focusing on bullet 2 in **Q1** on Student Book p. 266. One of the trickiest concepts for students to grasp is 'logical order'. Often they can recognise it, but there is no formula to produce it: each presentation has its own logic.

One way to test the concept may be to say that a logical order is one where no other arrangement of the details would sound better in that presentation, by that speaker. Recommend that students use this test whenever deciding on an order for a presentation.

As the details of each presentation on a school subject will vary, **PPT 9.3a–d** offers a short example of how **Q1** bullet 2 might be interpreted.

For **Q2**, suggest to students that they produce too many, rather than too few, details. When the student has found all possible details, given the time and sources available, an informed decision can be made on the overall structure of the presentation, and the student can select and order the material to best effect. It's always better to have to leave something out, than have to search for more information.

Building skills

It may be constructive to show **PPT 9.3e–f** before students tackle **Q3**. They can then can move on to trying the three specific techniques referred to in the bullet points.

Mention to students that these techniques are best used sparingly and with tact. The tone of the presentation relies as much on choice of language as any other factor: for example, any flippant use of humour may prove inappropriate in a presentation on a serious subject like a disease that is potentially upsetting to some in the audience.

On the other hand, in 'your favourite school subject' humour may well be appropriate, perhaps allowing the student to make some pertinent points that might otherwise land him/her in trouble!

Give extra support by working through **PPT 9.3e–f** more systematically. These offer three suggestions for how the presentation might begin and the effect of each one.

Give extra challenge by asking students to pick an obscure topic for a presentation and come up with a way of establishing a link in their opening between the subject and the listeners' experience, in order to engage the audience successfully. For example, they might choose 'medieval sports'. The student may have enthusiasm for field sports. He/she researches into the background to, say, archery and discovers that this, like many modern field sports, has its origin in the need for military training in the Middle Ages. This provides the opening link.

Developing skills

Run through the text about choice of endings on Student Book p. 267, and show **PPT 9.3g–h**, before tackling **Q4**. Allow pairs a few minutes to work through **Q4** and then take feedback. Conclusions should include the following:

- The speaker is urging the audience to take action in support of desirable change, so the purpose is persuasive.
- The direct appeal at the end suggests to the audience that they have the power to make a difference; this is a persuasive technique.

In **Q5**, numbering the sentences will help student to get to grips with the task. The students should recognise that this is essentially a list. Suggestions for improvement include:

- A simple reordering: for example, 6, 2, 4, 5, 3, 1, 7. This is provided on **PPT 9.3i**.
- Sentence 3 could clearly give more specific details on the books and equipment available.
- Sentence 2 might read: 'I've not been paid by any member of staff to say this, but our Maths staff have to be the best!'

Applying skills

Allow students at least 15 to 20 minutes to complete **Q6** individually. Their main focus should be on creating an effective beginning and ending, but clearly these must suit the overall structure of the presentation.

You could arrange a follow up session to hear some, or all, of these presentations, or perhaps have students present to each other in groups of five. Each student can then be peer-assessed by the others in the group, using the **Sound progress** and **Excellent progress** criteria on Student Book p. 267.

Towards A/A*	The best presentations will be shaped and structured assuredly. For example: • In an informative presentation, the audience will be led into the topic with something they can easily relate to, before being drawn into less familiar detail. • In an argumentative or persuasive talk, the line of argument will seem clear and natural, linking the reasons offered, so that each builds on the former in a seamless way, with the most appropriate details used to support each reason.

4 Using imagery, rhetorical techniques and humour for effect

Assessment objectives

AO3 Speaking and Listening

- **SL1** Articulate experience and express what is thought, felt and imagined
- **SL2** Present facts, ideas and opinions in a sustained, cohesive order
- **SL4** Use register appropriate to audience and context
- **SL5** Listen to and respond appropriately to the contributions of others

IGCSE examination

- **Component 5** Speaking and Listening Test (Individual task)
- **Component 6** Speaking and Listening Coursework (Individual activity)

Differentiated learning outcomes

- **All students must** use some techniques that engage the audience (Grade E/D).
- **Most students should** use a varied range of techniques to engage the audience (Grade D/C).
- **Some students could** show an assured use of a wide range of appropriate techniques to suit the needs of the audience (Grade A/A*).

Resources

- **Student Book**: pp. 268–9
- **PPT**: 9.4a–h

Other Student Book pages

- Structuring your presentation, pp. 266–7

Exploring skills

Introduce the idea that the use of imagery, rhetorical devices and humour can enliven even a rather factual informative presentation. These devices should not be overused, however, and each must always suit the overall tone of the presentation. There is no formula; students need to develop good judgement when using these techniques.

As a warm up on imagery, ask one half of the class to provide examples of similes and the other half to provide examples of metaphors on the subject of 'Getting up to go to school'. Spend 2 to 3 minutes sampling them and ask students to comment on their effectiveness or suitability.

> **(PPT) Give extra support by** reminding students of the difference between a simile and a metaphor, using **PPT9.4a**.

For **Q1** and **Q2**, allow students to work in pairs for 5 to 10 minutes. Then take brief feedback. If necessary, guide them to the following examples from the Band 1 sample response. These illustrate how good use of technical devices encourages listeners to develop ideas for themselves, thus becoming more involved in the presentation.

- Imagery – there are two prominent examples:
  - simile: 'like a god' – in Caliban's eyes, Prospero, with his magic, often whimsically hands out benefits or punishments.
  - metaphor: 'serpent' – the serpent has an obvious connection with the snake in the Garden of Eden. Even the island may be regarded as a kind of Eden, insofar as it features two innocents: Miranda and Ferdinand.
- Alliteration – 'He holds himself': the effort of exhaling the 'h' consecutively helps stress the words, suggesting Caliban's hatred of Prospero's authority.
- Repetition
  - 'He demands and he demands': the rhythm on the first syllables is slightly awkward, emphasising the burden Caliban feels himself to be under.
  - 'As if...': this occurs four times, but the student skilfully avoids overuse. The first use sets up the idea of Prospero's attitude: the next three demolish it.

- Minor sentence – 'Always craving more.': following the repetition of 'He demands' this reinforces how Prospero is never satisfied. By omitting the subject of the sentence, the student has made Caliban put the focus on the perpetual craving.

PPT 9.4b shows an alternative Band 1 extract, which also makes good use of the same technical devices.

> **Give extra challenge** by asking students to work out how the imagery examples, in **PPT 9.4c–d**, create their effects:
> - visual – creating an image through choice of detail
> - aural – use of alliteration and onomatopoeia in 't', 'g', 'cr', 'br', 'ck' and 'ar' suggesting sounds
> - kinaesthetic – assonance and alliteration in 'slipped' and 'shifted', the rhythm of the sentence suggesting the movement.

Building skills

Before students start **Q3**, spend 2 minutes recapping that repetition is often effective if done in threes, as with the 'as if' from the Caliban response on Student Book p. 268. For example: 'Despite having hideous blisters on his feet, Albert insisted on running again, and again, and again.' The second 'and again' suggests Albert is determined; the third might imply that Albert is very courageous – or that the speaker thinks he is an idiot, who will never learn!

Add that the speaker can modify the effect of the repetition by the way it is spoken. In the above example, the speaker might pause before the last repeat, and deliver the words as a kind of sigh. Invite some students to offer different interpretations. This should prepare students for improving the Band 3 sample extract in **Q3**.

Developing skills

For **Q4**, take 5 minutes to tell students that there are three main reasons for adding rhetorical questions (**PPT 9.4e** gives an example of each):

- to engage the audience, quickly
- to encourage the audience to consider the speaker's viewpoint for themselves
- to sound less dogmatic, as if the speaker is exploring the topic with the audience.

Then they can add their own to the sample response.

For **Q5** emphasise that the use of humour is risky because not everyone shares the same sense of humour. Irony, for example, can be cutting and so be inappropriate for some audiences. As a short extension, explore the examples in **PPT 9.4f–g**, which illustrate that care must be taken with irony.

Exaggeration can be presented to the students as an aspect of humour, since this is often the effect. Again, show that care must be taken by displaying **PPT 9.4h**.

Applying skills

Once students have written their presentation openings in **Q6**, allow time to hear a selection of these. Students will benefit from practising their delivery and judging the effect on their audience, while listeners will benefit from assessing the others' results. Listeners can use the **Sound progress** and **Excellent progress** criteria on Student Book p. 269 to give feedback on each presentation.

| **Towards A/A*** | High-attaining students will integrate the technical devices discussed so that they form a natural part of their presentation, and are not added as afterthoughts. In top grade presentations these devices will be appropriate in nature and tone. |

5 Delivering your presentation and answering questions

Assessment objectives

AO3 Speaking and Listening

- **SL2** Present facts, ideas and opinions in a sustained, cohesive order
- **SL3** Communicate clearly, fluently and purposefully as an individual and in dialogue with other speakers
- **SL5** Listen to and respond appropriately to the contributions of others

IGCSE examination

- **Component 5** Speaking and Listening Test (Individual task and discussion)
- **Component 6** Speaking and Listening Coursework (Individual activity)

Differentiated learning outcomes

- **All students must** use material in a straightforward manner and answer questions (Grade E/D).
- **Most students should** prepare material to be competent in delivery and when answering questions (Grade D/C).
- **Some students could** prepare material thoroughly to be assured in delivery and answering questions (Grade A/A*).

Resources

- **Student Book:** pp. 270–1
- **PPT:** 9.5a–g

Exploring skills

Draw the students' attention to the format of the individual task. The most common is the formal talk or presentation, but there are other ways of presenting material. Monologues, dramatic performances, role-play and media/news/documentary reports are all acceptable alternatives.

However, point out that the **Checklist for success** on Student Book p. 270 applies whatever the format. For example, the student may give a presentation as a TV news reporter, first giving the report and then answering questions as if from the studio presenter. He/she must look secure in his/her knowledge of the subject of the report.

Allow about 10 minutes for **Q1**, choosing one from the two options given here to allow for peer assessment:

- Two pairs – in one, the interviewee is interested in the food store job; in the other, the interviewee is uninterested. Each pair can then assess the other.
- Two students play the interviewers and two play the interviewees, with the whole group assessing what they saw. Remind students that it is not enough to say which interviewee was best; they must identify the specific features that made one successful – for example: clear, detailed responses to questions, evidence that the interviewee had researched the job; keeping good eye contact with the interviewer; enthusiastic tone of voice.

Building skills

Emphasise to students that, as always, the audience, whoever they are, in whatever context, are an integral part of the presentation. A presenter who appears confident gives the audience confidence, which means they relax and become more perceptive. They believe that:

- they are listening to someone who knows what he/she is talking about
- the presentation will be worth hearing.

Remind students that speakers deal with audiences in different ways: a stand-up comedian moves around and jokes with the audience; a presenter at an awards ceremony will be more serious.

Emphasise that reading from a script during a presentation will not be allowed! Stress that that even if a PPT or some other audio/visual aid is used (for example, to illustrate a presentation on painting), this should be an extra – it should never be the main focus of a presentation. If a student needs reminders, ask them to use a cue card. Not all students may be confident with these. They need to be given time to practise preparing and using a cue card effectively.

PPT — **Give extra support** by working through **PPT 9.5a–g** to help students prepare an effective cue card.

For **Q2**, ask students to work in groups of four. Two should deliver the sample extract individually to amuse and two make it sound sad. After each performance, the others discuss whether or not the approach was successful and explain which aspects of the delivery contributed to that success, or otherwise. Allow 10 minutes for this.

Give extra challenge by considering whether certain topics, by their nature, demand a particular approach. For example, can a presentation on world poverty ever be treated humorously? Or can one about a celebrity who is always making others laugh be treated seriously? In small groups, each student will suggest a topic, then the group will discuss the most appropriate way to present it.

For **Q3**, ask the students to focus on how a presentation with the three bulleted features would make the listeners feel: frustrated, bored, uncomfortable, irritable.

Developing skills

Allow 5 minutes for **Q4**. Discuss with students how these types of question are ones they should try to anticipate, because many end-of-presentation questions will involve either explaining or clarifying further detail.

Begin work on **Q5** by pointing out to students that a full answer is nearly always preferable to a brief one, but that they should develop judgement in knowing when to stop. The questioner doesn't want to hear another presentation! When they examine the two answers, they should see how the Band 1 sample response satisfies the questioner's immediate request and also offers sufficient extras: for example, alternatives, avenues for further consideration, to obviate the need for a follow up. The Band 3 sample response, though adequate, is rather general and closed: for example, the final assertion could be exemplified, not that many people would disagree with its view!

Applying skills

Remind students that, in tackling **Q6**, they need to observe the same requirements as outlined above for **Q5**, but, in addition, acknowledge that there may be some moral force behind the bulleted questions on Student Book p. 271. The speaker may need to be tactful in defending the view that watching movies like this is justifiable. The tone must be conciliatory, demonstrating tact in the style of delivery as well as the content. Advise them not to antagonise an audience when they want them to agree with them.

Remind students to prepare for questions in **Q7** that cover the areas dealt with in the presentation, then practise delivering these in a confident way. They need to appear confident, even if they are wishing the question hadn't been asked!

Give extra challenge by asking students to think of the most challenging, difficult questions they can. Some questioners may seek to trip a speaker up. Students should be prepared.

Towards A/A*	High-attainers will be thoroughly prepared. They will have material that is the result of wide research and carefully considered views. In addition, they will have anticipated a wide variety of questions, which they will answer in an assured manner speaking confidently and fluently.

6 Preparing for discussion

Assessment objectives

AO3 Speaking and Listening

SL3 Communicate clearly, fluently and purposefully as an individual and in dialogue with other speakers

SL4 Use register appropriate to audience and context

SL5 Listen to and respond appropriately to the contributions of others

IGCSE examination
- **Component 5** Speaking and Listening Test (Discussion)
- **Component 6** Speaking and Listening Coursework (Pair-based activity and group activity)

Differentiated learning outcomes

- **All students must** use material that is sufficient to continue discussions and answer questions (Grade E/D).
- **Most students should** prepare significant contributions to help sustain the discussion and answer questions (Grade D/C).
- **Some students could** prepare to lead in sustaining discussions and answer questions that invite further discussion (Grade A/A*).

Resources
- **Student Book**: pp. 272–3
- **PPT**: 9.5a–g, 9.6a

Other Student Book pages
- Responding to talk, seeing implications and summarising, pp. 278–9

Exploring skills

Emphasise to students that in a discussion everyone should take an active role. There are two reasons for this – namely, to demonstrate:

- that the student can express and defend ideas, and challenge alternative ones
- the student's listening skills, which will be dealt with more fully in Lesson 8.

Remind students that a cue card will be a useful memory aid. See **PPT 9.5a–g** for more about making a cue card.

Before students answer **Q1**, explain that preparation includes having a clear idea of the terms you are using for your discussion. Allow a few minutes to talk through what is meant by 'greatest', before they nominate any individuals. Offer these definitions:

- having an important position in society, wealth or status
- having extraordinary ability/high achievements
- being extremely kind, considerate or compassionate
- being extremely brave.

Ask students to consider each option. Do they have any alternative definitions? Are these suitable as criteria by which to judge any person they may nominate?

Allow 5 minutes for groups to answer **Q1**, giving time for students to consider carefully how their nominees meet the criteria and to agree their five choices. Then reflect that, in coming up with their reasons, they are in fact having an effective discussion. Elicit any good discussion techniques the groups used.

Give extra support by showing the grid in **PPT 9.6a** to targeted students. They can use their own version of this to weigh up the candidates for the 'greatest' people.

Building skills

Point out to students that, for **Q2**, the chair of the group, even if he/she remains neutral, will need to be aware of the main facts, of the likely views of those taking part, and of alternative views and courses of action that may not arise in the course of discussion.

Then allow 10 minutes for groups of three to work through the bullet points on Student Book p. 272. Make sure students understand the following points:

- Allowing each person to give a brief introduction of their position is useful, but keep it to 30 seconds each and stop them if they overrun. If not, the discussion can become a series of individual presentations, with no time for real discussion.
- Similarly, if speakers are to sum up their positions, these need to be done succinctly, so as to give everyone a fair opportunity. Most of the time must be spent in discussion. Of course, the chair needs to be seen to be tactful and fair in giving everyone an equal opportunity to speak.
- The chair's summary needs to be a synthesis of major points discussed and conclusions drawn, and should reflect the level of agreement, if any. Any personal view, in the concluding remarks, should demonstrate that the chair has given fair consideration to other views expressed, even if he/she doesn't agree with them.
- A unanimous conclusion may not be possible, but an acceptable one will be where the chair suggests the best compromise decision (and persuades others to accept it).

Q3 is best prepared in pairs, though each student should join a different group for Q4, as far as is practical. Allow 5 minutes for Q3 and give two short examples, such as:

- facilities need properly trained teachers to ensure students get the best from them
- computers in schools must be kept up to date and have decent technical support.

Ask students to spend 10 minutes on Q4, reminding them that each group member must create notes to support both positions.

> **Give extra challenge** by asking students to draw general conclusions about what they learned from the discussions in Q4 – for example, rather than making subject specific or personal points, they should look for the most effective methods of chairing and arguing.

Developing skills

Allow at least 5 minutes for Q5. Point out to students that challenging a view does not necessarily imply that you disagree with it. The main purposes of a challenge are:

- to test whether or not the speaker has carefully considered his/her position
- to help the challenger to understand the view more fully.

Allow at least 5 minutes for Q6. Either during feedback or before the task, make sure you elicit the following:

- Even a confident person copes better with a well-thought out view.
- 'Difficult' questions are usually ones for which you are not prepared.
- If you have supporting evidence, that will give you confidence.

Applying skills

There is much to do in this lesson and it is likely there will not be time to watch all the discussions from Q7, so a follow-up lesson will be needed. The remainder of this lesson could then be given over to preparation and some research. If a follow up is not possible, it may be better to watch one or two discussions, and ask the rest of the class to watch and comment on how well prepared the participants were.

> **Towards A/A*** | High-attaining students will have material that is thoroughly researched. They will also have developed the material beyond what might seem the anticipated limits of a discussion, in order to be ready to initiate/anticipate the development of that discussion, if necessary, possibly by the use of answers, which invite further consideration of the topic.

7 Developing and supporting ideas with confidence

Assessment objectives
AO3 Speaking and Listening
- **SL2** Present facts, ideas and opinions in a sustained cohesive order
- **SL5** Listen to and respond appropriately to the contributions of others

IGCSE examination
- **Component 5** Speaking and Listening Test (Discussion)
- **Component 6** Speaking and Listening Coursework (Pair-based activity and group activity)

Differentiated learning outcomes
- **All students must** use ideas they can develop through careful listening (Grade E/D).
- **Most students should** help sustain discussions through significant contributions and attentive listening (Grade D/C).
- **Some students could** respond to others and develop discussions through varied and appropriate contributions (Grade A/A*).

Resources
- **Student Book**: pp. 274–7
- **PPT**: 9.7a

Other Student Book pages
- Responding to talk, seeing implications and summarising, pp. 278–9

Exploring skills

Explain to students that however well prepared they are, they still need to be able to perform well under pressure. To some extent, frequent practice can build confidence, but in a robust discussion, a speaker must try to keep a clear mind on his/her position and know which details will support that position best. Add that not all discussions are adversarial. **Q2** exemplifies a supportive discussion. Even in such a discussion, however, a speaker needs to look confident: other participants are more likely to respect what a confident speaker is saying.

Allow 5 minutes for **Q1**, which explores the key skill of making points and addressing counter-points. In pairs, once they have made their lists, ask one student to make two points for the view, while the other counters them. Then they can reverse positions for a further two points. Tell students to be rigorous in listing strong points on both sides, regardless of which side they favour. This will help students to consider both sides and gain confidence in doing so.

Give them this example of someone who supports the view:
- **For**: competitive sport encourages people to be selfish, to believe winning is more important than any other factor.
- **Counter**: competitive sport recognises that we have a competitive nature and is a harmless way of satisfying that nature.

Start **Q2** as a class activity allowing 5 minutes. Point out that this is an exploratory discussion, in which both speakers ask questions not to win an argument but to gain a better understanding of the advertisements they are examining. The questions, however, can still be challenging. Both students question each other to support or challenge their analysis. They ask open questions, which raise possibilities. Whether or not lines of inquiry prove productive, is not the focus; it is the approach that matters: always looking for another view or idea.

Allow students 5 to 10 minutes to complete the grid for **Q3** individually or in pairs. Draw students' attention to the reasons for questions given on Student Book p. 275:
- requesting extra information
- encouraging someone to clarify or extend an idea
- challenging what someone has said.

Students should find:

1. Abi is asking Jenny for more information (but is also challenging her idea).
2. Abi is asking Jenny for more information.
3. Jenny is asking Abi to clarify an idea.
4. Abi is asking Jenny to clarify an idea.
5. Jenny is challenging Abi's idea.

> **Give extra challenge** by asking if all the examples fit neatly into the categories offered. In [1], is Abi challenging a point made by Jenny earlier, or is it her own point she is asking Jenny about? What is important here is that students should see that discussion is a dynamic activity requiring alertness on the part of the participants.

Building skills

Allow at least 10 minutes for **Q4**, which explores the vital skill of developing an idea effectively. Point out that students must be aware of the wording in a topic for discussion. For example, in the first statement, the word 'total' is very important. In this case, those who agree with it cannot concede that football is *ever* worth the time spent on it. Those who disagree must find points that show football *often* has value.

> **Give extra support** by an example and support this with **PPT 9.7a**.
> - Development of idea: all football offers is the chance for millions of people to waste 90 minutes of their time at least once a week.
> - Countering the idea: football gives people an opportunity to enjoy some valuable leisure time, often with friends.

Developing skills

In **Q5**, remind students that one way to find a counter-view is by focusing on a key word and then seek to qualify it. Allow the class 5 minutes to identify and then suggest the key word in each sentence in the statements on Student Book p. 276. Feedback should include:

- In statement 1: the key word is 'only'. Is there really no other place better?
- In statement 2: the key word is 'everything' – every *single* thing? How does the speaker know this?
- In statement 3: the key word is 'fool'. Does that mean everyone else is a fool?

> **Give extra challenge by** asking students to explain how the challenge to each key word works. In statement 1 – 'only': the speaker is vulnerable to challenge by precluding any other place: the speaker will be forced to find a wide range of reasons to defend the choice of place. In statement 2 – 'everything': the speaker has to find a huge range of detail to defend the position. In statement 3 – 'fool', the speaker risks alienating his listeners. Not a clever thing to do!

Applying skills

Run through the **Checklist for success** on Student Book p. 276 and then leave students to complete **Q6**. They will acquire confidence only when they prove to themselves that they can run and contribute to a discussion. Invite the class to comment on a few discussions, using the **Sound progress** and **Excellent progress** criteria on Student Book p. 277.

Towards A/A*	High-attainers will sustain discussions by developing and challenging arguments, showing assured listening skills in scrutinising others' language use; also in asking open questions and making suggestions that invite more contributions from others.

8 Responding to talk, seeing implications and summarising

Assessment objectives

AO3 Speaking and Listening

SL2 Present facts, ideas and opinions in a sustained, cohesive order

SL3 Communicate clearly, fluently and purposefully as an individual and in dialogue with other speakers

SL5 Listen to and respond appropriately to the contributions of others

IGCSE examination

- **Component 5** Speaking and Listening Test (Discussion)
- **Component 6** Speaking and Listening Coursework (Pair-based activity and group activity)

Differentiated learning outcomes

- **All students must** use the contributions made by others to develop their own contributions (Grade E/D).
- **Most students should** follow the contributions of others and respond with significant contributions of their own (Grade D/C).
- **Some students could** listen astutely, responding fully and appropriately to others (Grade A/A*).

Resources

- **Student Book**: pp. 278–9
- **PPT**: 9.8a–g

Other Student Book pages

- Developing and supporting ideas with confidence, pp. 274–7

Exploring skills

Start with this 3-minute activity to encourage careful listening. Read out the following sentence pairs once only. Each student, in silence, writes down the change in each. Students then swap notes with a partner, before you give the answers!

1. a) People always enjoy a love story and that is still true today.
   b) People always enjoy a love story and that is true today.

2. a) The easiest way to chop the leeks is to slice each leek longwise twice and then chop all the leek from top to bottom.
   b) The easiest way to chop the leeks is to slice each leek longwise twice and then chop the leek from top to bottom.

3. a) Deprived of the passion of summer, the scene looked like a photograph, accidentally taken in black and white.
   b) Deprived of the passionate summer, the scene looked like a photograph, accidentally taken in black and white.

These are not difficult; the aim is to prepare students to listen more purposefully than usual. Tell them that this skill is vital in discussions: when several speakers are all trying to make their points, they can be hard to follow.

Begin **Q1** by asking three students to read the discussion text on Student Book p. 278 out to the class. After students have answered the question, check that they understand that Lucy's contributions are closed, giving her listeners little to develop. Also that Kamal and Shabnam do at least follow up on comments made by the others. At this point, also draw attention to the **Top tip** which links back to Lesson 7.

PPT — **Give extra support** by showing **PPT 9.8a–d**, which offers a detailed analysis of the role of each person in the discussion text. These can be worked through with individuals, or could be a group activity.

Building skills

Before **Q2**, briefly discuss what 'imply' means. Explain that while some implications are fairly obvious, others can be subtle. You may like to offer these two additional examples:

134 • Lesson 8

- With tennis skills like that, she's unlikely to win Wimbledon.
- His latest painting would look good over that damp patch on my wall.

The implications students should note for **Q2** are:

- line 1: RE is sometimes cited as a waste of time by students
- lines 2–3: Mrs Bates dislikes Tejinder
- lines 4–5: this student sees this older teacher as out of touch with the modern world
- lines 6–7: any intelligent person can work out what's happening in the world themselves
- lines 8–9: older people's values are not relevant to these students.

All of these could be challenged by asking for evidence or asking for clarification.

> **Give extra challenge** by asking students consider this example: 'The 20th century didn't happen as far as our art teacher is concerned.' The implication is ambiguous: is it implying that the art teacher's ideas are old fashioned, or that he thinks 20th-century art was of poor quality? Set students to write three less obvious, more subtle examples of their own about school. They should test these with a friend.

Developing skills

Before groups discuss the topic in **Q3** on Student Book p. 279, explain that when summarising, there are three points to remember:

- Listen carefully.
- Identify the key points.
- Ensure you understand what the other speakers actually said; people get irate if misrepresented.

Point out that it is better to make brief notes frequently, although a quick decision will need to be made as to which to include in a final summary. Ask them also to note down points in their own words as far as possible: this will help them remember them and give them confidence that they have understood the points.

Allow 10 to 15 minutes for **Q3**.

PPT 9.8e–g offers an extension on listening skills, which can be done prior to **Q3**. Have a brief discussion of the points on **PPT 9.8e**. The passage on **PPT 9.8f** should be read to the class, ideally only once, but a second reading may be needed. Students should note three key points. They can then be shown the passage to confirm them. Alternative suggestions should be discussed briefly. Encourage students to trust their own judgements. Then run through **PPT 9.8g**.

Applying skills

As **Q4** is to be done in groups of three, it may be necessary to arrange a follow-up lesson, if all the discussions are to be heard. Students should be realising by now that effective listening is hard work, and you may decide that the practice is enough at this stage. As an alternative, sample a few trios and invite the class to comment, using the **Sound progress** and **Excellent progress** criteria on Student Book p. 279.

Towards A/A*	High-attaining students will show acute listening ability by making contributions that will encourage others to develop a discussion, while clearly demonstrating their own understanding. They will highlight key points, offer new ones, see and respond to implications, and perceptively summarise the contributions of others.

9 Leading a group discussion (C)(E)

Assessment objectives

AO3 Speaking and Listening

SL2 Present facts, ideas and opinions in a sustained, cohesive order

SL5 Listen to and respond appropriately to the contributions of others

IGCSE examination

- Component 6 Speaking and Listening Coursework (Group activity)

Differentiated learning outcomes

- **All students must** use contributions that help to move the discussion forward (Grade E/D).
- **Most students should** make significant contributions and take those of others into account (Grade D/C).
- **Some students could** sustain and direct discussions by making varied and pertinent contributions (Grade A/A*).

Resources

- Student Book: pp. 280–1
- PPT: 9.9a–b

Other Student Book pages

- Preparing for discussion, pp. 272–3

Exploring skills

Spend a few minutes going through the four leadership qualities bulleted in **Q1**. Also explain to students that confidence is a key factor in leading discussion; even very capable speakers may lack confidence. Students can, of course, gain confidence through practice, but they can give themselves some initial security by preparing well. Proper preparation is just as valuable for leading a discussion as for a presentation.

Students may not be required to have a particular view of the topic, but researching into it will enable the group leader to:

- suggest new lines for discussion
- recognise key points and keep the discussion focused on important factors
- see inconsistencies in other speakers' points more easily
- make summarising easier.

(PPT) **Give extra support** by allowing students 5 minutes to suggest a few phrases for each of the four leadership qualities named in **Q1** and to share them with the class. This will create a small bank of phrases for less confident students to hold in reserve. **PPT 9.9a** provides examples.

Building skills

Allow 5 to 10 minutes for pairs to read the sample discussion passage on Student Book p. 280 and then to answer **Q2**. Invite class feedback, eliciting from students that Jessica demonstrates all four leadership qualities:

- Initiating – for example, her opening question.
- Prompting – for example, she prompts Abdul and Sheri directly, by name.
- Directing – for example, she says: 'So you don't seem to agree at all. Is there any middle road?' She realises that Sheri and, in particular, Abdul, have entrenched positions, so she asks them to reconsider, to find some area for agreement.
- Summarising – in her final contribution. Abdul is likely to stick to his belief that there is no alternative and problems will be overcome. Sheri is likely to be more sympathetic to the suggestions. This is because Jessica's contribution hints that Abdul needs to accept that his rigid belief – that nuclear power will be made safe – is not really tenable.

Point out that in this example Jessica's last speech sums up what has been said, but that, in a longer discussion, her final questions could prompt others to further, more developed contributions. As it stands neither Abdul nor Sheri have offered developed arguments.

> **PPT** **Give extra challenge** by asking students to look at the three extra points, Abdul might make, as provided in **PPT 9.9b**. Invite them to suggest how Jessica would put each point to Sheri, to get a more developed response.

Ask students to consider the short discussion on Student Book p. 281 for 3 to 4 minutes and then to suggest answers to **Q3**. They should see that a leader would try to steer the discussion to consider pleasanter aspects of a place:

- by prompting Wayne to stop focusing on what he dislikes
- by directing Jane away from reacting to Wayne's negative comments.

Both need to be directed to make positive comments instead about where they would like to live and why.

Developing skills

Explain to students that, while the points raised by the three interested parties in the discussion about how to spend the money are important, for the discussion to be productive, the focus of **Q4** should be the performance of the chairperson. Students should, therefore, make brief notes on each chairperson as the discussion unfolds, rather than rely on memory and perhaps forget some useful aspects.

An obvious way is to make brief notes in the four categories of leadership quality outlined on Student Book p. 280. While in the chairperson role, the student should be taking notes for an acceptable outcome for his/her concluding comments, but should nonetheless be encouraged to reflect on his/her own performance.

Applying skills

Remind students that in **Q5** they may have to argue a view with which they disagree: for example, that exams are useful and should not be banned. Whichever viewpoint they are given to support, they must be committed to that view.

The student in the role of the chairperson will have to use all his/her skills to bring such opposing views to a conclusion acceptable to both parties.

If you wish to see all students attempt this, a follow-up lesson will be necessary. If there is a significant number of students in the class who still need to build confidence, you may prefer to sample several students in the chairperson's role, whose performances can act as models. As far as possible, select from across the ability range so as to reflect achievable standards for all students.

The **Sound progress** and **Excellent progress** criteria on Student Book p. 281 can be used by students to assess these performances.

Towards A/A*	The most successful candidates will be thoroughly prepared, in order to sustain a discussion by offering new ideas for consideration. Even if not an appointed chairperson, they will guide the direction of the discussion, through an assured ability to be concise and explicit in delivering their own views, while also making pertinent challenges to, and requests for clarification from, others.

10 Getting into role

Assessment objectives

AO3 Speaking and Listening

SL1 Articulate experience and express what is thought, felt and imagined

SL4 Use register appropriate to audience and context

IGCSE examination

- **Component 5** Speaking and Listening Test (Individual task and discussion)
- **Component 6** Speaking and Listening Coursework (Individual activity, pair-based activity and group activity)

Differentiated learning outcomes

- **All students must** use appropriate vocabulary and grammar to try to create believable roles (Grade E/D).
- **Most students should** use a variety of speaking styles to create believable roles (Grade D/C).
- **Some students could** select a wide range of appropriate speaking styles to create complex roles (Grade A/A*).

Resources

- Student Book: pp. 282–3
- PPT: 9.10a–c

Other Student Book pages

- Using imagery, rhetorical techniques and humour for effect, pp. 268–9
- Speaking in role, pp. 284–5

Exploring skills

In Lessons 4 and 5, reference was made to the fact that presentations and discussions do not always need to be presented formally. If students choose to include a role-play element, encourage them to do this, as it opens up a range of alternative methods of presentation.

Point out that gathering information, as suggested in the **Checklist for success** on Student Book p. 282, will provide a sound foundation for creating a convincing character. With this in mind, in **Q1** caution students about creating clichéd, superficial characters. On the other hand, they should avoid creating too much background material, which lacks focus.

PPT 9.10a–c offers some additional prompts for creating the background to the roles in **Q1**. Allow 5 minutes for this. When students have chosen and introduced their character to their groups for **Q2**, hold a brief plenary and ask each trio who created the most believable set of character details. Encourage them to identify what it was that made it successful, e.g. particular details or a combination of details.

Building skills

Introduce **Q3** by explaining to students that the purpose of a monologue is to convey the character's thoughts and, often, feelings to the audience. In some circumstances – film, for example – a voice-over can be employed, but it is usually more dramatic, and in role play more realistic, for a character to speak the monologue. The same applies here, even though the TV audience is not physically present. Encourage students to present the monologue so that the audience has a clear idea of what the character believes he/she has witnessed while the content, language and delivery also convey the character's distressed state. So they will need to work on varying their tone.

> **Give extra support** by spending 5 minutes on the following as a starting point. Students should write down these three sentences:
> - The robbers just burst in, shouting some very rude words.
> - I couldn't believe it. One of them stuck a gun right into a customer's face.
> - I thought they were going to shoot us all at one point.
>
> Ask them to speak each sentence to convey being each of the following: upset, shocked, frightened, angry.

Developing skills

For **Q4**, ask pairs to read the example role-play text aloud, preferably at least twice, so that they can hear the effect of the language. Pairs should conclude that:

- Neither character has much depth. Lisa attempts to sound understanding, but risks coming across as trite, even condescending in the way she offers tea in line 5. Katie moves to attack the school before properly questioning what happened. Explain to students that, in a role play, tension needs to be built up. If a character starts at too a high an emotional pitch, there is nowhere for the character to go, to develop.
- Clearly, the daughter has been excluded from school before the parent has been consulted or given a chance to appeal.

For **Q5**, point out that the way students deliver lines can affect the impact of the performance. Nonetheless, the students should pick up from the role play that:

- The dialogue doesn't really sound either natural or crafted for effect. Lisa needs to make her character sound firm, but conciliatory in tone; here it sounds rather condescending, especially in the last line. Katie needs to make her character a little more questioning: to find out Lisa's reasons for excluding Jiao, before moving to suggest the school is at fault.
- The scene is rather static: for example, Lisa's character, in remaining seated, suggests she does not respect Katie's character. In such a real-life situation, the characters may not move about, but in role play, movement can indicate aspects of character. Even if they are seated, they can alter position, point, hit the desk!
- Lisa's character could establish control early, by offering to explain what happened. Lisa, in asking what Katie would like, puts herself in a weak position, which Katie fails to exploit. Were she to ask Lisa to justify her decision in line 10, she would immediately gain the advantage, but her straightforward demand leads to a vague, unsupported attack on the school, which gives the advantage back to Lisa. One of them needs to assert control earlier.

> **Give extra challenge** by encouraging students to develop the characters by:
>
> - differentiating the language each uses: for example, Katie could use some slightly less accurate grammar to suggest a barely controlled anger
> - using facial expressions or body movements in place of, or to enhance, dialogue: for example, in Line 1, 'Lisa stands, walks to Katie, extending her hand, with a slight smile'.

Q6 offers students a chance to try out some of their ideas from **Q5** for themselves. They should improvise this same situation two or three ways, and be ready to incorporate the most successful approaches into their performance in **Q7**.

Applying skills

If practical, set **Q7** as homework and watch all groups in a follow-up lesson. Students need time to choose their own head teacher/parent interview topic and then prepare and practise the skills required, drawing on their role-play experience from **Q6**.

Students can then be asked to evaluate their performances using the bullets in **Q8** to guide them.

Towards A/A*	High-attaining students will create complex roles assuredly, which suggest implicit aspects of the character. They will do this by adopting the most appropriate speaking style, using a range from highly formal, correct standard English to informal, possibly ungrammatical or dialectal forms. They will also use appropriate non-verbal means, facial expressions and body movements to support their meaning.

11 Speaking in role

Assessment objectives

AO3 Speaking and listening

SL1 Articulate experience and express what is thought, felt and imagined

SL4 Use register appropriate to audience and context

IGCSE examination

- **Component 5** Speaking and Listening Test (Individual task and discussion)
- **Component 6** Speaking and Listening Coursework (Individual activity, pair-based activity and group activity)

Differentiated learning outcomes

- **All students must** use a range of vocabulary and sentence forms to match the character (Grade E/D).
- **Most students should** use a varied vocabulary and grammar to suit the character created (Grade D/C).
- **Some students could** assuredly adapt their speech and speaking style to convey the character created (Grade A/A*).

Resources

- **Student Book:** pp. 284–5

Other Student Book pages

- Using imagery, rhetorical techniques and humour for effect, pp. 268–9
- Getting into role, pp. 282–3

Exploring skills

Remind students that thorough preparation is always necessary for role play, especially as they will usually be working with others. A student must know what he/she will do *and* what everyone else will do. A group role play can easily be ruined by one student who is underprepared.

Q1 is demanding, so set students to tackle the Band 1 example response in pairs, and then feed back after 5 minutes. Elicit from students that in:

- sentence 1 – the mother reveals her own dilemma, but by not saying 'I' focuses on the problem, not herself
- sentence 2 – she acknowledges how this is a mutual problem, indicating an empathy with the other parent: 'Like you…' She is explicit in her feelings: 'I love him…want what's best for him…'
- sentence 3 – she shows in a simple, direct way how much anguish this causes her
- sentence 4 – she acknowledges that she is not the only one with this problem, but it is still a big worry
- sentence 5 – this is less an excuse for the son's behaviour, more a touch of desperation or hope that a solution can be found before too much damage is done.

> **Give extra support** by asking students to suggest the main emotion in each sentence. For example: sentence 1 – uncertainty; sentence 2 – love for her child; sentence 3 – anxiety; sentence 4 – empathy, sharing worry; sentence 5 – compassion for the son. Then ask them to see if any of the same feelings are explicit in the Band 3 example. Guide students to see that, despite the use of 'I', this example is less explicit and more general about feelings. There is no real sense of the personal anxiety, which is evident in the Band 1 example.

Building skills

To help pairs with **Q2** you might suggest some, or all, of the following prompts:

The government minister will probably argue on a national level – for example:

- Space research creates jobs, in associated industries.
- We cannot afford to be left behind other countries in this kind of research, not least for military reasons.

The shopkeeper may be more concerned with personal issues, for example:
- Problems like world poverty and hunger are more important.
- The money would be better spent on hospitals, education, decent housing.

Spend 5 minutes asking for suggestions as to what other arguments may be involved and how all these can be used. Also ask students to consider what the shopworker's opinion and treatment of the minister will be.

Warn them to avoid too many assumptions: for example, that the minister will necessarily be the more intelligent. Characters who confound the expectations of the audience can often be the most believable.

> **Give extra challenge** by modelling how to avoid creating characters who are stereotypical. For example, the minister may well push the government line effectively, but struggle to answer the shopkeeper's questions, relying heavily on prepared arguments. The shopkeeper may use relatively simple grammar, yet show high intelligence by asking some searching questions.

Developing skills

The main point for students to recognise from **Q3** is that the reporter is not acting like a camera: merely recording events. There is considerable personal involvement. She identifies with, and therefore speaks for, the other spectators. Features include:

- vocabulary often emotive – 'united in joy', 'outpouring of emotion', 'crying'
- judicious placing of repetition – 'long, long' emphasising that this is one of the longest races possible
- long, complex, yet controlled sentences that suggest the emotion is rushing out, but the reporter is still fully aware she is doing her job.

Indicate that to continue the report for **Q4** effectively, students need to include some, if not all, of the above features.

> **Give extra support** by suggesting the following details they could include: any moments in the race where people thought Alexandro was bound to give up, but didn't and details of how he managed to continue. What caused his pain in the first place? Had he tripped at the start and twisted his ankle? Was there a special reason why he was so determined to finish?

Applying skills

Introduce **Q5** by reminding students that, although this is a speech, they must *not* write a script, nor read it out. They may, however, prepare a cue card. Ask them to consider the following questions.

- How will the character wish the audience to view him/her? For example, do they wish to impress, dominate, evoke sympathy from, the audience?
- How will this affect their choice of language style for their character? Whether the character is modest, friendly or intelligent will also affect these choices.

Each student should deliver their speech in role to a partner and then ask them to identify from the performance what was convincing and what was unconvincing in terms of the character's personality and the words used. Students can also use the **Sound progress** and **Excellent progress** criteria on Student Book p. 285 to assess this.

Towards A/A*	Candidates will have a developed idea of the character and select the most suitable speaking style to match. They will use a wide variety of vocabulary and sentence structures to suit both the character and the context. Through entirely appropriate language usage and behaviour the candidate will give a convincing portrayal of a believable and unique character.

12 Interviews

Assessment objectives

AO3 Speaking and Listening

- **SL3** Communicate clearly, fluently and purposefully as an individual and in dialogue with other speakers
- **SL4** Use register appropriate to audience and context
- **SL5** Listen to and respond appropriately to the contributions of others

IGCSE examination

- **Component 5** Speaking and Listening Test (Individual task and discussion)
- **Component 6** Speaking and Listening Coursework (Individual activity, pair-based activity and group activity)

Differentiated learning outcomes

- **All students must** use some range of speaking styles when asking relevant questions and giving satisfactory responses (Grade E/D).
- **Most students should** use a variety of speaking styles when asking appropriate questions and giving detailed responses (Grade D/C).
- **Some students could** show assured command of spoken styles when asking penetrating questions or giving subtly balanced responses (Grade A/A*).

Resources

- **Student Book:** pp. 286–7

Other Student Book pages

- Getting into role, pp. 282–3
- Speaking in role, pp. 284–5

Exploring skills

Unless you have preset the viewing exercise as homework, you will need two recorded interview clips for **Q1**. YouTube offers a range of possible examples. For a politician, enter the name plus 'interview'; for a celebrity, enter 'celebrity interviews'.

Before showing each clip, give pairs 2 minutes to answer the following question. What would an interviewer expect to learn from:

- a politician?
- a TV personality?

Allow 3 to 4 minutes for feedback. Likely responses from the pairs are:

- from a politician – something about their policies
- from the TV personality – some human interest story.

Valid alternative expectations should be accepted: for example, a retired politician promoting their book or the idea that he/she achieved great things when in office.

After watching the clips, discuss whether students' expectations were confirmed or confounded by what they saw. They should note that:

- political interviews are likely to be searching, even robust; TV personality ones more friendly, less confrontational
- politicians usually have set points they wish to make, regardless of what they are asked; TV personalities may be more willing to disclose some personal aspects of their lives to appear human and likeable.

Emphasise to students that interviewing requires acute listening by both interviewer and interviewee.

Building skills

In answer to **Q2**, based on the teacher–student interview on Student Book p. 286, students should note in the first three interventions, how the teacher:

- helps Beata to start by posing a question that offers scope for a wide range of responses

- directs Beata to more specific details (regarding age, feelings)
- prompts Beata for more information (the reasons for her fear)
- uses existing knowledge of Moswen's background to prompt further detail (about speaking English)
- finally uses several ideas to prompt both speakers to give fuller accounts.

> **Give extra challenge** by organising students into threes. The trios should read through the **Q2** interview, but focus on what, for the teacher, would be the most effective facial expressions, body movements and tone of voice to help obtain the desired responses. Each takes the teacher role in turns. Then, as a class, decide who was most effective and why.

Developing skills

Stress that any interviewee that students choose to role-play must allow them to demonstrate their language capabilities fully. In the sample interview extract for **Q3**, neither the language nor the vocabulary is particularly complex, but both are appropriate to the event and the person recounting it.

Spend 10 minutes on this with students working in groups of four. Follow this with a class feedback session, eliciting these points:

- Effective sentences – there are two in particular:
  - sentence 4: having established the desperate predicament he was in, the writer uses the second person 'You', to get the audience to empathise
  - sentence 7 repeats the word 'survive' with 'could' to suggest hope and a possibility; with 'would' to express determination.
- The detail is appropriate and evocative focusing on the cold.
- The dream of his mother reveals his need for comfort in his extreme predicament, and also suggests his subconscious is creating the resolve he needs to survive.
- By combining precise factual detail with the personal emotion, the speaker has turned this from a simple survival story into a real person's account.

For **Q4** the interview will range beyond the initial question: for example, into how the champion achieved the success.

> **Give extra support** by asking students to think about something that they did better than they expected: for example, they scored a goal for the school football team, even though they started the match as a reserve. It need not be an Olympic sport or sport at all. The important thing is the feeling: that they did well, and could do very well if they tried. Then apply that feeling to an Olympic sport they like.

Search for clips on YouTube where Olympic sports people are interviewed, and use these as examples.

Applying skills

Q5 is best set as homework and sampled in a follow up lesson so that students have time to research, and predict and prepare for likely questions. This is a chance for you to assess how well they have understood the lesson, but some peer-assessment using the **Sound progress** and **Excellent progress** criteria on Student Book p. 287 is also desirable. This will work well if students have been set the research as homework previously.

Towards A/A*	As interviewers, high-attainers will listen intently. They will use language assuredly to follow up and develop interesting features, and to cover essential aspects of the topic. As interviewees, candidates will offer appropriate answers, assuredly judging how much information is required to suit the purpose of the interview.

1 Practice paper 1: Reading passages

Assessment objectives

AO1 Reading
- **R1** Demonstrate understanding of explicit meanings
- **R2** Demonstrate understanding of implicit meanings and attitudes
- **R3** Analyse, evaluate and develop facts, ideas and opinions
- **R4** Demonstrate understanding of how writers achieve effects
- **R5** Select for specific purposes

AO2 Writing
- **W1** Articulate experience and express what is thought, felt and imagined
- **W2** Sequence facts, ideas and opinions
- **W3** Use a range of appropriate vocabulary
- **W4** Use register appropriate to audience and context

Differentiated learning outcomes

- **All students must** use mark schemes to become familiar with the demands of the examination, allocation of timings, and marks.
- **Most students should** use mark schemes to become fairly confident in their use of time and in fulfilling the requirements of the grade descriptors.
- **Some students could** use the mark scheme to self-assess and improve their work as a matter of course.

IGCSE examination
- **Paper 1** Questions 1, 2 and 3

Resources
- **Student Book**: pp. 300–7
- **Worksheets**: 10.1a–f
- **PPT**: 10.1a–h
- **Revision videos for Paper 1**, extended response and writer's effects questions
- You will also need to download a copy of the **Paper 1 Mark Scheme** from the CIE website.

Exploring skills

Step 1 Ask students to read **An Introduction to Practice Paper 1** on Student Book p. 301. Read the section 'Which skills should I be using?' out loud. Ensure that students understand the terms:

- explicit meaning
- implicit meaning
- summary
- extended response
- writer's effects.

Working in pairs, students should use four colours to highlight the questions on the exam paper (**Worksheet 10.1a**) to show which questions are testing which type of reading. Use **PPT 10.1a** to show correct highlighting and explanations.

Use **PPT 10.1b** to brainstorm the reading and writing skills that students have learned in preparation for the exam, and then match them with the three questions in Paper 1.

> **Give extra support** by suggesting that students look for key words such as 'explain, using your own words' (for an explicit or implicit meaning question), 'feelings' (for an implicit meaning question), and 'language' or 'words and phrases' (for a writer's effects question).
>
> **Give extra challenge** by inviting students to create their own additional questions of each type, based on the Brady Barr reading passage.

Step 2 Ask students to read the 'Tips for success' on Student Book p. 301 and put their hands up when they have discovered a useful piece of information about how long to spend on each question in the exam. Explain that knowing the time allowed for the exam (it will be best to double check this on the CIE website) is useful as a guide to ensure they complete the whole paper and do not spend too much time on one question at the expense of others. It also gives the correct importance to high-tariff questions.

PPT Using **PPT 10.1c**, model for students how they should divide up the time available for each part of the question. Explain that they should use this as a rough guide to keep themselves on track.

Ask them to go through the paper in **Worksheet 10.1a** and annotate it to show how many minutes they should allow for each question.

Building skills

Step 3 Ask students to annotate the exam paper with the advice recommended in **Tips for success** on Student Book p. 301. This is a quick consolidation task of marking up questions to indicate how/where to manage time carefully, where to explain/where to use own words and so on.

Step 4 At this point you could use **Worksheet 10.1b** to take students through the mark scheme for this paper. (NB: Please supplement this bespoke mark scheme with the generic writing mark bands for Question 2 in the Paper 1 Mark Scheme on the CIE website, as CIE does not allow publishers to reproduce its mark schemes.)

PPT You could also use **PPT 10.1e** to go through the mark scheme, but just give an overview for now – don't go into detail (that comes at Step 8). (NB: as above, **PPT 10.1e** does not contain the generic writing mark bands for Question 2, so please have these to hand or add them to the PPT yourself.)

Step 5 Allow students 5 minutes to read Passage A in Question 1 (**Worksheet 10.1a**). Discuss the various strategies that they might use to tackle words that they are not familiar with. Allow a further 5 minutes' reading time.

> **Give extra support** by suggesting that students use **Worksheet 10.1c** to review reading techniques covered in Chapter 1.

PPT Then remind students about picking out key words in the questions and give them 5 minutes to do this.

Use **PPT 10.1d** to show the key words in each question.

Developing skills

Step 6 Students should then complete the exam paper. This could either be completed in one session, using all 90 minutes available, or you could split the session into two using the accurate timings as indicated by the mark allocations available. You could also introduce each question by looking at the mark scheme as per Step 4.

Applying skills

Step 7 Once students have completed the exam paper, there are a number of activities to encourage them to engage with the success criteria and to assess their own work

Paper 1, Question 1(d)
Response **A** = 6 marks
Response **B** = 4 marks

Paper 1, Question 2
Response **A** = 9 marks
Response **B** = 6 marks

Paper 1, Question 3
Response **A** = 4 marks
Response **B** = 1 marks

a) Use **PPT 10.1e** to show how marks are allocated and why. Then ask students to mark their own or a peer's answer.

b) Give students **Worksheet 10.1d** and ask them to rank the two sample responses to Question 1(d), the writer's effects question. Feed back using **PPT 10.1f**. Suggested marks for each response are shown in the panel on the left.

c) A similar activity could be completed using **Worksheet 10.1e**, which contains two sample responses to Question 2, the extended response task. Students could mark these responses, as directed. Feed back using **PPT 10.1g**.

d) Use **PPT 10.1h** to demonstrate a sample response to Question 3 and how a summary question is marked, and also refer to the Paper 1 Mark Scheme for this question on the CIE website.

Suggested marks for each response are shown on the left.

Step 8 Once students' responses have been reliably marked, hand out **Worksheet 10.1f** and ask students to conduct a self-review, looking at their own strengths and weaknesses and identifying targets for improvement.

2 Practice paper 2: Reading passages

Assessment objectives

AO1 Reading

- R1 Demonstrate understanding of explicit meanings
- R2 Demonstrate understanding of implicit meanings and attitudes
- R3 Analyse, evaluate and develop facts, ideas and opinions
- R4 Demonstrate understanding of how writers achieve effects
- R5 Select for specific purposes

AO2 Writing

- W1 Articulate experience and express what is thought, felt and imagined
- W2 Sequence facts, ideas and opinions
- W3 Use a range of appropriate vocabulary
- W4 Use register appropriate to audience and context

Differentiated learning outcomes

- **All students must** use mark schemes to become familiar with the demands of the examination, allocation of timings, and marks.
- **Most students should** use mark schemes to become fairly confident in their use of time and in fulfilling the requirements of the grade descriptors.
- **Some students could** use the mark scheme to self-assess and improve their work as a matter of course.

IGCSE examination

- **Paper 2**, Questions 1, 2 and 3

Resources

- **Student Book**: pp. 308–13
- **Worksheets**: 10.2a–f
- **PPT**: 10.2a–g
- **Revision videos for Paper 2**, extended response and writer's effects questions
- You will also need to download a copy of the **Paper 2 Mark Scheme** from the CIE website.

Exploring skills

Step 1 Ask students to read **An Introduction to Paper 2** on Student Book p. 308. Read the section 'Which skills should I be using?' out loud. Ensure that students understand the terms: extended response, writer's effects and summary.

Use **PPT 10.2a** to brainstorm the reading and writing skills that students have learned in preparation for the exam, and then match them with the three questions.

Step 2 Explain that these question types are always fixed in place on the paper: for example, Question 1 is always the extended response question. Ask students why this is to their advantage. Note: Question 2 is described as the 'language question' in the Cambridge IGCSE syllabus, but as it focuses solely on assessment objective R4 (see above), it is referred to in these materials as the 'writer's effects question'.

Give extra support by revisiting the Student Book (Chapters 4, 5 and 6) to remind students what these terms mean: extended response, writer's effects and summary.

Give extra challenge by asking students to make a quick poster explaining each question type, including key skills, example questions and giving top tips.

Step 3 Ask students to read the section titled 'Tips for success' on Student Book p. 308. Explain that knowing the time allowed for the exam is useful to ensure students complete the whole paper and do not spend too much time on one question at the expense of others. It also gives the correct importance to high-tariff questions.

Using **PPT 10.2b**, model for students how they should divide up the time available for each part of the question. Advise them to use this as a rough guide to keep on track. Ask them to go through the exam paper in **Worksheet 10.2a** and annotate it to show how many minutes they should allow for each question.

Step 4   Ask students to annotate the exam paper with the advice recommended in **Tips for success** on Student Book p. 308. This offers consolidation of marking up questions to indicate how to manage time carefully, where to explain/where to use own words, etc.

Building skills

Step 5   At this point you could use **Worksheet 10.2b** to take students through the mark scheme created for this practice paper. (NB: You will need to supplement this bespoke mark scheme with the generic marking criteria for Question 2 and the generic Quality of writing marking criteria for Question 3 in the Paper 2 Mark Scheme on the CIE website, as CIE does not allow publishers to reproduce its mark schemes.)

You could also use **PPT 10.2c** to go through the mark scheme, but just give an overview for now – don't go into detail (that comes at Step 8). (NB: as above, **PPT 10.2c** does not contain the generic writing mark bands for Question 2 and Question 3, so please print these from the CIE website or add them to the PPT yourself.)

Step 6   Allow students 10 minutes to read the passages in the exam paper (**Worksheet 10.2a**). Discuss the various strategies that they might use to tackle words that they are not familiar with. Allow a further 5 minutes' reading time.

> **Give extra support** by suggesting that students use **Worksheet 10.1c** to review reading techniques covered in Chapter 1.

Then remind students about picking out key words in the questions and give them 5 minutes to do this. Use **PPT 10.2d** to show the key words in each question.

Developing skills

Step 7   Students should then complete the exam paper. This could either be completed in one session, using all 105 minutes available, or you could split the session into two or more parts using the accurate timings as indicated by the mark allocations available.

If approaching the paper in parts, remind students to use only Passage B to answer Question 3. You could also introduce each question/section by looking at the mark scheme as per Step 5. Before beginning, students may like to watch the revision videos that talk through the extended response and writer's effects questions on Paper 2.

Applying skills

Step 8   Once students have completed the practice exam paper, there are several activities to encourage them to engage with the success criteria and to assess their work:

Paper 2, Question 1
Response **A** = 7 marks (Reading 4, Writing 3)
Response **B** = 19 marks (Reading 14, Writing 5)
Response **C** = 13 marks (Reading 9, Writing 4)

Paper 2, Question 2
Response **A** = 10 marks
Response **B** = 6 marks

Paper 2, Question 3
Response **A** = 7 marks (Reading 5, Writing 2)
Response **B** = 10 marks (Reading 7, Writing 3)

a) Use the annotated version of the mark scheme in **PPT 10.2c** to show how marks are allocated and why. Then ask students to mark their own or a partner's answer.

b) Give students **Worksheet 10.2c** and encourage them to mark the three sample responses to Question 1 (extended response). Ask them to identify the different types of content outlined in the first part of the mark scheme: A (What happened), B (How she coped) and C (Advice to the young people). Feed back using **PPT 10.2e**. Suggested marks for each response are given in the box on the left.

c) Set a similar activity using **Worksheet 10.2d**, which offers two sample responses to Question 2 (writer's effects). Students identify which band each response falls into using the Band criteria in the Paper 2 Mark Scheme on the CIE website. Feed back using **PPT 10.1f**. Suggested marks are given in the box on the left.

d) Give students **Worksheet 10.2e** and ask them to mark the two sample responses to Question 3 (summary). Ask them to identify the different points of content outlined in the mark scheme. Feed back using **PPT 10.2g**, which has the points of content annotated onto the responses. Suggested marks are shown on the left.

Step 9   Once students' responses have been reliably marked, hand out **Worksheet 10.2f** and ask them to conduct a self-review. Encourage them to look at their own strengths and weaknesses, and to identify targets for improvement. Brighter students may be able do this independently, but weaker ones may need to do this as a guided task.

3. Practice paper 3: Directed writing and composition

Assessment objectives

AO1 Reading
- R1 Demonstrate understanding of explicit meanings
- R2 Demonstrate understanding of implicit meanings and attitudes
- R3 Analyse, evaluate and develop facts, ideas and opinions

AO2 Writing
- W1 Articulate experience and express what is thought, felt and imagined
- W2 Sequence facts, ideas and opinions
- W3 Use a range of appropriate vocabulary
- W4 Use register appropriate to audience and context
- W5 Make accurate use of spelling, punctuation and grammar

Differentiated learning outcomes

- **All students must** use mark schemes to become familiar with the demands of the exam, allocation of timings, and marks.
- **Most students should** use mark schemes to become fairly confident in their use of time and in fulfilling the requirements of the grade descriptors.
- **Some students could** use the mark scheme to self-assess and improve their work as a matter of course.

IGCSE examination
Paper 3 Sections 1 and 2

Resources
- **Student Book**: pp. 314–17
- **PPT**: 10.3a–e
- **Worksheets**: 10.3a–g
- **Revision videos for Paper 3**, composition tasks
- You will also need to download a copy of the **Paper 3 Mark Scheme** from the CIE website.

Exploring skills

Step 1 Ask students to read **An Introduction to Paper 3** on Student Book p. 314. Read the 'Which skills should I be using?' section out loud.

Ensure that students understand that they must complete the directed writing task in Section 1 and then *just one* of the four composition tasks in Section 2 – two tasks in total for Paper 3. It is important they that play to their strengths when selecting which type of composition question to answer (description or narrative). Look through the exam paper on **Worksheet 10.3a** to reinforce the sequence of these questions with students.

Building skills

Step 2 Use the task on **Worksheet 10.3b** to revisit the different conventions the two types of writing that students have learned in preparation for Section 2 of the exam.

Step 3 Ask students to read 'Tips for success' on Student Book p. 314. Remind students that timing is crucial on Paper 3, as for the other papers. However, as there are only two equally weighted questions on this paper, their time allocation is more straightforward at one hour per task. Ask them to go through the exam paper in **Worksheet 10.3a** and annotate it to show how many minutes they should allow for each question.

Step 4 Ask students to annotate the exam paper with the advice recommended. This is a quick consolidation task of marking up questions to indicate how/where to manage time carefully, where to use ideas from the text and where to use your own words and ideas, and so on.

At this point you could use **Worksheet 10.3c** to take students through the mark scheme created for this paper. (NB: You will need to supplement this bespoke mark scheme with the generic marking criteria for Section 1 (Writing) and Section 2 in the Paper 3 Mark Scheme for 2015 onwards on the CIE website, as CIE does not allow publishers to reproduce its mark schemes.)

PPT

Alternatively, also use **PPT 10.3a** and **PPT 10.3b** to introduce the mark schemes for Sections 1 and 2 respectively, just as an overview. You will go into detail at Step 7. (NB: As above, **PPT 10.3a** does not contain the generic mark scheme for Writing in Section 1 and **PPT 10.3b** does not contain the generic mark schemes for Section 2, so please print these from the CIE website or add them to the PPT yourself).

As students work through slides, encourage them to see the patterns in the mark descriptors. Colour has been used to help them to track the development of specific skill areas across the bands for directed writing.

As an extra activity, students could colour-code the Section 1 Writing mark scheme downloaded from the CIE website to show similar progression of the strands across the descriptors. Then they could add more tips to their copies of the paper.

Developing skills

Step 5 Students should then complete the exam paper. This could either be completed in one session, using all 120 minutes available or in two equal shorter sessions. You could also introduce each section by looking at the mark scheme as per Step 5 above. Students may wish to watch the Paper 3 video clips before they begin, which talk through the two types of composition task in detail.

Applying skills

Step 6 Once students have completed the exam paper, there are several possible activities to encourage them to engage with the success criteria and to assess their own work.

PPT

a) Use **PPT 10.3a** to show how marks are allocated in Section 1 and why. Then ask students to mark their own or a partner's answer. Repeat this process for Section 2 using the generic composition mark schemes you have downloaded or printed from the CIE website.

Paper 3, Section 1

Response **A** = 22 marks (Reading 9; Writing 13)

Response **B** = 11 marks (Reading 4; Writing 7)

---

b) Use **Worksheet 10.3d** to encourage students to consider two sample responses to the directed writing task (Paper 3, Section 1). Students could annotate the responses using the 'Pro', 'Con' and 'Additional content' headings used in the marking guidance and then check their ideas using the lists provided in **PPT 10.3c**. They could also identify which of the bands for Reading each response should be placed in, before you reveal the allocated marks (shown on the left). Students should also refer to the generic Writing mark scheme on the CIE website to guide their decisions.

Paper 3, Section 2

Question 2

Response **A** = 15 marks (Content & structure 8; Style & accuracy 7)

Response **B** = 24 marks (Content & structure 12; Style & accuracy 12)

Question 3

Response **A** = 20 marks (Content & structure 10; Style & accuracy 10)

Response **B** = 16 marks (Content & structure 8; Style & accuracy 8)

---

c) A similar activity could be completed using **Worksheets 10.3e–f**, which contain sample responses to the composition task (Paper 3, Section 2), with two examples of each type of writing (description and narrative). These can be marked individually or ranked overall to show the range of marks available.

Students could use 'Content and structure' band descriptors from the Paper 3, Section 2 mark scheme downloaded from the CIE website to annotate the responses, circling each new point and underlining the development given. They could also highlight the start of all new paragraphs or sections and the use of any linking words or phrases in each response, to help them to judge structure.

Students could use highlighters and follow the colour-coding key used in the 'Style and accuracy' mark scheme slide in **PPT 10.3b** to highlight evidence for their judgements about style and accuracy, using the CIE band descriptors.

Use **PPTs 10.3d–e** to assess the sample responses:

- **Worksheet 10.3e / PPT 10.3d** = sample responses to Question 2 (descriptive composition)
- **Worksheet 10.3f / PPT 10.3e** = sample responses to Question 3 (narrative composition)

Suggested allocated marks are shown on the left.

Step 7 Once students' responses have been reliably marked, use **Worksheet 10.3g** and ask students to conduct a self-review looking at their own strengths and weaknesses, and identifying targets for improvement.

Worksheet 1.2: Locating information: scanning

Student Book **Q3** Using the extract from *Q & A* by Vikas Swarup, fill in this table to explore how the writer suggests the house is unpleasant.

Words read	Is this about a house?	Are the words unpleasant?	Other thoughts
I live in a corner of [the city]	No, about an area		But corner sounds like a trap – not nice
in a	Yes, 'in' suggests we are going to get a description of a house next		
cramped		Yes, means too small for comfort	
hundred-square-foot	Yes, about its size		I'm used to a bigger room so I would not like this
shack	Another word for a house	This word means not well made or temporary, so yes	
which has (a) no natural light			
or (b) ventilation			
with a corrugated metal sheet serving as a roof over my head			
It vibrates violently			
whenever a train passes overhead			
There is no running water			
and no sanitation			

Worksheet 1.4a — Explicit meaning (1)

Student Book **Q2** Using a dictionary, fill in the table below to explore the explicit meaning of the writer's words and their effect on the reader.

Word	Precise meaning	How this affects me	What the writer wanted to achieve
infinite	Endless, not possible to calculate	Makes clear how vast her imagination is	Understanding of the girl's character
stuffed	Very full	Large number of objects in house made clear	Understanding of the girl's home environment
yellowed			
dusty			
artificial			
museum-like			
calm			
wrapped			
separated			

© HarperCollins Publishers 2013

151

Chapter 1
Key reading skills

Worksheet 1.4b: Explicit meaning (2)

Student Book Q2 Using a dictionary, fill in the table below to explore the explicit meaning of the writer's words and their effect on the reader.

Word	Precise meaning	How this affects me	What the writer wanted to achieve
infinite	Endless, not possible to calculate	Makes clear how vast her imagination is	Understanding of the girl's character
stuffed	Very full	Large number of objects in house made clear	Understanding of the girl's home environment
wild			
loud			
messy			
unbiddable			
scalped			
attenuated			
insectile			
brassy			
adorned			

Chapter 1 Key reading skills

152 © HarperCollins Publishers 2013

Worksheet 1.5 — Implicit meaning: character

Student Book **Q3** Using the extract from *Great Expectations*, fill in the table below to explore how Dickens establishes the two characters.

Pip: What is said/done	Effect: What it tells us about him	Effect: What it suggests about his relationships

The Man: What is said/done	Effect: What it tells us about him	Effect: What it suggests about his relationships

© HarperCollins Publishers 2013

Worksheet 1.6a — Implicit meaning: setting (1)

Task Change the 'happy' atmosphere of this piece of writing – first to 'miserable', then to 'scary' – by altering the words and phrases that have been underlined.

Happy

I looked up at the <u>shining sun</u> in the sky and, feeling <u>happiness</u> deep in my heart, <u>laughed</u> out loud. The trees <u>swayed gently</u>, <u>birds sang</u> from the branches, and I felt <u>a warm glow</u> envelop me. I began to <u>walk lazily</u> through the forest, <u>smiling</u> at the <u>beauty</u> that surrounded me. <u>Pausing</u> at the bank of a stream, I <u>gazed</u> at the <u>glistening</u> waters before <u>jumping lightly</u> to the other side. I found myself in a field of <u>bluebells</u> and a <u>soft aroma drifted to</u> my nose. As my mind filled with <u>peace</u>, I <u>reclined on</u> the ground and <u>drifted into sleep</u>.

Miserable

I looked up at the _____ in the sky and, feeling _____ deep in my heart, _____ out loud. The trees _____, _____ from the branches, and I felt _____ envelop me. I began to _____ through the forest, _____ at the _____ that surrounded me. _____ at the bank of a stream, I _____ at the _____ waters before _____ to the other side. I found myself in a field of _____ and a _____ _____ my nose. As my mind filled with _____, I _____ the ground and _____ .

Scary

I looked up at the _____ in the sky and, feeling _____ deep in my heart, _____ out loud. The trees _____, _____ from the branches, and I felt _____ envelop me. I began to _____ through the forest, _____ at the _____ that surrounded me. _____ at the bank of a stream, I _____ at the _____ waters before _____ to the other side. I found myself in a field of _____ and a _____ _____ my nose. As my mind filled with _____, I _____ the ground and _____ .

Worksheet 1.6b: Implicit meaning: setting (2)

Student Book Q4 Complete the tick chart to show the different ingredients used to create the mood. Try to add five more words or phrases from the extract from *Set in Stone* that are used to create the mood.

Student Book Q5 Then, in the end column, write words or phrases of your own that would make the approach to the house exciting and optimistic.

Words or phrases	Time of year	Time of day	Weather	Land-scape	Objects	Actions	What is said/ sounds	Exciting words or phrases
darkness		✓						
branches								
mossy earth								
trickle of water								
faint mist								
wrought-iron gates								
a loud grating squeal								

© HarperCollins Publishers 2013

Worksheet 1.7a — Emotive language (1)

Student Book **Q6** Fill in the chart to explore emotive language and its effects.

Word/phrase	Effect on the reader	Reason why the writer wants that effect
collapse	We think of something losing all power, strength and natural order.	They want us to understand that the cod population is very severely affected by the over-fishing – it is not just a minor change.
stripped bare		

Worksheet 1.7b: Emotive language (2)

Student Book **Q6** Fill in the chart to explore emotive language and its effects.

Word/phrase	Effect on the reader	Reason why the writer wants that effect
collapse	We think of something losing all power, strength and natural order.	They want us to understand that the cod population is very severely affected by the over-fishing – it is not just a minor change.
stripped bare		
scandal		
victims		
dying		
horrific		
suffer		
plough		
fragile		
devastating		
contaminated		

© HarperCollins Publishers 2013

157

Chapter 1
Key reading skills

Worksheet 1.8a: Sensory language (1)

Student Book **Q1** Fill in the chart to explore sensory connotations and their effect.

Word/phrase →	Explicit meaning →	Sensory connotations →	Effect
All around me was darkness	No light, cannot see	Fear, menace, blindness	Character feels scared. Place is frightening. Something bad is going to happen.
a wailing shriek			
I could smell the coolness of the mossy earth			

Student Book **Q2** Fill in the table to highlight the different words and phrases used to stimulate the senses in the beach description.

See	Hear	Touch	Taste	Smell
slush-grey and ice-white gulls toddlers wrestle	scream waft	sticky	salt	candy-floss

Chapter 1 Key reading skills

158 © HarperCollins Publishers 2013

Worksheet 1.8b — Sensory language (2)

Student Book **Q4** Fill in the table to explore different word types and their sensory effect.

Word/phrase	Noun	Adjective	Verb	Adverb	Effect
Slush-grey		✓			Precise colour, makes us picture dirty snow. This does not sound positive and adds to the feeling of unease or unhappiness.

Worksheet 1.9 Synthesis

Student Book Q2 Underline and number all the different phrases that show the problems of extreme weather conditions. The first example has been done for you.

> Extreme winds, such as those found in hurricanes, tornadoes, and some thunderstorms can <u>overturn caravans</u> (1), tear off roofs and topple trees causing extreme distress to many people and financial hardship to whole communities. Some of the strongest tornadoes can demolish houses completely, leaving people homeless and vulnerable to disease and criminal harm. People may be knocked down or struck by debris and many places may lose electricity. Flooding and storm surges can destroy buildings and roads, contaminate water supplies, halt other essential services and drown people. Large hail stones can damage cars and roofs, and destroy crops, but rarely kill people. Heat waves can lead to drought, which causes crop loss as well as health issues and death from dehydration.

Student Book Q3 Now reread the extract and put the phrases that you have numbered under headings. Write your headings in the boxes provided; you don't have to use all the boxes. Decide whether each phrase needs a new heading or if can be placed under an existing heading. The first heading and example have been done for you.

Destruction of property		
1		

160 © HarperCollins Publishers 2013

Worksheet 2.1a: Sentence functions

Student Book Q1 Your teacher will provide you with a set of playing cards like the ones below, where each card refers to a specific sentence function:

Dec = Declarative

Int = Interrogative

Imp = Imperative

Ex = Exclamatory

Describe how to get from your home to school using all four sentence functions. Play the appropriate card for each sentence. For example, if you say 'Turn left out of my house', you would play the 'Imp' card ('Imperative').

Aim to use up all your cards.

Do not use any sentences that you can't define as one of the four types listed above.

| Dec | Int | Imp | Ex |

Worksheet 2.1b: Types of sentence

Task 1 For each of the following sentences, decide whether the sentence is:
- simple
- compound
- complex.

Explain your answer.

Sentence	Sentence type	Why is it this type?	What does the sentence convey?
The river Nile was incredibly wide, and we saw crocodiles basking in the midday sun.			
They seemed to be smiling!			
Even though we were travelling light, we were dripping with sweat.			
My PC is making a very strange noise and I'm a bit alarmed at the smoke coming from the back.			
I simply had to leave.			
Despite all the setbacks we had earlier in the construction, the finished product was perfect.			
The rain was pouring and the wind was howling, but we still soldiered on through the forest to the campsite.			
The girl with the flaxen hair was quietly, softly, murmuring to herself.			

Task 2 For each of the sentences above, highlight the following features:
- subjects (green)
- verbs (pink)
- subclauses (orange)
- connectives (blue).

Task 3 What overall meaning does each sentence convey? For example:
The first compound sentence conveys a scene of peace and calm by having two balanced clauses providing extra detail for the reader.

Worksheet 2.2: Using sentences to create an effect

Student Book Q3 You are going to continue writing an extract from a short story called 'The Pursuit'. A man has escaped from his captors and is on the run in an unfamiliar country. You need to vary the types of sentence you use to make this extract exciting to read. You could use the structure below to formulate your ideas and to practise using different types of sentence for different purposes:

> **The Pursuit**
>
> *The man stopped. His breathing was heavy. Then, he heard steps. It was them! He had no choice. He began to climb the tower. He dragged himself up the stone stairs, despite the pain from his wounded leg.*

Next use a simple sentence telling the reader how long the man had been running:

Then use a complex sentence containing '**, which**', telling the reader more about the tower and the view that could be seen:

Now use a simple sentence telling the reader that the man is not going to give up:

Finally, show the man's relief as he nears the top and watches his pursuers turn back. Try using '**, although**' to tell the reader that there was no way he could carry on any further that day:

- Check that you have used the correct punctuation at the end of each sentence and that your commas are in the right places.
- Ask a partner to evaluate your choices of different sentence types and functions.

Worksheet 2.3a: Getting commas right

Commas are used:

1. to **separate items in a list**.

    The colours in a rainbow are red, orange, yellow, green, blue, indigo and violet.

    There is no comma between the last two items as there is an 'and'.

2. to **separate parts of a sentence**. If you are writing a complex sentence, then a comma separates the main clause (second clause in the example) from the subordinate clause (first clause in the example).

    Despite the fact that the rain had stopped, the man continued to hold an umbrella above his head.

    Notice that there is a subject and a verb in both clauses and that one can stand alone and one cannot. Where the two clauses meet is the place for a comma!

    When deciding whether to use a comma, ask yourself the following questions:
    - Are there two or more clauses?
    - Which clause can stand alone?

    Insert a comma before or after the main clause.

3. to **add more information**.

    'I'm not standing for this!' yelled the manager, aggressively pointing at the whole team.

    Here we learn more about the manager, but it is not a clause.

Task 1 List all the members of your family. There is .... and me.

Task 2 Where should the comma be in these sentences?

- The queue to the football stadium snaked through the town which meant that the traffic was at a standstill.

- Having waited until the lights had changed Anya cycled straight across the junction.

Task 3 Use a comma to add more detail about the speakers to the following conversation.

- 'I do believe that we have met before,' said the man ....

- 'Do you play cricket?' said the second man ....

- 'Yes, for the local team, but only when I can,' replied the first man ....

- 'Ah, that will be it. I was here last month. You thrashed us,' replied the second man ....

Worksheet 2.3b: Getting apostrophes right

> **Apostrophes** are used:
>
> 1. to **show possession with a noun**, for example:
>
>   *Bella's basket, the girl's football, Miko's flute, the box's lid, the dogs' leads, the women's cell phones.*
>
>   (Do **not** use apostrophes in straight plural forms of nouns, for example: *I bought some apples and mangoes.*)
>
> 2. to **shorten words in contracted forms**, for example:
>
>   *can't* instead of *cannot*
>
>   *don't* instead of *do not*.
>
>   When you are writing these shortened forms, check where the letters are that you have missed out and mark the spot with an apostrophe: *shouldn't*. If you cannot see how the word has been shrunk, don't use an apostrophe.

Task 1 Add some more examples of using apostrophes to show possession:

....

....

....

....

Task 2 Shorten the following:

- would not = ...
- could not = ...
- will not   = ... (careful here)
- it is   = ...
- there is   = ...
- she has   = ...
- we have   = ...

Think of three more examples, if you can:

- .... = ...
- .... = ...
- .... = ...

Worksheet 2.3c: Punctuation of speech

This worksheet will help you to use the rules of **punctuating speech**:

1. Put speech marks around the actual words spoken, including any punctuation – this might be a comma, an exclamation mark, a question mark or a full stop.
2. Use a new line for each new speaker. When the speech is not a question or exclamation, put a comma before the closing speech mark.
3. If the speaker comes first, add a comma afterwards and then the speech inside speech marks. Begin speech with a capital letter and end with a full stop.
4. You can place the speaker mid-sentence if you wish. If the sentence of speech continues on, do not give the first word of the speech a capital letter.
5. If someone speaks more than one sentence but the speaker is mentioned in between, use a full stop and then a capital letter to start the next part of the speech.

Student Book Q2 Read the text below and rewrite it using these five rules for punctuating speech. The text in bold is correctly punctuated. You could add clearer descriptions of who is speaking too.

I ran up the corridor towards the exam room. Out of breath, I turned the handle and burst in. 'You're late!' hissed my teacher. But I was just... You're late she said again. Sit down he whispered. Sorry. I was given the exam paper. The clock said 10:07. I had been seven minutes late.

One hour and fifty two minutes later pens down was thundered across the room. I left as soon as I could. I didn't want twenty questions about where I had been from everyone. But it was unavoidable. What happened to you she said. Nothing I said back. But you were so late. I didn't think they would let you take the examination. Neither did I said someone.

....
....
....
....
....
....
....
....
....

Now continue the dialogue:

....
....
....

Worksheet 2.3d: Colons, semi-colons, brackets and dashes

> Remember that often:
> - a **colon** signals to the reader: *and I'm going to tell you why*
> - a **semi-colon** signals to the reader: *and I'm going to tell you a little bit more about that*
> - **brackets** signal to the reader: *don't forget that*
> - a **dash** signals to the reader: *know what I mean?*

Task 1 Choose a character: politician, comedian, charity worker or TV presenter. Decide on the type of punctuation you think would convey their role and personality. For example:

> *I am a politician and I am going to tell you exactly why I believe I am right so I will be using the colon.*

Next choose an issue of importance to your character – global warming, rights for young people, improved transport systems or the rise of celebrities.

- My chosen character: ....
- Punctuation to suit this character: ....
- My chosen issue/topic: ....

Write a short speech using punctuation to help to convey your meanings:

....
....
....
....
....
....
....
....
....
....
....
....

Task 2 When you have finished writing your speech, work with a partner to evaluate the impact of the punctuation – *has it emphasised the character of your speaker?*

Task 3 Now choose a different character or a different issue to demonstrate how that particular person might use punctuation to have an effect on an audience.

Worksheet 2.4a: Structuring a paragraph

A paragraph needs to keep the same topic throughout. To keep your writing on the right track, it can be helpful to use the pronouns 'this' and 'it' within second, third and later sentences. This requires you to explain the topic or to provide new information about it.

- **Step 1**: introduce your topic in the first sentence.
- **Step 2**: use the word 'This' to start your second sentence.
- **Step 3**: use the word 'it' in your third sentence.

For example:

The rain came on Thursday. This was unfortunate because it meant the cycling trip we had planned had to be cancelled. The forecast says that we might get a break from it on Sunday, so I'm keeping my fingers crossed that we can go then.

- Step 1: introduce topic of paragraph
- Step 2: use the word 'This' to start your second sentence
- Step 3: use the word 'it' in your third sentence

Task 1 Can you find the topic and then follow its trail in the following paragraph?

My class started trampoline lessons yesterday for the first time. This was very scary for me and my friends because we did not like heights and we thought it looked very dangerous. However, it turned out to be great fun and we can't wait to do it again next week.

Task 2 Try writing a three-sentence paragraph using 'This' and 'it' for one of the following topics. Annotate your work to show the trail in your writing.

- The chemistry experiment
- The horse that escaped
- A new baby brother

....
....
....
....
....
....
....

Remember, you could start with a time reference, for example: *Last week our chemistry teacher showed us what happened when an acid is mixed with an alkali.* Then, you can use a time reference to start the next paragraph: *Yesterday, we saw what happened when you mix acid with water*

Worksheet 2.4b: Using connectives

Student Book Q3 Try each of the following connectives in the gaps of the paragraphs below. You could cut them out. Decide whether each connective is a 'definite match', 'possible match' or 'complete contradiction'. Then choose which one helps to make the paragraph cohesive or achieves flow from the previous one. There is more help with this on Student Book p. 47.

At first,	Firstly,	Therefore,	In contrast,
What is more,	Next,	Secondly,	Consequently,
However,	In addition,	Later that day,	Finally,
As a result,	Although	Moreover,	Furthermore,

Paragraph 1

.... it was incredibly busy at the airport.

.... there were long queues up to my desk.

Apparently, the traffic in the city was terrible. ....

there was a student demonstration which closed the main road.

Paragraph 2

.... most passengers made it on time,

.... one family, poor things, had a nasty shock

when they handed me their tickets. They'd got the wrong day!

Worksheet 2.4c: Constructing an argument

Use the cards below with the connectives cards from **Worksheet 2.4b** to play 'argument dominoes'. Match each point below to a connective and then that connective to the next point in order to structure the argument text appropriately.

Argument – A new power station in your area

It will bring lots of new jobs.	There will be more pollution.	The area will be well landscaped.	The beautiful landscape will be ruined.
Local businesses such as catering companies will thrive.	New modern housing will be built for the families of the workers.	An increase in traffic will bring pollution and congestion.	Peace and quiet will be lost forever.
The power station will be an eyesore and house prices will drop.	The local school will be lost.	The local community will be exploited and their concerns ignored.	A new road will be constructed so lorries can transport raw materials to the power station.
Less pollution is created by modern power stations.	The local tourist industry will collapse.	The school will be expanded and improved.	Noise from the plant will be 24 hours a day, 7 days a week.

Worksheet 2.5: Vocabulary choices

Student Book Q3 This task supports your understanding of word classes and shows how this can help to improve your vocabulary choices.

- Write down alternative words for the nouns, adjectives, verbs and adverbs that are listed below.
- Then think of a few of your own to complete each table. (A thesaurus will help you with this – try to use a thesaurus regularly when you are writing to improve the originality of your work.)

Nouns: these are objects/things, proper names, emotions/ideas, places, for example: *mango, table, Aisha, love, Santiago*.

Everyday nouns	A more unusual choice
house	dwelling, abode, cardboard box
dog	
car	

Adjectives: these qualify or add more information to a noun (telling us something's quality, size, colour, for example: *tiny green* kiwi fruit; *wonderful* film).

Everyday adjectives	A more unusual choice
small	miniscule, microscopic, insignificant
clean	
full	

Verbs: these express actions or states, for example: (to) leave, (to) think, (to) run.

Everyday verbs	A more unusual choice
walk	stroll, wander, march
clap	
call	

Adverbs: these usually describe or modify verbs and adjectives, for example: leave *quickly*, Fernando is *extremely* fast.

Everyday adverbs	A more unusual choice
very	enormously, stupendously, enviably
slowly	
accurately	

© HarperCollins Publishers 2013

Worksheet 2.6 — Formal and informal language

Student Book **Q1** Annotate the following examples A and B, explaining the features that are typical of 'formal' or 'informal' writing. Use a highlighter, red pen or pencil to mark the features of formal and informal writing that you see.

Example A

> Well, you wouldn't believe it, Carlos, but there's me, kicking a ball around in our backyard when the Real Madrid boss trots by!

Example B

> Dear Mr Mourinho,
>
> Thank you for your kind invitation to attend a training session with the first team on Monday 23 March. I would be delighted to come, and would like to thank you for noticing my skills when you passed by our house last week.
>
> Yours sincerely,
>
> Didier Brillianti

Student Book **Q3 and Q4** Can you see the difference between the active and the passive voice? Use your highlighter to mark the verb and then see if there is a subject who performs the verb. If not, then the writing is likely to be passive.

By whom? *By whom?*

> The shark <u>was observed</u> at 7 a.m. breaking the surface of the water approximately half a mile from the shore. Local coastguards <u>were alerted</u> and the shark <u>was guided</u> out to sea to safer areas before any harm was done to tourists.

By whom?

> *I saw the shark at around seven this morning in the sea, I guess about half a mile or so out. I called the coastguards and they guided it out to sea before it could do any damage.*

Worksheet 2.7a: Different language for different audiences

Task This worksheet introduces a range of scenarios that require the use of specific types of language. Work in groups of three and explore what words and phrases are most appropriate to use for each role and situation.

When you have completed the role plays, discuss:
- Which scenario was the most difficult and why?
- How would you describe the ways in which your language changed to suit each role?

Scenario 1:	A birthday party for five year olds
Roles:	One parent (host) and two 5-year-old guests
Action:	Two guests arrive and are taken to the party room for the birthday tea. Host needs to take coats and check that guests like cake and chocolates.

Scenario 2:	A dinner party for senior colleagues from work
Roles:	Host hoping to get a promotion and two senior colleagues from work
Action:	Host needs to welcome guests and check that Italian cuisine is acceptable to all.

Scenario 3:	An end of year celebration for teenagers finishing examinations
Roles:	Teacher (host) and two 16-year-olds
Action:	Teacher needs to welcome the teenagers and show that this evening is for them to enjoy and relax after five years of hard work.

Scenario 4:	A fire drill in a department store
Roles:	Shop assistant and two shoppers who are wearing new clothes
Action:	Shop assistant needs to give clear instructions to the shoppers to get them into the car park and lined up at the assembly point as soon as possible. The shoppers are not sure about wearing the clothes they have not paid for and want to change back into their own clothes.

© HarperCollins Publishers 2013

Worksheet 2.7b: Matching content to audience

Student Book Q3 It is important to select the appropriate content and style to match the audience you are writing for. Look again at the newspaper article on Student Book p. 54, and then consider the different text which needs planning – a letter. Here is the key information to bear in mind: you have been asked to plan...

> '... a letter to David Field, the zoo director, expressing your support for the zoo's endangered species programme, and your concern about the decline in the zoo's elephant population.'

First, complete the table shown below.

- Add any further layout or presentational features of the article or letter.
- Read the task above again, and decide the purpose/s of the letter.
- Focus on the style of the letter once you know its purpose and audience.

Text features	Newspaper article	Letter
Presentation	Headline and photo	Address and opening greeting – 'Dear...'
Purpose	To inform	
Style and key features	No reference to first person Lots of facts and stats	Written from 'I' point of view (in the 'first person') Tone still quite formal but personal as letter is to one named individual

Student Book Q4 Using your notes from the table and bearing in mind what you have learned about the tone, style and content that needs including, continue the example letter from Student Book p. 55.

Original: Dear Mr Field,

There was a newspaper article about the birth of the elephant at the zoo.
It was pleasing to see the work done by the staff...

Your version: Dear Mr Field,

I was delighted to read..

....

....

....

....

....

....

....

Worksheet 2.8 Voice and role

Student Book Q1 We can tell a lot about people from what they say and how they say it. Work in groups of four to read the statements from four people below. Who are they? What is their role? How do we know?

Once you have shared your ideas, match the statement to the role and make sure you can explain your match referring to the language being used for each one.

> Naturally, we were very proud to see our lad up on stage. To think it was only two years ago that he left home and started his career. We took so many photos!

actor Sunil

Why have I chosen this role?
....
....
....

> I felt so nervous. Of course, we'd rehearsed for weeks but nothing prepares you for curtain up. Waiting in the wings felt like an eternity. I didn't think it went that well, to tell the truth.

theatre reviewer

Why have I chosen this role?
....
....
....

> Sunil Vaswani's landmark performance in the central role was a revelation. He combined a certain vulnerability and power at the same time and spoke Shakespeare's verse with clarity and control.

interviewer

Why have I chosen this role?
....
....
....

> So, Sunil – this is your first major stage role and it looks like you nailed it, according to the reviews. Does this mean you'll be looking for parts in films soon?

Sunil's mum

Why have I chosen this role?
....
....
....

Student Book Q4 The following diary entry contains a mixture of past and present tense narrative. As you read through, think about the reason for the changes and the impact it has on the reader. Does this change the tone of the writing? Does it give us a clear picture of the writer?

Day 1: preparing for the competition

[Past tense] → <u>Got up at 8 a.m.</u> and <u>went down</u> to join all the other students for breakfast.
I'd made a sort of friend with a girl called Sonya last night – at least I
thought I had, but this morning she <u>ignored me and spent</u> all [Past tense]
breakfast with her nose in a dictionary. This <u>made</u> me laugh.
[Present tense] If you <u>don't know</u> the spellings by now, then you never will. [Past tense]
Mind you, I <u>was so nervous I couldn't</u> eat anyway.

Breakfast just made me think of cooking-related spellings; 'restaurant'
(remember the 'au'!), 'lasagne', 'cucumber' (not 'queue cumber'!!),
and 'temperature' all <u>kept on going through</u> my head.
[Present tense] <u>Am I</u> going mad? <u>Is it</u> all worth it? I was about to text Mum and Dad, [Past tense]
but then <u>in came</u> the organiser – a thin, severe looking man in a grey suit
[Past tense] – and <u>told</u> us Round 1 was going to start in 10 minutes in the Main Hall.

Worksheet 3.1 Analysing Hillary Clinton's speech

Student Book **Q3** Use this worksheet to discuss parts of the speech. Underline, highlight or annotate significant words and sentences in the part of the speech your group is allocated.

1	Mrs Mongella, Under Secretary Kittani, distinguished delegates and guests: I would like to thank the Secretary General of the United Nations for inviting me to be part of the United Nations Fourth World Conference on Women. This is truly a celebration – a celebration of the contributions women make in every aspect of life: in the home, on the job, in their communities, as mothers, wives, sisters, daughters, learners, workers, citizens and leaders.
2	It is also a coming together, much the way women come together every day in every country. We come together in fields and in factories. In village markets and supermarkets. In living rooms and board rooms.
3	Whether it is while playing with our children in the park, or washing clothes in a river or taking a break at the office water cooler, we come together and talk about our aspirations and concerns. And time and again, our talk turns to our children and our families. However different we may be, there is far more that unites us than divides us. We share a common future.
4	By gathering in Beijing, we are focusing world attention on issues that matter most in the lives of women and their families: access to education, health care, jobs and credit, the chance to enjoy basic legal and human rights and participate fully in the political life of their countries.
5	There are some who question the reason for this conference. Let them listen to the voices of women in their homes, neighbourhoods and workplaces. There are some who wonder whether the lives of women and girls matter to economic and political progress around the globe. Let them look at the women gathered here and at Huairou – the homemakers, nurses, teachers, lawyers, policymakers and women who run their own businesses.
6	It is conferences like this that compel governments and people everywhere to listen, look and face the world's most pressing problems.

Worksheet 3.2a — Analysing dialogue

Task 1 Working in groups of three in role as director, Sandra and Mum, read the following dialogue from a play. The director's notes are for guidance only – you can present the characters in your own way if you prefer.

Sandra: (*eagerly*) It's so exciting! My plane leaves in 24 hours …

Mum: Are you sure you've packed properly? Have you got your visa, travel sickness pills…? You need to prepare properly.

Sandra: (*not listening*) …and soon I'll be in Paris! I'm so looking forward to it.

Mum: You'll need your phrase book, too. And an umbrella – it's bound to rain. I was looking at the forecast and, although it says it'll be sunny, you never know. Your father and I went to Berlin last year and we got drenched on the first morning.

Sandra: Oh, stop fussing. I'll be fine. Travel is about freedom, not boring plans and 'what ifs'.

Director's note: *Mum is starting to panic.*

Director's note: *Sandra is staring at the poster as if in a dream.*

Director's note: *Sandra nods without understanding what has been said.*

Director's note: *Mum doesn't know what she is saying and starts to cry.*

Director's note: *Sandra cannot see the pain on her Mum's face and carries on oblivious.*

Task 2 Once you have finished your reading, discuss what you have learned about the two characters and which parts of the dialogue gave you the best clues.

Student Book Q1 Prepare an answer to the following questions:

- What is this dialogue about?

  ....

  ....

- How are Sandra and her mother's reactions to the trip different?

  ....

  ....

Then explore the following question by looking at the text and covering the names of the speakers:

- Would you know who was speaking if their names weren't shown?

  ....

  ....

- How?

  ....

- Was this easy to do?

  ....

© HarperCollins Publishers 2013

Worksheet 3.2b — Continuing the dialogue

Student Book Q4 Continue the dialogue between Sandra and her mum. Remember to follow the instructions on Student Book p. 67.

Sandra: (*eagerly*) It's so exciting! My plane leaves in 24 hours…

Mum: Are you sure you've packed properly? Have you got your visa, travel sickness pills…? You need to prepare properly.

Sandra: (*not listening*) … and soon I'll be in Paris! I'm so looking forward to it.

Mum: You'll need your phrase book, too. And an umbrella – it's bound to rain. I was looking at the forecast and, although it says it'll be sunny, you never know. Your father and I went to Berlin last year and we got drenched on the first morning.

Sandra: Oh, stop fussing. I'll be fine. Travel is about freedom, not boring plans and 'what ifs'.

....
....
....
....
....
....
....
....
....
....
....
....
....
....
....
....

Worksheet 3.3 Diary writing

> **Content** is *what* the writing is about:
> - What subjects has the writer chosen to write about?
> - Why do you think this was important to the writer?
> - Why does it make the diary interesting to read?
>
> **Structure** is about *how* the information has been organised:
> - Have incidents or ideas been grouped together for any reason?
> - Have they been described in chronological order or are very important incidents placed first?
> - What information about the writer do we get from the sequence of events?
>
> **Style** is about the *particular words, sentences and paragraphs* the writer chooses:
> - Are the choices linked to who they are and where they live or what they do?
> - Or are they linked to what effect the writer wants to have on the reader?
>
> Diaries are often personal and written privately to explore feelings and emotions that might not be shared elsewhere. How does the writer achieve this and what does it feel like to read it?

Student Book Q2 Discuss the content, structure and style of the first diary with a partner.

Monday, 11 March

What a day it's been! I overslept and missed the school bus and then, when I finally arrived, I found out the whole class was on a science trip and they had already left. I felt such a fool. I had to sit on my own outside the head teacher's office all day. It was so boring!

I'm back home now, sitting in my room. I haven't told mum or dad I missed the trip. If I do, they'll go mad. Dad's home. I'd better pretend I'm asleep.

Student Book Q4 Look at the second diary below and compare it with the first extract in terms of how the writer has used content, structure and style.

Yesterday, it was cloudy and rainy all day, the crocodiles starved of any sunlight and barely any warmth... then today we awoke to a totally different morning: back to the scorching heat and the crocodiles returning in droves to bask on the sandbanks, while the Goliath Heron, too hot even to finish washing, just sat down in the river and stayed there (and who could blame it?). I had to take a cold shower at midday, just to fortify myself for the onslaught of the afternoon heat.

Tonight, as might be expected, the thunder and lightning are raging again, huge storm clouds fomented in the heat of the day, now towering overhead... and the rain continues, and the bugs multiply, and the flowers prepare to launch into their reproductive cycles once again... the tiny pretty blue *commelina* flowers are already blooming everywhere you look (including on our nascent lawn) and the *sansevieria* we transplanted into our garden (both on the balcony and outside) are sending up a proliferation of shoots, the new spikes breaking the surface of the earth like spiky aliens, and reaching up towards the light...

Worksheet 3.4a — Features of report writing

Writers make choices about how they present information. You task is to decide whether those choices were correct in the example below.

Task 1 With a partner, decide how Texts 1 and 2 below are different. Which is the most suitable to report a crime?

Text 1

At about six o'clock I was walking up to my house when I saw a man emerge from the side door. It was my neighbour, Mr Jacobs. He hadn't seen me. He quickly climbed the fence between our houses, and disappeared.

When I opened my door and went inside I noticed that the tin of money with all my savings had gone. That is when I phoned you. It must have been 6.15 by then.

Text 2

Six o'clock. I'm walking to my house. I see a man come from the side door. It's my neighbour! Mr Jacobs hasn't seen me. What is he doing? He's climbing the fence between our houses and now he's disappeared.

I'm opening the door and I'm going inside. And I'm noticing that the tin of money with all my savings is gone. So I'm phoning you and it's 6.15.

Task 2 How are Texts 3 and 4 below different? Which one is better suited to a report on a school event?

Text 3

The school fund-raising day was a great success thanks to you all. Three things made the day a great success: the weather, your hard work and the generosity of visitors and parents.

The day began with clear blue skies, but it wasn't too hot. As our families arrived, it began to get really busy. I was working on a stall selling cold drinks. We soon ran out and needed more supplies desperately! I must thank Kiki who cycled all the way to the shop and back with baskets full of lemonade and soda. She's been my best friend since Grade 2 and now you all know why. In fact, just as we restocked, the Mayor appeared and we were able to serve him a wonderfully cool drink.

Text 4

I was working on a stall selling cold drinks – we soon ran out and needed more supplies desperately. Big thanks must go to Kiki who cycled all the way to the shop and back with baskets full of lemonade and soda. She saved my life! She's been my best friend since Grade 2 and now you all know why.

The school fund-raising day was a great success thanks to you all. The day began well, with clear blue skies, but not too hot, and as our parents and families arrived it began to get really busy.

Worksheet 3.4b: Content, structure and style of report writing

When writing reports, you need to consider the Purpose, Audience and Form, as well as the Content, Structure and Style. If you were writing a report on a rugby match, your notes might look like this:

> Purpose: to tell readers what happened at the Italy v France match.
>
> Audience: rugby fans.
>
> Form: report – less than 600 words with 1 photograph, headline.
>
> Content: first half, the lead taken by Italy, the penalties, the injury. Second half, the comeback by France, the 'try against all odds', the closing score, the disputed sending off.
>
> Structure: chronological, four paragraphs. Factual, simple sentences and some personal comment in longer, complex sentences.
>
> Style: mainly informal, talking to an audience that are familiar with technical terms, the main players, the rules. Give personal views of the players' skills and the management of the teams.

Student Book **Q2** Use the following table to record your ideas about the school fundraising report.

Form:	Report in school magazine about a charity day
Purpose:	
Audience:	Students our age
Content:	It gives clear information, but it also covers...
Structure:	It could be in time sequence, but could also jump around to topics such as the weather, money raised and number of people there.
Style:	

© HarperCollins Publishers 2013

181

Worksheet 3.5a: News report or feature article?

Student Book **Q1** Sort these headings into those that come from news reports and those that come from feature articles.

Temperatures dip to –30° for coldest night on record

Why are our winters getting colder?

ICE CAUSES CHAOS ON MOTORWAYS

Snow go – 36 hours stuck on train

How to predict cold winters

Worksheet 3.5b (1): Material for feature writing

Student Book Q4 Highlight the ideas and facts from these two articles that you will use in your own feature article.

Mountain Goat Kills Hiker
by Alex Robinson 19 October 2010

ROBERT BOARDMAN, 63, was hiking with his wife and friend in Olympic National Park on Monday when he was attacked and killed by a mountain goat. The trio was hiking up a popular switchback trail and decided to stop for lunch when the goat approached them and started acting aggressively.

Boardman tried to scare the goat off, but instead of running away, it charged him goring him badly in the leg. More hikers came to try to help Boardman, but the goat stood over the man's body and wouldn't let any other hikers come to his aid.

An hour after the attack, rescuers finally arrived at the scene but Boardman died from his injuries. Park officials eventually shot and killed the goat.

Apparently, that specific goat had shown aggressive tendencies in the past. 'It has shown aggressive behaviour, however, nothing led us to believe it was appropriate to take the next level of removal,' park spokeswoman Barb Maynes told the Associated Press. 'This is highly unusual. There's no record of anything similar in this park. It's a tragedy. We are taking it extremely seriously and doing our best to learn as much as we can.'

The goat is being examined by scientists to see if it had any diseases that could have caused it to act so aggressively.

Why do men love 'dangerous' dogs?

Robert Crampton

There are two problems trying to interview aggressive men with aggressive dogs, one practical, the other ethical. The practical problem is that genuinely aggressive men with genuinely aggressive dogs don't want to be interviewed, still less photographed. These Bill Sikes characters tend to disappear, swearing, with Bull's Eye around a corner as you approach. Appearances can in any case be deceptive. You find some likely-looking candidate togged up in Lonsdale and adidas, teeth missing, shaved head, 80 lb of canine energy straining at the leash, and he turns out to be a sweet guy with a sweet dog.

One such was Lee Randall, 36, an asbestos remover by trade, whom I met in Bow in East London, his American boxer Che at his feet. 'Some people are scared of her, but it's not the dog, it's the owner. It's like a baby, or a computer. You get out what you put in. It's the same as anything. A dog is only aggressive if it's taught to be.' Che is fine around people, says Randall, although squirrels are another matter.

Randall wouldn't want to be seen walking around with a toy poodle, but that doesn't mean he has a boxer to be aggressive, or macho, or as a status symbol. It means he has a boxer because he likes the way boxers look and behave. It's a similar story with Staffordshire bull terriers, the most popular dog in London, according to the Kennel Club. A lot of people think they're ugly, but beauty is in the eye of the beholder. A lot of people think Staffs must be nasty too, because of the way they look, but they're actually renowned for their good temperament, especially around children.

Worksheet 3.6a: Comparing formal and informal letters

Student Book **Q1** Compare the two letters – one informal and the other formal.
- Use the table below to note down the features you identify.
- Then summarise the differences and similarities in the space provided.

Informal letter	Formal letter
Content – what is the letter about? Why has it been written?	**Content** – what is the letter about? Why has it been written?
Structure – how has the information been organised?	**Structure** – how has the information been organised?
Style/tone – describe the language used and the 'voice' of the writer	**Style/tone** – describe the language used and the 'voice' of the writer

The two letters are similar in the way that they both ....

....

....

....

However, the two letters are different because ....

....

....

© HarperCollins Publishers 2013

Worksheet 3.6b: Comparing the different styles

Student Book **Q2** Use the table below to compare the letter writers' use of structure and style in more detail.

Informal letter	Formal letter
What kind of vocabulary is used?	What kind of vocabulary is used?
Are there abbreviations? Give examples.	Are there abbreviations? Give examples.
What do you notice about the sentences?	What do you notice about the sentences?
Is punctuation used?	Is punctuation used?
How does the letter open/close?	How does the letter open/close?

Chapter 3 Key writing skills

© HarperCollins Publishers 2013

Worksheet 3.7: Stages in the analysis

Task Cut out the five cards below. Then place them in order and explain the structure of the analysis text on Student Book p. 81.

---

new time and general point

---

more specific, but not completely explained

---

what happened is described

---

how the specific problem occurred

---

analysing the consequences – looking ahead

Worksheet 3.8: Using well-chosen evidence

Task Cut out these two sets of cards for students to use in a matching pairs activity. Give each student one set of three cards from the top batch and one set of three cards from the bottom batch. They have two minutes to match the two sets.

100g dark chocolate per day could reduce the risk of a heart attack or stroke by 21% (*British Medical Journal* research)	Dr Miles Better: 'Eating chocolate is fine, provided it is in moderation and you stick to dark chocolate.'	I bought a large bar of chocolate recently and finished it all in one go, and I felt really guilty, especially when the dentist told me a week later that I needed two fillings!
100g dark chocolate per day could reduce the risk of a heart attack or stroke by 21% (*British Medical Journal* research)	Dr Miles Better: 'Eating chocolate is fine, provided it is in moderation and you stick to dark chocolate.'	I bought a large bar of chocolate recently and finished it all in one go, and I felt really guilty, especially when the dentist told me a week later that I needed two fillings!
100g dark chocolate per day could reduce the risk of a heart attack or stroke by 21% (*British Medical Journal* research)	Dr Miles Better: 'Eating chocolate is fine, provided it is in moderation and you stick to dark chocolate.'	I bought a large bar of chocolate recently and finished it all in one go, and I felt really guilty, especially when the dentist told me a week later that I needed two fillings!
100g dark chocolate per day could reduce the risk of a heart attack or stroke by 21% (*British Medical Journal* research)	Dr Miles Better: 'Eating chocolate is fine, provided it is in moderation and you stick to dark chocolate.'	I bought a large bar of chocolate recently and finished it all in one go, and I felt really guilty, especially when the dentist told me a week later that I needed two fillings!
100g dark chocolate per day could reduce the risk of a heart attack or stroke by 21% (*British Medical Journal* research)	Dr Miles Better: 'Eating chocolate is fine, provided it is in moderation and you stick to dark chocolate.'	I bought a large bar of chocolate recently and finished it all in one go, and I felt really guilty, especially when the dentist told me a week later that I needed two fillings!

Expert comment	**Personal anecdote**	**Factual information**
Expert comment	**Personal anecdote**	**Factual information**
Expert comment	**Personal anecdote**	**Factual information**
Expert comment	**Personal anecdote**	**Factual information**
Expert comment	**Personal anecdote**	**Factual information**

Worksheet 3.9: Using facts, statistics, expert opinion and anecdote to persuade

Task Put each statement into the right column then create one of your own before analysing their effect.

- Up to 70% of parents would walk their children to school if cars were banned.
- Just a ten-minute walk twice a day would provide all the fresh air and exercise needed, according to Dr Langham from the University of Liverpool.
- Without traffic, serious injuries outside the school could be minimised.
- Yet again my daughter was forced to walk round a car parked up on the pavement in order to get to the school gates, forcing us into the road.

Fact	Statistics	Expert opinion	Personal anecdote
This has the effect of:	This has the effect of:	This has the effect of:	This has the effect of:

Worksheet 3.10a: Structuring an argument

Task Allocate two students to read the script out to the whole class.

Student 1: *Bike rental schemes allow people to rent a bike between two different places and can be an economical and convenient way to get from A to B.*

Student 2: *Our local council raised over a million pounds last year by installing ten 'docking stations' and a hundred bikes. This was a lot cheaper than repairing the entrance to the tube station, which cost half a million. Several commuters to the city centre found that the bikes had improved their punctuality to work and their overall fitness – and saved them money.*

Student 1: *However, following a particularly wet summer, others were not impressed. Many of the students that were targeted for the bike rental scheme chose to keep warm and dry by taking the bus to college, leaving the bikes untouched on most days. A lot of effort went in to researching who would use the bikes, but it did not prove accurate. Many students felt that a minibus service from the edge of town would be more useful.*

Student 2: *So, all in all, we have to ask ourselves: is it worth it? Considering the minimal set-up costs of the bike scheme and the initial successes for some commuters, it must be viewed positively, and with predictions of a sunny Spring this year, we can only hope that students are persuaded to give the bikes a go.*

Worksheet 3.10b — 'For' and 'against' an argument

Student Book Q10 Cut along the dotted lines to create two 'heading' cards and 10 'argument' cards. Divide the 'arguments' cards into two piles under the appropriate heading – i.e. those for and those against the argument.

For pedestrianisation	Against pedestrianisation
Joni Muller, 35, mother of 2 young children: 'I would definitely go into town to shop if there weren't any cars – it would be so much safer.'	even when weather is bad, people won't be allowed to park
safer – less traffic	more space, no cars, trucks, vans
difficult for senior citizens who are less mobile	10% drop in sales when similar scheme introduced in nearby town
encourage families, healthy – less pollution, car fumes	difficult for shop owners to take deliveries
estimated 70% improvement in air quality according to research local government group	shopkeeper, Raj Kapoor, 52: 'At the moment my older customers can park nearby, but that will change. I worry they won't bother to come in.'

© HarperCollins Publishers 2013

Worksheet 3.11: Comparing two information texts

Use the table below to compare the two informative texts. Give examples of the techniques each writer has used and describe the effect of each.

Feature	TrakkMeNow	Dragon Hunter King 2020
Is the text written in the first, second or third person? Give an example. Why is it written in this way?		
How would you describe the tone of the text? Give an example. Why is this tone used?		
What kind of language is used? Give an example. What effect does this have?		
Which sentence types are used? Give examples. What effect do they create?		

Worksheet 3.13: Creating atmosphere

Student Book **Q5** Make your own notes on how the writer creates a mood in the two extracts. You will need to consider what the writer has done to create a vivid picture in your mind.

Use the table below to make notes about the effect of the writer's choice of language.

Quotation	Technique	Mark out of 5?	How does it help create mood?
I gasped at the myriad colours of the spider	use of the senses (sight)		
which sparkled in the raindrops	use of the senses (sight)		
falling like a shattered necklace through the amber branches ...	use of imagery, comparing raindrops to jewels		
My companion stepped back,	use of movement		
blood draining from her face,	use of imagery creating vivid picture		
as the spider fixed her with its tiny black eyes,	use of the senses (sight)		
its body no more than an inch or two away	use of the senses (sight)		
on the twisted limbs of a tree which bent over us ...	use of the senses (sight)		

© HarperCollins Publishers 2013

Worksheet 3.14: Varying sentences in descriptive text

Student Book Q5 Once you have your strip of paper, take responsibility for improving that sentence. Should it be shorter for impact and surprise, or should it be longer providing interesting details?

Once you have made your improvements, work with your other group members to put the whole text back together and see if you think it works better by creating tension and atmosphere.

Suddenly, after two hours, the performance came to an abrupt end as he sang the last words of his final song and disappeared off stage.

We stared wide-eyed towards the stage as the arena lights came on and bathed us in brightness.

The place seemed ordinary now and was no longer the magical site of a few minutes before.

But the lights went down once again and everyone exploded into excited cries.

A beam of yellow picked out a thin figure at the side of the stage who was holding a guitar, a without warning a beautiful melody began.

Worksheet 4.1 Summarising information

Task 1 Come up with one word or phrase that summarises each of these groups of words.

Broom, vacuum cleaner, bleach, mop, duster	
Iron, silver, brass, copper, steel	
Earwig, grasshopper, butterfly, ant, wasp	
Charles Dickens, Shakespeare, J.K. Rowling, Agatha Christie, C.S. Lewis	
One Direction, The Beatles, Spice Girls, Coldplay, Take That	
Football, tennis, hockey, rugby, athletics	
Violin, trumpet, drum, cello, piano	

Task 2 Using your own words as much as possible, rewrite each sentence below as a concise summary. Try to use no more than ten words for each one.

1 My mum's sister really liked working her way through as many books, magazines, newspapers and text books as she could possibly get her hands on.

2 The shop my dad runs sells pens, paper, ink cartridges, etc., and it is always full of people who just love shopping there.

3 At the end of the working week, when it's got dark and the stars are coming out, I like to just sit back, have a long, cool drink and watch some of the nonsense that is on the television.

4 My dad's father is really old – nearly 80 years old – but he still likes going out all the time and meeting his friends, his family and the people that he used to work with.

© HarperCollins Publishers 2013

Worksheet 4.2: Locating, selecting, ordering and summarising

Task Read through this extract from a travel brochure about Tokyo.

Then, using up to 75 words, summarise the different things a tourist can do when visiting Tokyo.

Remember to:
- skim the passage, looking out for information on what a tourist can do
- scan it to select key phrases
- underline these, and then number them into a logical order
- write your summary, putting the information into your own words.

While lustrous skyscrapers, flashing neon and a wave of people burst frenetically across the streets of Tokyo, its extensive parks and gardens recline in tranquil beauty. This is a land of wonder, where natural and man-made beauties merge in harmony as ancient and modern collide. We only use hotels on the Yamanote loop railway line, which makes it easy for you to embark on a city tour – for which we can provide comprehensive and insightful pre-departure notes.

Get up early for the amazing Tsukiji fish market and enjoy a sushi breakfast. Then take a stroll through the huge Ueno Park to the impressive National Museum or the Imperial Gardens, gazing across at the moated palace. Explore historic Asakusa with its temples and traditional handicrafts before plunging into the grandiose shopping and entertainment districts of Shinjuku, Shibuya and Ginza. There is so much to see and do (and buy), that you will want to spend plenty of time delving into Tokyo.

The city is also a good base for exploring some of Japan's best sights, the most famous being the conical perfection of Mount Fuji. Capped with snow and swathed in cloud, she looks down to Hakone with its sculpture park, volcanic hot springs and scenic Lake Ashi. Buddhist temples speckle the seaside town of Kamakura, once the country's capital, and there are pleasant walks around the area, whilst in Nikko you can see splendidly carved temples and shrines. The historical side of the country is fascinating and it is really worth visiting these reminders of its past. A peaceful boat trip to the Izu Islands, which reach down into the Pacific, reveals images of forgotten Japan; with beaches, hot springs and hidden shrines, these pretty isles are rarely visited by westerners.

Visiting Tokyo will be an experience you will cherish forever.

Worksheet 4.3 Selecting and summarising

Student Book **Q3** Show your selection and summary skills. Fill in this table by finding the key information from the second part of the passage.

What the author did to try to get out of danger	
What happened to him and his canoe	
Extension: Details that are irrelevant	

Student Book **Q5** Develop your selection and summary skills. Complete this mind map on the dangers of tidal canoeing, and how Mitchinson tries to cope with them, by finding the key information from both extracts.

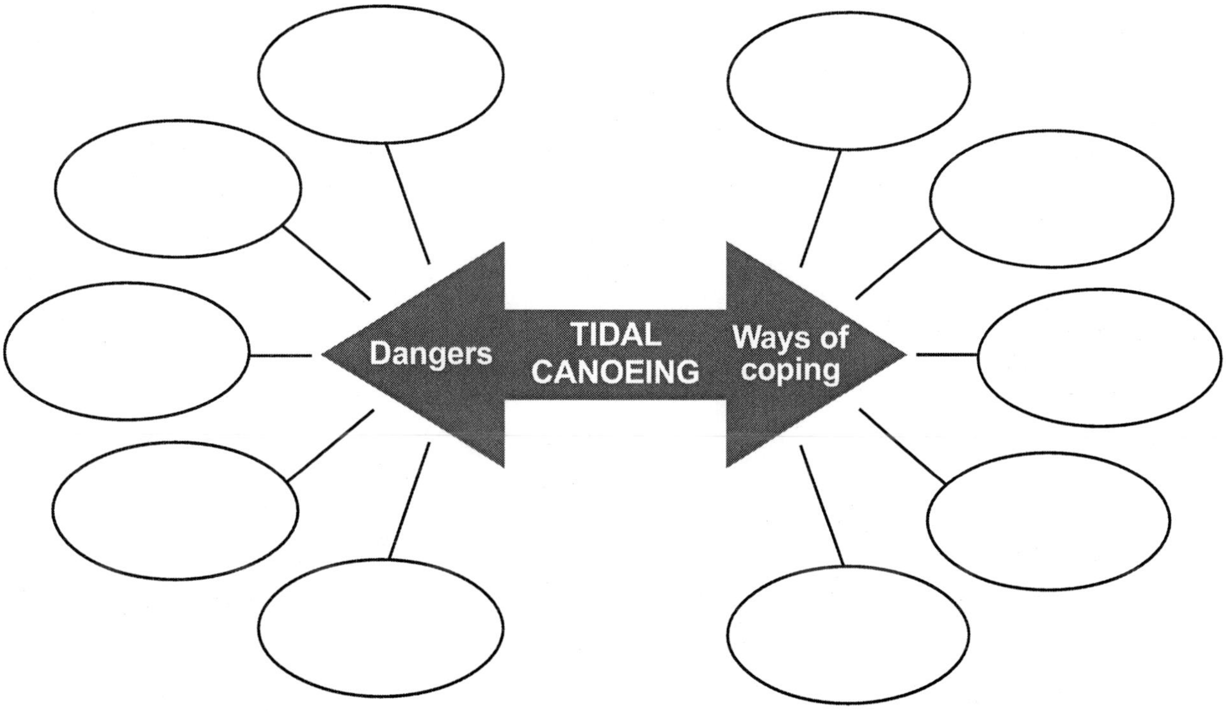

© HarperCollins Publishers 2013

Worksheet 4.4a: Rewriting in your own words

Student Book Q2 Using Passage A, part 2, note down key phrases that show the problems with the Himalayan roads and how the bus services attempt to cope with them. Then rewrite each key phrase in your own words.

Original	My own words
'buried under massive mudslides at 30-kilometre intervals'	Roads often covered by fallen mud

Student Book Q3 Using Passage B, find seven problems with road travel and write them in your own words.

Seven problems in my own words
1
2
3
4
5
6
7

Chapter 4 Summary questions

198 © HarperCollins Publishers 2013

Worksheet 4.4b — Analysing summary responses

Student Book **Q5** Read through Answers 1 and 2. Which would gain full marks and why?

Task: Write a summary of the problems of road travel as described by the author.

Answer 1

Problems with road travel: Passage B

When waiting for a bus, people pestered the author to buy things. Because she was white, her different colour made her feel conspicuous. She had to push her way onto the bus, due to there being so many passengers. With over-crowding and un-shaded windows, the journey was hot and uncomfortable. This was increased by other passengers' behaviour, such as tugging or poking her, and the presence of frightened animals. In addition, there were no toilet facilities, which was a problem for the author as she had an upset stomach due to travel sickness.

Answer 2

In Passage B, there is no room to sit because the bus is so crowded so she ends up yanking on a young girl's hair. People try to sell her things, such as orange juice, t-shirts, stereos and biscuits. People keep pulling and prodding her. I think this would be horrible because I hate being on a crowded bus. Because the bus is so busy she has to squeeze in between two other women. She also felt odd because everyone looked at her. There were never white faces around so she stood out. There are also animals everywhere, like chickens, which is disgusting! She reaches Sanya Juu just after sunset and she tries to find a bathroom. The journey was bad because she needed the bathroom on the bus and there wasn't one. Also, because it's so crowded, the bus got really hot. It was also hot because the sun poured through the glass windows.

© HarperCollins Publishers 2013

Worksheet 5.1 — How do we make inferences?

Task Use this worksheet of suggestions to create a poster showing other students what they can look at to help them to draw inferences. You could use examples from the extract on Student Book p.132 (also given below) or select an extract of your own.

> The waitress smiled gently when we told Her that we were nervous about the storm approaching Florida. 'I remember when I lost my home in 1984,' she began. 'It had been pretty wild for a few hours so we'd already boarded up the windows and brought the livestock in. Suddenly we got a call to evacuate our homes, and we all piled into the truck when a huge gust of wind swept out of nowhere and took the house roof clean off. My golf clubs had been standing inside my hallway and the next day I found them clear half a mile away, in a field, sticking out of the grass like sentries!'

	People	Places
What the writer tells us about	<ul><li>facts</li><li>facial expressions</li><li>body language</li><li>what characters do and say</li><li>reactions of other characters</li></ul>	<ul><li>the time of year</li><li>the time of day</li><li>the type of landscape or buildings</li><li>the sensory prompts</li></ul>
What people say	<ul><li>the words chosen</li><li>the tone of voice</li><li>the pace of their words</li></ul>	<ul><li>The words chosen</li><li>The tone of voice</li><li>The pace of their words</li></ul>
What people /animals do	<ul><li>how they move</li><li>the pace of their movements</li><li>the purpose of their actions</li></ul>	<ul><li>how they move</li><li>the pace of their movements</li><li>the purpose of their actions</li></ul>
The reactions of people/animals to each other	<ul><li>how they interact</li><li>what mood they are in with each other</li></ul>	<ul><li>how they interact</li><li>what mood they are in with each other</li></ul>

Worksheet 5.2: Proms – comprehension questions

Student Book Q2 Complete the table below with synonyms for the words given.

Word	Meaning
shimmering (sequins)	shining and catching the light
(beautifully) manicured (nails)	
slicked back (hair)	

Student Book Q3 Read this passage and then complete the grid below to answer this question:

How did the teachers behave at the prom?

Add two more examples to the table from the passage.

> We were stars for the night! Some teachers were like paparazzi. They lined the red carpet, all dressed up themselves, lenses zooming, making us blink with the flashes and calls for smiles. Others formed a human shield, bossily holding back the cheering Year 7s, as if they were bouncers at a film première, keeping us away from mere mortals.

Word	Meaning	Inference
Like paparazzi	Taking photographs	
formed a human shield		Protective of the prom goers – didn't want the photos spoilt

© HarperCollins Publishers 2013

Worksheet 5.3: Understanding writer's effects questions

Student Book **Q3**   Read through the first table, which shows you how to explore and explain the word 'wide-eyed'. Then, using the second table, try to follow the same process in order to explain what the word 'enlightened' means.

'Wide-eyed'	Your ideas
Who are 'wide-eyed'?	The students
What is the context or situation?	The students are looking at their teacher, waiting for him/her to tell them about Paris.
What other similar words or phrases come to mind?	'Wide' links to 'big'. If your eyes are open, you're looking, and it says in the text that they're 'staring'. The dentist says 'Open wide' so he can look in your mouth. If your eyes are open wide, they must be open as much as they'll go. The more 'open' your eyes, the more you can take in. You'd only do this if you were looking at something interesting or shocking.
So what might the word mean?	'Wide-eyed' means looking at something with complete attention, perhaps in shock or wonder.

'Enlightened'	Your ideas
Who are 'waiting to be enlightened'?	
What is the context or situation? *(Also think about what the students 'want' from their teacher.)*	
What other similar words or phrases come to mind? *(Think about what we link 'light' to: the light at the end of the tunnel; a light bulb above a head in a cartoon; the effect of lighting something up.)*	
So what might the word mean?	

Worksheet 5.4a: How words and phrases suggest ideas and emotions

Student Book **Q2** Complete the table below, exploring the meaning of words from the text and how they suggest helplessness.

Word/phrase	Meaning	How it suggests 'helplessness'
'**plucked** from a beautiful big bungalow'	Taken suddenly without warning or forcefully.	The verb 'plucked' suggests the writer was like a small creature or item taken from above without knowing. The word suggests he has been aggressively removed from his home, which adds to the feeling of helplessness.
'**dumped** in a crumbling house'	Dropped without care.	
'**forced** to live in a crowded dormitory'		

Student Book **Q5** Complete the table below, exploring the meaning of words from the text and how they suggest an unsuitable place for learning and education.

Word/phrase	Meaning	How it suggests an unsuitable place for learning
'It is **cramped**, noisy and dirty'		
'It has a classroom with **ramshackle** desks'		
'a **cracked** blackboard'		

© HarperCollins Publishers 2013

Worksheet 5.4b — Exploring parts of a sentence and word classes

Task 1 It is important that you understand the different **parts of a sentence**. Sentences should contain a **subject** (what the sentence is about), a **verb** (what the subject is doing, or what is happening to the subject), and an **object** (something affected by, or affecting, the subject).

For example:

- The car   sped down   the road.
  (subject)   *+ verb*   *+ object)*
- The woman   drank   a cup of tea.
  (subject)   *+ verb*   *+ object)*
- The newspaper was read by   the man.
  (subject)   *+ verb*   *+ object)*

Label the subject, verb and object in these next three sentences.

A	The house had a large garden.
B	The boy dropped his pen.
C	The cheese was eaten by the mouse.

Task 2 When exploring the different parts of a sentence, it's also important that you understand the different **word classes**:

- **verbs** (doing words)
- **nouns** (things, people, places words)
- **adjectives** (words describing a noun)
- **adverbs** (words describing a verb).

Look at the example below, then label the remaining three sentences to show the different word classes.

- The naughty girl ran quickly through the quiet museum.
      ⇩   ⇩   ⇩   ⇩   ⇩   ⇩
    adjective noun verb adverb   adjective noun

A	The man walked slowly downstairs and put on his muddy boots.
B	The big lion hungrily opened its mouth and showed its sharp teeth.
C	Sleepily, the woman closed her eyes and dreamt of a beautiful island.

Worksheet 5.5: Exploring a writer's effects further

Task Read the following story extract and complete the tasks.

> The house stood alone on the moors, glaring out across the barren landscape. Its smashed windows were like the eye sockets of a skull, and ivy clambered across the brickwork. Abandoned for a decade, no one went near the building; too many rumours and stories warned away even the most curious local.
>
> Inside, the floorboards were rotting away, and a damp, oppressive smell filled the air. Here were shadows and nightmares. Even in summer, the house felt cold inside; an icy, unwelcoming atmosphere seeped out of the walls. There were still signs of the tragedy of ten years ago: a blood stain across the kitchen floor, a bullet hole in the wall and the rusting padlock on the cellar door.

Pick out three powerful verbs and say what their effect is:

1 ....
2 ....
3 ....

Identify a simile and say what mood or atmosphere it creates: ....

....

....

....

Pick out three powerful adjectives and say what their effect is:

1 ....
2 ....
3 ....

Identify a short sentence and say what mood or atmosphere it creates: ....

....

....

....

© HarperCollins Publishers 2013

Worksheet 5.6a — Analysing a writer's effects

Student Book Q5 Read through the following extract and add further annotations which respond to the effects or feelings created.

Think about symbolic ideas, where what is described reflects bigger or wider issues.

> Fourwinds, the house at which I was to take up employment, apparently lay in a very isolated spot (1), for I could see no sign of habitation, no plume of smoke (2) from a shepherd's humble croft. I felt very conscious of travelling from one stage of my life to the next: every step away from the road carried me farther from London, my mother and sister, the art school and my friends there; each tread brought me nearer to the house and its inhabitants, of which, and of whom, I knew very little.

Annotations:

(1) the writer is alone

(2) repetition of 'no' is negative and empty

(3) ....

(4) ....

(5) ....

Student Book Q6 Share your annotations with a partner. Then, using the feedback, write your own short response to the paragraph describing what effect is created by the selected words and phrases. Is the effect still one of unease or do you sense other feelings now?

Worksheet 5.6b: Using the language of analysis

Task *How does the writer create an unhappy atmosphere in the extract below?*

> It had been four long, empty, miserable days since she had last seen Sam. She waited by the silent telephone, hoping desperately for it to ring. The house was cold and the curtains had been left drawn, letting in none of the summer sunlight from outside. It felt more like winter. The ticking of the clock seemed to echo around the house, reminding her, every second, that he was gone. Their last words had been full of anger and bitterness, emotions that still left a cruel taste in her mouth. He wasn't coming back.

Use the vocabulary bank below to complete the analysis. You don't have to use all the phrases, and some can be used more than once.

_____ the author creates an unhappy atmosphere is by describing the house, 'It felt more like winter'. This _____ conveys how it is cold and dark, which _____ the character's misery. The fact that she doesn't open the curtains also _____ that she doesn't want to face the world.

_____ , the house seems lonely: 'the silent telephone' and 'the ticking of the clock seemed to echo'. The _____ 'silent'_____ a lack of hope or comfort, whilst the verb 'echo' and _____ 'ticking' helps the reader to imagine how the house feels empty.

_____ creates an unhappy atmosphere by describing the woman, 'desperately'. This _____ _____ that she is feeling terrible, and this _____ the reference to 'four long, empty, miserable days', where the _____ of adjectives stretches out the sentence to show how her life seems to have stopped. _____ by the short sentence, 'He wasn't coming back', which seems very final and _____ that she has given up.

Sentence starters	Explanation phrases	Connectives	Techniques
One way in which	suggests	In addition	adjective
The author	implies	Furthermore	adverb
In this text	conveys	The author also	short sentence
	reflects	This is added to by	onomatopoeia
	is emphasised by		list

© HarperCollins Publishers 2013

Worksheet 6.1: What voice and tone?

Task 1 For each of the following tasks draw a line to match the voice or tone you think is most appropriate to each task.

Then, explain your answers.

Task	Voice and tone
1 Write a letter to the Managing Director of a large retail chain of fashion shops protesting about the company's use of real fur in their clothes.	A Analytical, clearly thought through, more of an impersonal tone but very well informed on the facts and details.
2 Write a report for a national newspaper about the problem of rubbish being left by climbers on Everest and how this affects the environment.	B Strong, emotional and personal tone, demonstrating your own commitment and feelings about the subject. Supported by facts and examples, but passionately committed to one point of view.
3 Write a description of a journey, real or imagined, into a place or landscape that is completely different from your own, and include how it makes you feel.	C Personal, direct tone that links clearly to reader/audience who might share similar viewpoints. Ideas clearly expressed; perhaps use of rhetorical devices and good examples to back up opinion.
4 Write a speech to be given to your school in which you argue that people of your age should be given more respect by older people.	D Vivid and detailed with a real sense of wonder and surprise, perhaps even shock; possibly reflective and thoughtful, too.

Task 2 Now, write the **opening paragraph** for each of these tasks, in the appropriate voice, tone and style.

Worksheet 6.2 Understanding the passage

Task Reread the passage about Anthony Smith, and answer the questions below.

Find the relevant words or phrases from the passage, and then write your answers in the spaces provided.

What is Anthony Smith intending to do?

What might be considered unusual about this?

What reasons does Anthony Smith give for going on the trip?

Student Book Q2 Highlight the **key words** in the question below that will help you answer it.
Think about:
- the task and its purpose
- the audience
- the form
- whose voice you will write it in.

> *Imagine you are Anthony Smith's grandson. You have been invited onto a news programme to talk about your grandfather. Write a conversation that you then have with the presenter. You should include:*
>
> - *what your grandfather is intending to do*
> - *your concerns about the trip*
> - *the reassurances your grandfather has given you.*

© HarperCollins Publishers 2013

Worksheet 6.3a — What's implied?

Student Book Q3 Below are a number of descriptions from the story. Select the inference you think is closest in each case. Bear in mind that aspects of each of the choices might be partially correct.

1 **What image of Salvadorean society is provided by the description of the Suns, Shades, Ant-hill and Balcony people?**
   - A Salvadorean society is very split between the haves and have-nots.
   - B All Salvadoreans behave like animals at football matches.
   - C There are distinct groups, each with their different behaviours, attitudes and levels of wealth.
   - D Salvadoreans are passionate about football.

2 **What are the author's feelings about the crowd?**
   - A He feels bored watching them.
   - B He finds them funny and comical.
   - C He feels sorry for the poor, and despises the rich.
   - D He thinks they are fascinating and, in the case of certain groups, frightening.

3 **What can we infer about Alfredo from what we are told?**
   - A He's very 'streetwise' and knows how to look after himself and the writer.
   - B He's selfish and greedy.
   - C He's very poor.
   - D He is proud of his fellow people and wants to show them off to the writer.

Worksheet 6.3b: Journal or diary writing plan

Student Book Q7 Use the writing frame below to help you structure your journal response to the passage about the football match. Remember that you are writing as Alfredo.

Today, of course, was the day of the big match. I went there and took ....
....
....
....

It was incredibly exciting and...
....
....
....

Of course, there were the usual touts but ....
....
....
....

As we entered the stadium, it was clear that my friend Paul........................
....
....
....

The crowd was divided as it is usually. I felt..
....
....
....

Taking Paul to the match made me realise that..
....
....
....

As for Paul...
....
....
....

© HarperCollins Publishers 2013

Worksheet 6.4: The four elements of the task

Task The task about the 'Call Me!' scheme provided information about the role of the writer, the content, a parent's concerns about the scheme, the form, audience and purpose. But how do these affect your actual answer?

In your group of four, each take one of the elements below. Note down what each requires you to think about when you write your final answer. Some suggestions have been included to get you started.

Form – newspaper article	Purpose – to argue
What are the conventions of newspaper articles? For example: • Headline or title	What are the features of effective 'argument' texts? For example: • Points backed up by evidence
Audience – other members of the school (probably mostly students)	**You – the writer** (a student)
What are the implications? For example: • Familiar references? ('the school hall', 'our teachers')	How will you write? What style? What voice? • The scheme is something you care about as you're part of the school

Worksheet 7.1: Features of narratives and descriptions

Student Book **Q2** Complete the relevant columns in the chart below, listing the key conventions of good narratives and good descriptions. You can work with a partner.

	Conventions of good narratives	Conventions of good descriptions
Structure	Structure to add interest Strong opening that hooks the reader Use of flashbacks Surprising ending	Ideas are very developed and detailed
Style	Vividly paints picture of setting in reader's mind using imagery	

Add the following features into the correct column. Some features might go in both. Some might not fit at all (e.g. they may be more relevant to non-fiction texts).

Conventions to add to structure or style	
Similes	Exciting plot or events
Rhetorical questions	Conclusion that sums up viewpoint or the issue discussed
Patterns of threes	Facts and figures, graphs and tables
Metaphors	Past tense (usually)
Clear viewpoint or opinion	Present tense (for writing about the current situation)
Includes evidence or logical reasons for viewpoint	Direct speech and conversation
Strong sense of character	

© HarperCollins Publishers 2013

Chapter 7 Composition questions

Worksheet 7.2: Developing a narrative response

Student Book Q4 Read the following composition task.
- Highlight or underline the key words, and decide on the form and focus of the task.
- Discuss the questions below it with a partner, but then make your own notes in the spaces provided.

Narrative writing

'The lost umbrella on the bus'. Use this as the title of a narrative.

Now fill in these 'development boxes' to help you plan your answer.

Possible content	Specific details
What is the basic overall content I will include? (e.g. my key ideas)	What specific details will I include? (e.g. what the umbrella looks like, and if/why that might be important)

Style and structure	Originality
What stylistic conventions of language or structure will I include? (e.g. time-shifts, imagery)	What might make my answer different or original? (e.g. an unusual 'angle', how I begin or end the story)

Chapter 7 Composition questions

Worksheet 7.3a — Overall effects

Student Book Q4 Read the passage below and then:
- underline the **three similes**
- circle the **two metaphors**.

> The midnight lake shone like a huge, silver brooch, and around it, in the swaying grasses, glow-worms glittered like miniature diamonds. The moon, which hung from the sky's dark neck, was an enormous locket which I felt I could reach out and touch. I was poor in terms of money but living in such a beautiful place, I was like the richest prince on earth.

Student Book Q5 Read the passage below and then:
- highlight **any imagery** you notice
- **think about what** common idea or topic **links it all together**.

> There was a wild rush to get to the front to see the band. Like bees racing towards their favourite lily, we sped towards the stage. From the sides of the arena, other people swarmed over the barriers like soldier ants or a tide of beetles swallowing up the space.

The common idea or topic that links all the imagery together is:

....

....

....

© HarperCollins Publishers 2013

Worksheet 7.3b: Linking imagery

Task Use some of the best similes or metaphors below to write your description.

- Enormous, towering skyscrapers like huge trees reaching for the sky
- Narrow roads twisting like dirty rivers full of creatures battling along
- Ambitious business-people are reptiles fighting for survival.
- At night new people emerge like glowing insects desperate to attract a mate.

City = jungle

The city was like a jungle as I went to work today. Above me ....

....

In my office ....

....

Worksheet 7.4a: Making a spider diagram

Student Book **Q1** Complete the spider diagram from the Student Book adding additional 'legs' and further sections to create as many ideas as possible. A few more ideas have been provided for you.

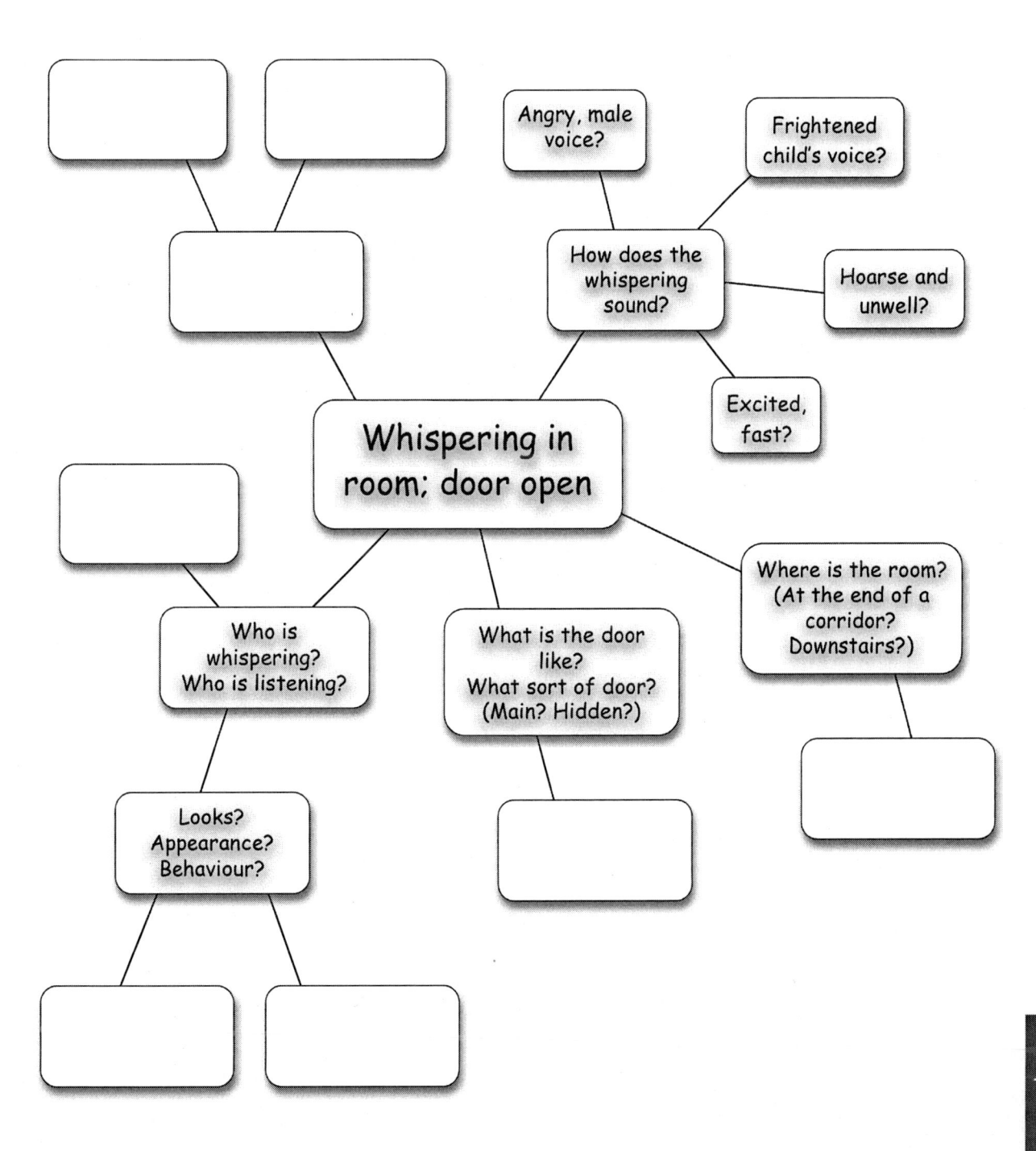

Central idea: Whispering in room; door open

- **How does the whispering sound?**
  - Angry, male voice?
  - Frightened child's voice?
  - Hoarse and unwell?
  - Excited, fast?

- **Who is whispering? Who is listening?**
  - Looks? Appearance? Behaviour?

- **What is the door like? What sort of door? (Main? Hidden?)**

- **Where is the room? (At the end of a corridor? Downstairs?)**

© HarperCollins Publishers 2013

Chapter 7 Composition questions

Worksheet 7.4b: Focusing on movements

Student Book Q7 Complete the following tasks, which will help you to write your own effective descriptive paragraph.

- Write a first version of your paragraph using the following prompts.

  I knelt down very slowly and carefully on the ....

  ....

  I began to ....

  ....

  At that moment ....

  ....

- Now choose one of the following questions (or one of your own) to build into your paragraph. Decide where it would go.
  - What was that sound?
  - Whose voice could I hear?
  - Was that a man or woman speaking?
  - What should I do?
  - Should I stay or leave?
  - What would happen if they heard me?

- You will already have written in sentences, but you can create effects with short and long sentences, and by varying prepositions (*alongside, beside, near, above, below, next to, underneath*).

  Write a final version of your paragraph here, adding further sentences and prepositions to create detailed descriptions of movement and positions.

Worksheet 7.5: Elements of narrative writing

Student Book Q3 — The cards below describe different elements of successful narrative writing. Decide which elements apply to the two extracts in **Q3** on Student Book p. 201.

You may be asked to cut out and attach the relevant card(s) to the extracts or you may be asked to stick them to the relevant part of the extract on the board.

flashback	surprise	suspense
withholds information	visual detail	sense of character
sense of place	action	direct speech

© HarperCollins Publishers 2013

Worksheet 7.6 (1)

My narrative: 'The Escape!'

Task   Generate ideas, plan, and write a narrative with this title: **'The Escape'**

Stage 1: Write your ideas for the story in the spaces around the title in the spider diagram. Think about the five Ws: Who, What, Where, When and Why.

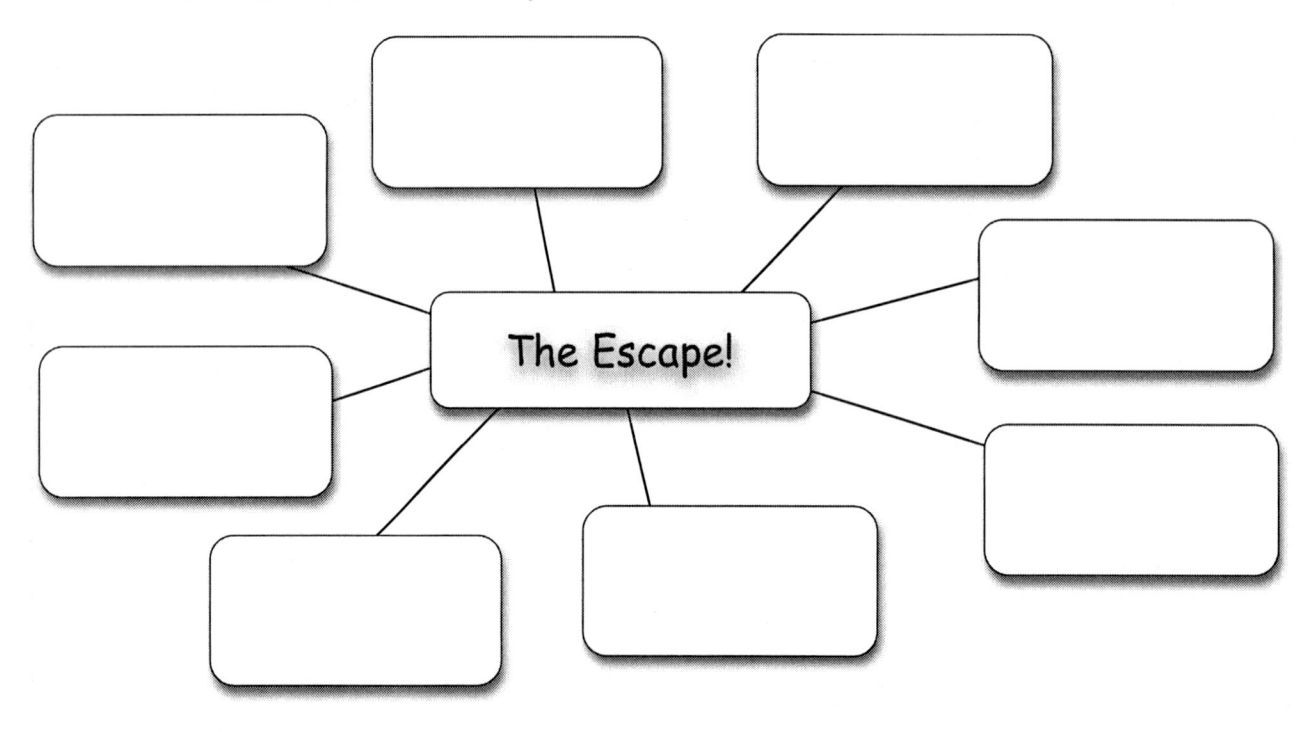

The Escape!

Stage 2: Write down your **key idea or ideas** for the story in the table below. These do not need to be your final decisions, but it means taking your best ideas from the spider diagram and beginning to shape them:

Main character + information about them	
Other character/s	
Setting/locations	
Basic story ideas	

Worksheet 7.6 (2) My narrative: 'The Escape!'

Stage 3: Structure/plan your narrative.

Introduction	
Development/ complication	
Climax	
Resolution	

Stage 4: Write your narrative, making sure...
- your characters are clearly-drawn and believable
- you have the right balance of dialogue and action
- you have a vivid setting and descriptions that add to the atmosphere
- you vary sentences for effect
- you use vivid and relevant vocabulary
- you spell correctly, punctuate clearly and write legibly.

Worksheet 8.1a — 'Snake' by D.H. Lawrence

Student Book Q7 Read the whole text of D.H. Lawrence's poem 'Snake'.

Focusing on the second half (from 'And truly I was afraid...'), highlight:

- further physical descriptions of the snake, especially those using imagery
- words, phrases or lines that indicate the poet's emotions.

Write a brief account of how the situation develops in the second half of the poem, and how the poet feels by the end. You might like to comment on his reference to 'the albatross'. (Look up the poem 'The Rime of the Ancient Mariner' by Samuel Taylor Coleridge if you do not understand what is being referred to).

'Snake' by D.H. Lawrence

A snake came to my water-trough
On a hot, hot day, and I in pyjamas for the heat,
To drink there.

In the deep, strange-scented shade of the great dark carob-tree
I came down the steps with my pitcher
And must wait, must stand and wait, for there he was at the trough before me.

He reached down from a fissure in the earth-wall in the gloom
And trailed his yellow-brown slackness soft-bellied down, over the edge of the stone trough
And rested his throat upon the stone bottom,
And where the water had dripped from the tap, in a small clearness,
He sipped with his straight mouth,
Softly drank through his straight gums, into his slack long body,
Silently.

Someone was before me at my water-trough,
And I, like a second comer, waiting.

He lifted his head from his drinking, as cattle do,
And looked at me vaguely, as drinking cattle do,
And flickered his two-forked tongue from his lips, and mused a moment,
And stooped and drank a little more,
Being earth-brown, earth-golden from the burning bowels of the earth
On the day of Sicilian July, with Etna smoking.

The voice of my education said to me
He must be killed,
For in Sicily the black, black snakes are innocent, the gold are venomous.

And voices in me said, If you were a man
You would take a stick and break him now, and finish him off.

But must I confess how I liked him,
How glad I was he had come like a guest in quiet, to drink at my water-trough
And depart peaceful, pacified, and thankless,
Into the burning bowels of this earth?

Was it cowardice, that I dared not kill him?
Was it perversity, that I longed to talk to him?
Was it humility, to feel so honoured?
I felt so honoured.

And yet those voices:
If you were not afraid, you would kill him!

And truly I was afraid, I was most afraid,
But even so, honoured still more
That he should seek my hospitality
From out the dark door of the secret earth.

He drank enough
And lifted his head, dreamily, as one who has drunken,
And flickered his tongue like a forked night on the air, so black,
Seeming to lick his lips,
And looked around like a god, unseeing, into the air,
And slowly turned his head,
And slowly, very slowly, as if thrice adream,
Proceeded to draw his slow length curving round
And climb again the broken bank of my wall-face.

And as he put his head into that dreadful hole,
And as he slowly drew up, snake-easing his shoulders, and entered farther,
A sort of horror, a sort of protest against his withdrawing into that horrid black hole,
Deliberately going into the blackness, and slowly drawing himself after,
Overcame me now his back was turned.

I looked round, I put down my pitcher,
I picked up a clumsy log
And threw it at the water-trough with a clatter.

I think it did not hit him,
But suddenly that part of him that was left behind convulsed in undignified haste,
Writhed like lightning, and was gone
Into the black hole, the earth-lipped fissure in the wall-front,
At which, in the intense still noon, I stared with fascination.

And immediately I regretted it.
I thought how paltry, how vulgar, what a mean act!
I despised myself and the voices of my accursed human education.

And I thought of the albatross
And I wished he would come back, my snake.

For he seemed to me again like a king,
Like a king in exile, uncrowned in the underworld,
Now due to be crowned again.

And so, I missed my chance with one of the lords
Of life.
And I have something to expiate:
A pettiness.

Taormina, 1923

Worksheet 8.1b: Dangerous ideas in the wild

Student Book Q11 Have any of the texts you have read about 'danger in the wild' made you think of good ideas for descriptive or narrative writing?

Perhaps the words/phrases below will help you think of some ideas.

When you have reflected on these, fill in five possible titles/ideas at the bottom of the page.

CHASE secret hunted flight **storm**

BEAST fangs CAVE *POISON* desert

Blood LOST FOUND *stranger* Mist

Fog river *dust* HAWK MANEATER

FOREST backpack *waves* villagers

rope ICE FALL *rocks* **Job**

journey Holiday *raft* track

My ideas/titles	Further details
1	
2	
3	
4	
5	

Chapter 8 Approaching written coursework

Worksheet 8.2a: Trying out structures

Student Book Q3 Write your key points or ideas onto the strips below and then move them into an order that you feel would work best for your chosen piece.

Worksheet 8.2b — Key assignment points

Student Book **Q3** Look at this example of points prepared for the Komodo dragon assignment – an article for the school magazine. Cut the list up into strips and order them in the way you think would work best in an assignment.

Physical appearance: lizard with yellow, forked tongue; length = 2–3 metres; weighs 70kg

---

Habitat: found on Indonesian islands of Komodo, Rinca, Flores; prefers hot, dry places

---

Current situation: under threat and considered at risk; around 1100 left in natural environment

---

Main fascination with Komodo dragon; it's rare, like a dinosaur; I've always been fascinated by lizards

---

Character: its bite can be venomous and though Komodo dragons are usually shy, some reports of attacking humans

---

Reputation: popular in zoos due to fearsome reputation

Food/prey: carnivorous; use their tails to knock down prey, such as deer, goats and pigs

Worksheet 8.3: Evaluating my story idea

Student Book **Q2**
- Write down your story idea in up to 75 words in the box.
- Then use the **Checklist for success** below to see if you have covered all the key elements needed.
- Redraft your idea, if necessary.

My story ideas

Checklist for success

Does my story...?	Yes	No/needs more work
Have just one or two main characters?		
Include a problem or difficulty that has to be overcome?		
Have a simple plot that readers can follow?		
Have one main location or setting?		
Include an effective beginning and ending?		

© HarperCollins Publishers 2013

Worksheet 8.4a: Pandas: annotated article

Student Book Q1–3: These annotations will allow you compare your own analysis of the arguments, techniques and style used by Chris Packham in his article.

Pandas – worth saving?

I don't want the panda to die out. <u>I want species to stay alive – that's why I get up in the morning. I don't even kill mosquitoes or flies</u>. So if pandas can survive, that would be great. <u>But let's face it</u>: conservation, both nationally and globally, has a limited amount of resources, and I think we're going to have to make some hard, pragmatic choices.

[Love of animals] [Informal and chatty]

<u>The truth is, pandas are extraordinarily expensive to keep going.</u> We spend millions and millions of pounds on pretty much this one species, and a few others, when we know that the best thing we could do would be to look after the world's **biodiversity** hotspots with greater care. Without habitat, you've got nothing. So maybe <u>if we took all the cash we spend</u> on pandas and just bought rainforest with it, we might be doing a better job.

[Argument 1] [Vocabulary] [Informal and chatty]

Of course, it's easier to raise money for <u>something fluffy</u>. <u>Charismatic megafauna like the panda do appeal to people's emotional side, and attract a lot of public attention</u>. They are emblematic of what I would call **single-species conservation**: ie a focus on one animal. <u>This approach began in the 1970s with Save the Tiger, Save the Panda, Save the Whale, and so on, and it is now out of date</u>. I think pandas have had a valuable role in raising the profile of conservation, but perhaps 'had' is the right word.

[Argument 2] [Vocabulary]

<u>Panda conservationists may stand up and say, 'It's a flagship species. We're also conserving Chinese forest, where there is a whole plethora of other things.'</u> And when that works, I'm not against it. <u>But we have to accept that some species are stronger than others. The panda is a species of bear that has gone herbivorous and eats a type of food that isn't all that nutritious, and that dies out sporadically</u>. It is susceptible to various diseases, and, up until recently, it has been almost impossible to breed in captivity. They've also got a **very restricted range, which is ever decreasing, due to encroachment on their habitat** by the Chinese population. Perhaps the panda was already destined to run out of time.

[Gives the other side of the argument] [Argument 3] [Vocabulary]

Extinction is very much a part of life on earth. And we are going to have to get used to it in the next few years because climate change is going to result in all sorts of disappearances. The last large mammal extinction was another animal in China – the Yangtze river dolphin, which looked like a worn-out piece of pink soap with piggy eyes and was never going to make it on to anyone's T-shirt. If that had appeared beautiful to us, then I doubt very much that it would be extinct. But it vanished, <u>because it was pig-ugly and swam around in a river where no one saw it</u>. And now, sadly, it has gone for ever.

[Informal and chatty]

… I'm saying we won't be able to save it all, so let's do the best we can. And at the moment I don't think our strategies are best placed to do that. We should be focusing our conservation endeavours on **biodiversity hotspots**, spreading our net more widely and looking at **good-quality habitat maintenance** to preserve as much of the life as we possibly can, using hard science to make educated decisions as to which species are essential to a community's maintenance. It may well be that we can lose the cherries from the cake. But you don't want to lose the substance. Save the Rainforest, or Save the Kalahari: that would be better.

[Vocabulary]

Worksheet 8.4b: Putting the counter-arguments

Student Book Q3
- You already have your group list of arguments that Chris Packham makes in his article. Your **top five** can be added to the left-hand column below the sample.
- But what about **counter-arguments**? These are arguments which directly deal with Packham's points and give the **opposing point of view.** In your groups, come up with ideas **against** Packham's and add them to the right-hand column.

Arguments FOR (Packham's views)	Counter-arguments AGAINST
Pandas can't survive naturally, so let them die.	This is not a good message to send to people who care about animals as it makes us/them seem helpless.

© HarperCollins Publishers 2013

Worksheet 8.4c: Pandas: a counter-argument

Task The text below gives a counter-argument to the article written by Chris Packham, which argued that pandas might not be worth saving.

Read through the article and discuss with a partner:
- What arguments does Mark Wright give for saving the panda?
- What evidence is there that he has some sympathy for Chris Packham's viewpoint? Why do you think he admits he has sympathy?
- How does Mark Wright make a direct connection with his readers through the language he uses?
- How effective, overall, do you think Wright's arguments are, compared with Chris Packham's?

Should pandas be left to face extinction?

This week, TV naturalist Chris Packham said pandas might not be worth saving. Mark Wright from the World Wide Fund for Nature is one of the many who disagree.

No, says Mark Wright

You are reading this because it is about giant pandas. We could have this argument about the frogs of the rainforest, and the issues would be identical, but the ability to get people's attention would be far lower. So in that sense, yes you could argue that conservationists capitalise on the panda's appeal.

And, to be fair, I can understand where Chris is coming from. Everywhere you look on this planet there are issues to be addressed and we have finite resources. So we do make really horrible choices. But nowadays, almost exclusively, when people work in conservation they focus on saving habitats.

Chris has talked about pandas being an evolutionary cul-de-sac, and it's certainly unusual for a carnivore to take up herbivory. But there are many, many other species that live in a narrowly defined habitat. When he says that if you leave them be, they will die out, that's simply not true. If we don't destroy their habitat they will just chunter along in the same way that they have for thousands of years.

And besides, in terms of its biodiversity and the threats it faces, I think that the part of China where pandas live should be on the preservation list anyway. The giant panda shares its habitat with the red panda, golden monkeys, and various birds that are found nowhere else in the world.

The giant panda's numbers are increasing in the wild, so I don't see them dying out, and I haven't heard anything to suggest that other biodiversity isn't thriving equally.

It is true, though, that there are some cases where preserving an animal is not the best use of resources. If you asked 100 conservationists – even at WWF – you would probably get 90 different answers, but look at what happened with the northern white rhino in Africa, which we're pretty sure has died out. We lament its loss. But at the same time it had got to the stage where the likelihood of success was at a critically low level. If you were doing a battlefield triage system – the rhino would probably have had to be a casualty.

Otherwise, charismatic megafauna can be extremely useful. Smaller creatures often don't need a big habitat to live in, so in conservation terms it's better to go for something further up the food chain, because then by definition you are protecting a much larger area, which in turn encompasses the smaller animals.

And of course they are an extraordinarily good vehicle for the messages we want to put out on habitat conservation. Look at Borneo, where you instantly think of the orang-utans. In the southern oceans, you think of the blue whale. Then there are polar bears in the north. There are things you pull out from the picture because people can relate to them. And it does make a difference.

Dr Mark Wright is chief scientist at the World Wide Fund for Nature (WWF)

Worksheet 8.5a: Do you agree or disagree?

Student Book **Q2**
- Look at the grid below based on Chris Packham's panda article and his arguments.
- Try to make your own decisions about whether you agree or disagree with his points, and add your own comments. If you cannot decide, use the bank of comments underneath the grid and place them in the right space – then make your decision as to which you agree with.

Original point in article	Agree?	Disagree?
Should just buy 'rainforest' with charity money not panda habitat.		
Pandas are useful for promoting conservation, but they don't have much use otherwise.		
Pandas are only supported because they are seen as 'fluffy'.		
(Your own idea)		
(Your own idea)		

Possible views for the 'agree' or 'disagree' column – can you place them?

- Some well-loved creatures don't look very 'fluffy' – for example, rhinos and elephants could be considered ugly by some, yet people want to save them, so why not pandas?
- Images of pandas that show them hugging suggest they are almost like humans, and this misrepresents how animals behave.
- We mustn't judge animals on their 'use'; they give pleasure in lots of ways that can't be measured, such as watching how they behave and move.
- If we buy general rainforest, the chances are we'll save thousands of species – insects, plants, and other less well-known creatures, which in their own way are just as appealing as pandas.
- Pandas do have a very specialist diet, which means that in normal circumstances they would probably die out – that's how nature works!

Worksheet 8.5b: Options for responding

Student Book **Q6**
- Look at the three options for responding to the 'panda texts' and make notes on the one you think you could develop.
- Or, come up with your own, original idea and provide details about it.

Options	Notes and details (how you would use the texts you have read)
A proposal for a new television series about nature conservation and whether it is worthwhile	
An analytical article for a newspaper weighing up the facts, arguments and viewpoints	
The script of a conversation between you and your parents in which you ask for them to pay the subscription to a wildlife conservation magazine or organisation. They refuse, saying it's a waste of money.	
Your own idea	

Worksheet 10.1a (1) Practice Paper 1 Reading Passages (Core)

Reading Passages (Core) 1 hour 45 minutes

Answer **all** questions.
Dictionaries are **not** permitted.
The number of marks is given in brackets [ ] at the end of each question or part question.

**Read Passage A carefully, and then answer Questions 1 and 2.
Answer all questions using your own words as far as possible.**

Passage A

Brady Barr has a TV series on The Geographic Channel. Here is an article that he wrote for the channel's website about filming a particularly dangerous episode.

It was day three for our team in a snake cave on an island in Indonesia. On the previous two days we had seen many pythons, but all small, so we weren't expecting to see anything unexpected on day three. We were only going in to get some pick-up shots and move to the next filming location. 5

The cave was literally a chamber of horrors, probably the worst place I have worked in the ten years I have been at Geographic. The cave was filled with the usual customers (scorpions, roaches, maggots, spiders, millions of bats, lizards, and snakes), but it was the unbelievable amount of bat guano 10
that made it unbearable. There were places where you had to wade through chest-deep liquefied bat guano. The stuff was like quicksand, almost sucking you down and making progress very slow and cautious. This bat guano soup along with low oxygen levels eventually prevented our expedition from going deeper 15
into the cave.

On day three, about 200 feet (60 meters) into the cave, walking along the right-side wall where the fecal soup was the shallowest, I spied a large python partially exposed in a crack in the left wall, on the opposite side of the cave across the deepest 20
part of the fecal river.

[With cameras rolling] I frantically waded across the middle deepest portion of the fecal river (waist deep on me) and to the other side of the cave, where I was successful in grabbing the last few feet of the snake's tail before it escaped into the wall. 25

By this time Dr. Mark Auliya, a python expert working with me on this project, arrived to assist me in pulling this large snake out of the wall. I handed over the tail to Mark while I attempted to free more of the large snake's body from the crevice as Mark pulled. 30

After a brief power struggle, the python popped out of the crack in a blur of coils and quickly started to wrap us up. In the waist-deep fecal soup, the darkness of the cave and myriad of coils, it was difficult to locate the head, which was our major concern. With Mark still holding the tail, the big snake wrapped 35
its powerful coils around Mark's body once and around both of my legs down low at least once, and maybe two coils. The

snake's head was horrifyingly all over the place, popping in and out of the fecal soup and making securing it almost impossible. Before we could formulate a plan to get out of the quicksand-like fecal soup, where drowning was a serious issue while trying to subdue a giant snake, it bit me.

I felt the snake attach to my leg right below my left buttock, which sent me literally through the roof with pain. These guys are armed with dozens of strongly recurved razor-sharp teeth. After securing its hold, it threw the weight and power of its muscular body into the bite and started ripping downward. The power of these snakes is beyond comprehension ... remember, they are constrictors, and power is the name of their game.

Since the bite was occurring underwater, no one but me really knew what was occurring, and I was in such indescribable pain I couldn't convey much information, other than guttural screams. I was so completely incapacitated by the pain I couldn't even attempt to remove the snake from my leg. I was terrified that the snake was going to pull me off my feet with its coils around my legs and drag me underwater, yet after what seemed like an eternity the snake released its bite yet continued to hold me with its coils. It most likely needed to get a breath of air, since the bite occurred under the water. After letting the team know that it released its bite, we still could not locate the head after frantic searching.

This was the time I was most concerned, and without doubt one of the scariest moments I have ever been a part of, because the horror of taking another bite was simply overwhelming. I really did not think that I could remain conscious if I took another bad bite, and I knew that another bite was coming for someone if we didn't secure the head.

Prayers answered—the snake relinquished some of its coils, and I finally spotted the head at the surface of the water a long way away. Mark quickly dragged the snake to the opposite side of the cave, the shallow side, and I threw a bag over its eyes and quickly secured the head. We immediately placed the large snake into a capture bag, and then Mark inspected my wounds. They were bad; it was a horrific bite.

They have so many teeth that produce these deep ripping wounds, it's excruciating if you are on the receiving end. When the team discovered how severe the injuries were, we immediately exited the cave and cleaned the wound. Infection was really the biggest concern. Snake bites are always bad because they have such unclean mouths, but to receive a bite in a cave environment in a liquefied slurry of bat feces simply has to be the absolute worst of all septic situations. We were in a very remote area, so I had to hike out many kilometers to our truck.

The entire sequence was filmed. It is chilling footage to watch. It was an epic snake capture, one to go down in the history books.

Worksheet 10.1a (3) Practice Paper 1 Reading Passages (Core)

Question 1

(a) Explain, **using your own words**, why the writer describes the cave as a 'chamber of horrors' in paragraph 2. [2]

(b) Why do you think Brady described himself as 'frantically' wading after the snake when he sees it in paragraph 4. [2]

(c) Why was it so important to get out of the quicksand in paragraph 6? [1]

(d) (i) Reread paragraph 6 ('After a brief... bit me'). Explain, **using your own words**, what the writer means by the words in italics in **three** of the following phrases:

   (a) the python popped out of the crack in *a blur* of coils (lines 31–2)

   (b) *wrapped* its powerful coils around Mark's body (line 35)

   (c) The snake's head was horrifyingly *all over the place* (line 38)

   (d) *popping in and out* of the fecal soup (line 39).

(ii) The snake moves around a great deal in this section of the account. Explain how the words and language in **each of the phrases you have chosen** help you to imagine its movement. [6]

Phrase selected a), b), c) or d)	The meaning of the words in italics	How the words and language in the phrase help you imagine the snake's movement

(e) Explain, **using your own words**, what the writer means by:

   (i) 'guttural screams' (line 52, paragraph 8) [2]

   (ii) 'deep ripping wounds' (lines 75–76, paragraph 11) [2]

   (iii) 'chilling footage' (line 85, paragraph 12). [2]

(f) Which two-word phrase in paragraph 9 tells you that Brady could not bear the idea of being bitten again? [1]

(g) Explain, **using your own words**, what Brady meant by 'an epic snake capture, one to go down in the history books' in paragraph 12. [2]

[Total: 20]

Worksheet 10.1a (4): Practice Paper 1 Reading Passages (Core)

Question 2

Imagine that you are a Geographic Channel viewer. You have just watched Brady's television series for the first time and were horrified by the scene that he described in the extract when you saw it on screen. You have also read his account on the web page.

Write a **letter of complaint** to the channel's website trying to persuade them not to make programmes that involve the 'hunting' of dangerous animals for entertainment.

In your letter, you should include:

- what you disliked about the incident shown
- what you think in general about such television programmes.

You should base your ideas on what you have read in Passage A, but do not copy from it.

Be careful to use your own words. Address each of the two bullets.

Begin your letter of complaint like this: 'As soon as I switched off the Brady Barr TV episode featuring the python, I had to write...'

You should write about 200–300 words.

Up to 10 marks are available for the content of your answer and up to 5 marks for the quality of your writing.

[Total: 15]

Worksheet 10.1a (5): Practice Paper 1 Reading Passages (Core)

Read carefully Passage B, a transcript of a blog posted on a forum for viewers of The Nature Channel, and then answer Question 3 (a) and (b).

Passage B

Just flick on the television on any given night of the week and you will be faced with a mind-boggling array of documentaries focusing on all manner of exotic beasts from every corner of the globe – and they're just the presenters! No, seriously, I now have access to virtually any creature, in any location from Pole to Pole.

Progress indeed, you may say. In my childhood we were lucky if we saw the occasional lemur peeling a grape on Animal Magic or a rogue elephant knocking down the set on Blue Peter. They were glamorous strangers imported for our viewing pleasure and usually accompanied by a zoo keeper in a smart uniform. How we laughed at their strange features and 'aahed' at their cute habits when they were let out of their boxes for a few minutes of air-time...

After our bed-time our parents watched their once-a-week dose of some exceedingly dull programme with close-up film of insects constructing elaborate dens and birds jumping off cliffs. The voice over was factual, often very knowledgeable, but awfully sensible ... frankly I didn't mind that I wasn't allowed to stay up.

Nowadays young and old can see anything, anywhere, doing everything – including quite a few things that frankly put me off my dinner! We see animals in their natural environments, living, dying, just as nature intended. It can be tough to watch but it is reality. Modern nature programmes often tell a story. We get involved with a family or a character. Recently we had to delay dinner just to check whether a little meerkat lived or died!

Of course the presenters are a bit more high profile than I'm used to. They seem to be as much on show as the animals but they really know what they're talking about and they certainly have a gift when it comes to making things interesting. I do wish they wouldn't do stupid things though: putting your hand in something's mouth doesn't strike me as setting a great example! I think I preferred it when the presenter just kept a polite distance and whispered to the camera.

You know we ought to think ourselves lucky. From the comfort of our sofa we can share the lives of all sorts of amazing creatures in a way that generations past could not even imagine. Perhaps soon we won't even need zoos at all – now that would be progress!

Worksheet 10.1a (6): Practice Paper 1 Reading Passages (Core)

Question 3

Answer the questions in the order set.

(a) Notes

What do you learn about the changes in wildlife themed television shows according to Passage B?

Write your answers using short **notes**.

You do not need to use your own words.

Up to 10 marks are available for the content of your answer.

(b) Summary

Now use your notes to write a summary of what **Passage B** tells you about the changes in wildlife themed TV shows.

You must use **continuous writing** (not note form) and **use your own words** as far as possible.

Your summary should include all 10 of your points in **Question 3(a)** and must be 100 to 150 words.

Up to 5 marks are available for the quality of your writing.

Worksheet 10.1b (1) Practice Paper 1 Marking guidance

Paper 1 (Reading Passage – Core), maximum raw mark 50

NB : All Examiners are instructed that alternative correct answers and unexpected approaches in candidates' scripts must be given marks that fairly reflect the relevant knowledge and skills demonstrated.

Question 1

(a) Explain, **using your own words**, why the writer describes the cave as a 'chamber of horrors' in paragraph 2. [2]

- Because it is an enclosed area full of nasty creatures/things like guano which people don't usually like – so they are 'horrors'.

Give 2 marks for a clear explanation; 1 for a glimmer.

(b) Why do you think Brady described himself as 'frantically' wading after the snake when he sees it in paragraph 4? [2]

- Because he is very worried that it will get away.
- Because they have only seen small pythons up until now and he's keen to see it.
- This will make good TV so he doesn't want to miss the chance of filming it.

1 mark each for first two points or 2 for third point.

(c) Why was it so important to get out of the quicksand in paragraph 6? [1]

- Because it almost sucks you down/slows you down.

Award a maximum of 1 mark for any.

(d) (i) Reread paragraph 6 ('After a brief... bit me'). Explain, **using your own words**, what the writer means by the words in italics in **three** of the following phrases:

    (a) the python popped out of the crack in *a blur* of coils (lines 31–2)
    (b) *wrapped its powerful coils* around Mark's body (line 35)
    (c) The snake's head was horrifyingly *all over the place* (line 38)
    (d) *popping in and out* of the fecal soup (line 39).

- (a) 'blur' suggests cannot be seen distinctly as moving so fast
- (b) 'wrapped' suggests that the snake's body went around all sides of the man and enclosed him/you couldn't see him anymore
- (c) The head was moving so quickly and erratically that it seemed to be everywhere/changing location constantly
- (d) It was going in and out of the water quickly/emerging/submerging

(ii) The snake moves around a great deal in this section of the account. Explain how the words and language in **each of the phrases you have chosen** help you to imagine its movement. [6]

Award 1 mark for a partial explanation of each phrase. Award 2 marks for an explanation of each phrase which shows clear appreciation of the effect of the writer's use of language. Paraphrase of chosen phrase = 0 for explanation. Explanation must also be predominantly in the candidate's own words.

For example:
- 'Blur' makes me think that you can't see the snake when it moves. *(1 mark)*
- 'Blur' makes me think that the snake is going so quickly that you can't focus on it. *(2 marks)*

Worksheet 10.1b (2) Practice Paper 1 Marking guidance

(e) Explain, **using your own words**, what the writer means by:

    i) 'guttural screams' (line 52, paragraph 8) [2]

- Calling out loudly in a harsh, unpleasant way/not really words, just sounds

    ii) 'deep ripping wounds' (lines 75–76, paragraph 11) [2]

- The holes made by the snake were very deep but also irregular and long, splitting the skin

    iii) 'chilling footage' (line 85, paragraph 12). [2]

- The film made you shiver/feel upset/cold

Give up to 2 marks for an explanation in own words of each of the three phrases.

(f) Which two-word phrase in paragraph 9 tells you that Brady could not bear the idea of being bitten again? [1]

- 'Simply overwhelming'

(g) Explain, **using your own words**, what Brady meant by 'an epic snake capture, one to go down in the history books' in paragraph 12. [2]

For example:
- Epic – a big exciting story

Or
- One to go down – will be worth re-telling/remembering/not be forgotten

Give up to 2 marks for an explanation in own words of one of the points above.

[Total: 20]

Worksheet 10.1b (3): Practice Paper 1 Marking guidance

Question 2

General notes on task

The most successful extended responses are likely to provide a clear and convincing account of what was unpleasant about the incident described in the passage. There will be a sensible and convincing attempt to give their objections to this kind of TV programme.

Less successful responses are likely to be over-reliant on the contents of the original passage and to lift sections of it with little attempt to analyse why it was shocking or inappropriate. There will be unconvincing objections.

Look for and credit an attempt to write in an appropriate register.

Marking criteria for Question 2:

Table A, READING: (Using and understanding the material)

Use the following table to give a mark out of 10 for Reading.

Band 1	9–10 marks	Uses and develops several ideas, both factual and inferential, from the passage. Demonstrates and develops suggestions about why the material could be upsetting and unacceptable.
Band 2	7–8 marks	Refers to several details from the passage and makes some reference to the horrifying nature of the incident. Shows some awareness of how it could affect the viewer.
Band 3	5–6 marks	Repeats some details from the passage about the incident. Shows incomplete understanding of the nature of the incident. Focuses on the question and on the passage, but uses material simply and partially.
Band 4	3–4 marks	There is some relevance to the question with a tendency to retell the original rather than to focus on the requirements of the question. Makes simple references to why it is shocking.
Band 5	1–2 marks	There is an attempt to use the passage. May retell the story or give occasional relevant facts. There may be examples of misunderstanding or lack of clarity.
Band 6	0 marks	Very little/no relevance, or the response copies unselectively or directly from the passage. General misunderstanding of task and passage.

Table B, WRITING (Core tier)

Your teacher will give you a copy of the **Paper 1, Question 2** writing mark bands, which award up to 5 marks for the quality of your writing.

Add the marks for Reading and Writing to give a total mark out of 15 for Question 2.

[Total: 15]

Worksheet 10.1b (4): Practice Paper 1 Marking guidance

Question 3

Answer the questions in the order set.

(a) Notes

What do you learn about the changes in wildlife-themed television shows according to **Passage B**?

Write your answers using short notes.

You do not need to use your own words.

Up to 10 marks are available for the content of your answer.

Give 1 mark for each point below up to 10 marks.

1. Wider choice of shows
2. Wider range of animals
3. Wide range of locations
4. They're not accompanied by keepers now
5. They're not kept in boxes and just let out for show
6. Subject matter of the shows is wider (nothing off limits – 'reality shown')
7. Shows often contain a story
8. Presenters less formal
9. Presenters more high profile
10. Shows more engaging
11. Risk taking by presenters is more common

(b) Summary

Now use your notes to write a summary of what **Passage B** tells you about the changes in wildlife themed TV shows.

You must use continuous writing (not note form) and **use your own words** as far as possible.

Your summary should include all 10 of your points in **Question 3(a)** and must be 100 to 150 words.

Up to 5 marks are available for the quality of your writing.

[Total: 15]

Your teacher will give you a copy of the **Paper 1, Marking criteria for Question 3(b)** Table A, Writing (concision, focus, use of own words). Use the table to give a mark out of 5 for the quality of your writing.

Worksheet 10.1c — Reading techniques

In Chapter 1 of the Student Book you learned a wide range of reading skills. These included how to work out the meanings of words even if you are not familiar with them.

You were advised to go back and read the rest of the sentence to help you work out what a word meant.

For example: You are struggling with the word 'marsupials'.

The sentence it comes from is: 'Marsupials are one my favourite types of creature – especially kangaroos with their little joeys.' What can you learn?

1. What type of word is 'marsupials'? Is it a verb, noun, adjective or adverb?

   It says that marsupials are their favourite type – so it would seem to be a collective noun.

2. Are there any descriptions or extra information that help you to work out what 'marsupial' means?

   It says that kangaroos are marsupials – so now it seems that it's a word to describe the family of mammals that kangaroos belong to.

3. Does the word come from another language that you know the meaning of?

   It's actually from Latin – 'marsupium' means pouch.

4. Can the word be broken down into prefixes or suffixes that you know the meaning of?

   The suffix '-ial' usually means 'of the kind of' or 'like'.
   For example, 'he's very jovial'.

Task

Try this example:

What does hazardous mean?

Sentence:

It was a good trek although the rope bridges were slightly hazardous and I almost fell through the slats once.

1. What type of word is 'hazardous'? Verb, noun, adjective or adverb?

2. Are there any descriptions or extra information that help you to work out what it means?

3. Does the word come from another language that you know the meaning of?

4. Can the word be broken down into prefixes or suffixes that you know the meaning of?

Worksheet 10.1d: Sample responses to Paper 1, Q1(d) (Writer's effects question)

Put the following sample student responses to Question 1(d) of Paper 1 (the writer's effects question) in rank order. The middle column contains the students' answers to part (i) and the right-hand column contains their answers to part (ii).

Use the mark scheme to give them a mark.

	Suggested rank	Suggested mark
Sample student response A		
Sample student response B		

Sample student response A

Phrase selected a), b), c) or d)	The meaning of the words in italics	How the words and language in the phrase help you imagine the snake's movement
a)	'Blur' suggests that it was not possible to see distinctly.	It was moving very quickly.
b)	'Wrapped' means to cover something up completely including all sides.	It was moving to surround him by weaving around him over and over.
d)	'Popping in and out' means that it moved suddenly without notice emerging then retreating.	It moved suddenly up and down breaking the surface of the liquid.

Sample student response B

Phrase selected a), b), c) or d)	The meaning of the words in italics	How the words and language in the phrase help you imagine the snake's movement
a)	Wrapped is when you put paper round something.	The snake is folded like paper round the man.
b)	All over the place means everywhere.	There are lots of snakes everywhere.
d)	Pop means that someone visits quickly.	The snake only comes out for a short time then disappears.

Worksheet 10.1e: Sample responses to Paper 1, Q2 (Extended response task)

Read the two sample student responses to the extended writing task on Paper 1.
- Which is a Band 1 and which is a Band 3 response for Reading?
- What marks would you give them for Writing?

	Band 3 or Band 1?	Suggested mark
Sample student response A		
Sample student response B		

Sample student response A

To the producer of Brady Barr's recent 'snake hunt' episode

I have some questions for you:

- Is going into a cave of quicksand with low oxygen levels sensible?
- Is grabbing a snake by it's tail in any way responsible behaviour?
- Is focussing on loud complaining about the bite which followed and then focusing the rest of the show on the presenter's fears of infection in any way abut animals?
- Is dragging the terrified snake and putting it in a bag an act of conservation or education?

I don't think so. Have you learnt nothing from the death of Steve Irwin?

In my opinion TV channels like yours are there to help us to understand animals – their lifestyles and how to live alongside them. They are not there to show acts of stupidity or acts of cruelty for no reason other than to give viewers (and the presenter if you ask me) a thrill.

This programme will stick in my mind for a long time – and not for any god reason.

Yours, disgusted of Woking

Sample student response B

Dear Sir

I have just had to turn of the TV after a rubbish hour I thought that your TV company was dedicated to looking after wild animals – not hunting them down for entertainment. I have watched the national geographic channel on and off for a few months now and often enjoy the great films of animals in their homes but this was soo bad.

That Brady Barr just enjoys the sport of loking for things and then showing off. I mean, he goes into a cave knowing it's dark and wet and full of mess – scorpions, roaches, maggots, spiders, millions of bats, lizards, and snakes and then he complains because he gets bitten! Please! To be honest my brother and sister were really scared. I wouldn't be suprized if they don't get nightmares tonight. When that snake was running around in the dark it was horrible. And of course it hurt. So tax payer's money was then spent rushing him to hospital – It was his own falt.

TV is supposd to be fun.

Worksheet 10.1f — Paper 1 Self-review

Task Now that you have marked your own response to Practice Paper 1, you should be able to identify your strengths and weaknesses and set targets for improvement. Complete the table below in order to record your findings and conclusions.

Question	Mark	At my target level?	Could be improved	Specific weakness(es)
1 (a)				
1 (b)				
1 (c)				
1 (d) (i)				
1 (d) (ii)				
1 (e)				
1 (f)				
1 (g)				
2				
3 (a)				
3 (b)				

Targets (try to set one for each question type)
1 Explicit meaning
2 Implicit meaning
3 Summary
4 Writer's effects
5 Extended response

Worksheet 10.2a (1): Practice Paper 2 Reading Passages (Extended)

Reading Passages (Extended)   **2 hours**

Answer **all** questions.

Dictionaries are **not** permitted.

The number of marks is given in brackets [ ] at the end of each question or part question.

Part 1

Read **Passage A** carefully and then answer **Questions 1** and **2**.

Passage A

One minute I was asleep, strapped in snugly under my blanket, with three weeks of adventure drifting in front of my eyes in hazy flashes; a grin playing on my lips as I re-lived the dopey smile of a sloth hanging sideways whilst I zip-wired past high in the tree canopy. The next I was wrenched awake by the scream of metal tearing from metal and a glimpse of stark white skeletal fingers of lightning reaching for the trembling wings of the plane.

It must have been hours later – my watch had broken on impact (which I'm told was at about 1:30 a.m.) and there were now shadows being cast on the jungle floor from a distant, cloud-strangled sun. I shivered, irritably shrugging as water dripped warm, but not warm enough, onto my sodden clothes from the tendrils of my fringe hanging down over my face. I was upside down, still strapped in, suspended in the triangular haven of my seat. Apart from the obvious tunnel of snapped branches and stretched creepers which signalled my arrival, there was nobody and nothing to be seen of the rest of my fellow passengers or our plane. There was a huge temptation to stay there, safe, almost warm, drifting in and out of consciousness. If I had done so, I wouldn't be writing this now. They found my seat, still attached to two others, days from anywhere and largely hidden from sight by the high tree canopy which had opened to embrace me and then resealed itself with hardly an outward sign of intrusion. Luckily my dad's voice – loud and jolly – rang in my mind: 'Up and at 'em. Slackers never get anywhere!'

It's best not to think too much if you're scared, I always find. It's got me through some nail-biting moments, though most of those were self-imposed: white water rafting through rapids, kayaking down swollen rivers, climbing telegraph poles… But this time I was in the middle of nowhere, in the midst of a jungle that I knew to be full of all sorts of things that forest rangers tell you not to go near and I had no idea what to do next!

Except, actually, if I sorted through the junk in my mind, I probably did have some idea of what to do. Yes! Find water and follow it. My basic survival training – now a long time ago – slowly drifted back into my consciousness. Think! Think! I grumbled at myself. I'd been on so many guided walks of jungles and National Parks. Surely I knew something useful! I unbuckled and fell to the ground, glad of the soft mulch below but still letting out a scream to rival the howler monkeys' calls around me.

Worksheet 10.2a (2): Practice Paper 2 Reading Passages (Extended)

Of course, moving in any direction proved to be less than easy. My eyes were bloodshot (from the change in air pressure as the plane descended I was later told) and my head ached as if a hammer was clanging against an anvil lodged inside it. I was covered in cuts and scratches and I could see instantly that one deep wound looked dangerously open and was already inhabited by maggots. (Later I was able to tip gasoline on it, an excruciating but effective trick I remembered from treating our dog when it had a tick.) I later found that I had various fractures and minor injuries – but miraculously nothing major. I ached, and any movement felt like the day after a workout with a demon as my own personal trainer! I fought to block out the pain and the voice telling me to give up and take a rest. I had to get out of there. I had to!

It was easiest to float in the water, swimming when I had the energy, trying not to think about the crocodiles and turtles that I had so joyously fed with bread only days before as we toured these very waters. I sang to myself, silly bits and pieces of pop songs I had on my iPod, and I pictured my mum and dad's faces, imagining the warm smell of shepherd's pie waiting for me at home. I conjured up rosy scenes of Christmas mornings around the tree, of my – totally fictional – wedding day to come; anything to keep me going, anything to keep me focused on a happy ending. I found myself offering small bribes: you can rest for a few minutes if you get to that bit of sandy outcrop; if you see three heron you can stop and find some shade for an hour. I would count steps, strokes, heliconia flowers – anything to mark the passing of time and distance. I took shelter on ledges parallel to the water, my back to the river bank, hopeful that nothing would clamber out and find me huddled in its favourite resting spot.

Question 1

Imagine that you are the author of Passage A. You have been asked to give a speech at the Graduation ceremony of a local High School.

Write your speech, in which you:

- explain what happened to you and how you coped with the challenges that you faced
- use your experience to inspire and motivate the audience to make the most of themselves.

Base your speech on what you have read in Passage A, but be careful to use your own words. Address each of the two bullets.

Begin your speech 'Imagine waking up strapped upside down in a plane seat, high up in the tree canopy after the most terrifying experience of your life... this was what happened to me...'

You should write between 250 to 300 words allowing for the size of your handwriting.

Up to 15 marks are available for the content of your answer and up to 5 marks for the quality of your writing.

[Total: 20]

Worksheet 10.2a (3): Practice Paper 2 Reading Passages (Extended)

Question 2

Reread the descriptions of:

(a) the plane journey and crash in paragraph 1, beginning 'One minute I was asleep...'

(b) waking up after the crash in the tree canopy in paragraph 2, beginning 'It must have been hours later...'

Select **four** powerful words and phrases from each paragraph. Your choices should include imagery. Explain how each word or phrase selected is used effectively in the context.

Write about 200 to 300 words, allowing for the size of your handwriting.

Up to 10 marks are available for the content of your answer.

[Total: 10]

Worksheet 10.2a (4) Practice Paper 2 Reading Passages (Extended)

Part 2

Read **Passage B** carefully and then answer **Questions 3(a)** and **(b)**.

Passage B

'A very long shift': a day in the life of the trapped Chilean miners

The 33 men trapped nearly half a mile under Chile's Atacama Desert are suffering terrible privations – but they are also experienced miners who know that to survive, they must be organised. The Guardian's Jonathan Franklin reports.

Day in the San José mine begins at 7:30 a.m., when a makeshift lighting rig powered by truck batteries and a portable generator flickers into life, casting a weak light on the refuge where the men have now spent 44 days. In the hours after the shaft was sealed the miners used truck headlamps to light their way, but in the following days electrician Edison Pena wired up a series of lamps which provide between eight and 12 hours of light to provide a semblance of day and night.

Breakfast begins to arrive at 8:30 a.m. via a delivery system known as the 'pigeons' – the 3-metre metal tubes that are packed with food, medicine and letters and lowered 700 metres through a 8.8 cm communications shaft. The food takes over an hour to arrive, with deliveries every 20 to 30 minutes. At the bottom of the mine, three men are tasked with receiving the 'pigeons', unpacking bottled water, hot sandwiches and morning medicines, then stuffing the latest letters and messages into the torpedo-shaped tube, which slowly rises out of sight.

After breakfast the men clean their living area. 'They know how to maintain their environment. They have a designated bathroom area and a garbage area, and are even recycling,' said Dr André Llarena, an anaesthesiologist with the Chilean navy. 'They put plastic stuff away from biological [wastes], in different holes. They are taking care of their place.' Morning showers require the men to climb aboard a bulldozer-type mining vehicle that rumbles 300 metres up the tunnel to a natural waterfall where they shower, shampoo and clean off the ubiquitous rust-coloured mud. Showers and breakfast are followed by morning chores, some under instruction from mining engineers above ground, others in obedience to common sense.

Nineteen-year-old Jimmy Sanchez, the youngest of the group, is the 'environmental assistant', who roams the caverns with a handheld computerised device that measures oxygen, CO_2 levels and air temperature, which usually averages around 31°C. Every day Sanchez takes the reading from the gas detector and sends his reports to the medical team outside the mine. Another group of men reinforce the mine walls and divert streams of water seeping into their refuge. Several of the drilling

Worksheet 10.2a (5) Practice Paper 2 Reading Passages (Extended)

and communications tubes connecting the men to the surface use water as lubricant, meaning a constant stream of muddy gunk trickles into their world. 40

> 'Dermatological infections, toothaches, constipation and withdrawal from tobacco addiction have caused problems.'

Throughout the morning, some of the men maintain regular security patrols to scan the perimeter of their sleeping and living 45 quarters, alert for signs of another rockfall. Others spend hours working with long-handled picks to lever loose large rocks that threaten to fall from the ceiling. What the miners most fear is that a small rockfall could suddenly trigger a full-scale collapse, leaving them trapped in an even more confined space. 50
Food deliveries and meals take up much of the day. Lunch delivery starts at noon and takes a full hour and a half to deliver the hot meals.

Question 3

Answer the questions in the order set.

(a) Notes

What are the hardships faced by the trapped miners in **Passage B**?

Write your answer using short **notes**.

You do not need to use your own words.

Up to 15 marks are available for the content of your answer. [15]

(b) Summary

Now use your notes to write a summary of what **Passage B** tells you about the hardships faced by the trapped miners.

You must use **continuous writing** (not note form) and **use your own words** as far as possible.

Your summary should include all 15 of your points in **Question 3(a)** and must be 200 to 250 words.

Up to 5 marks are available for the quality of your writing. [5]

[Total: 20]

Worksheet 10.2b (1): Practice Paper 2 Marking Guidance

Paper 2 (Reading Passages – Extended), maximum raw mark 50

Note: all Examiners are instructed that alternative correct answers and unexpected approaches in candidates' scripts must be given marks that fairly reflect the relevant knowledge and skills demonstrated.

Question 1

Imagine that you are the author of Passage A. You have been asked to give a speech at the Graduation ceremony of a local High School.

Write your speech, in which you:

- explain what happened to you and how you coped with the challenges that you faced
- use your experience to inspire and motivate the audience to make the most of themselves.

Base your speech on what you have read in Passage A, but be careful to use your own words. Address each of the three bullets.

Begin your speech 'Imagine waking up strapped upside down in a plane seat, high up in the tree canopy after the most terrifying experience of your life... this was what happened to me...'

You should write between 250 to 300 words allowing for the size of your handwriting.

Up to 15 marks are available for the content of your answer and up to 5 marks for the quality of your writing. [Total: 20]

For this question, 15 marks are allocated to assessment of Reading Objectives R1 to R3 (see syllabus); 5 marks are allocated to assessment of Writing Objectives W1 to W4 (see syllabus).

General notes on possible content

Note: there are two parts to a complete answer.

The first part will deal with the events as described in the passage but a good candidate will infer strengths and character traits from the passage and will integrate these into their speech.

The second part may well be integrated into the account of events and should be clearly rooted in, related to and derived from the passage but will take into account the more mundane situations likely to be encountered by the average 16 year old.

Candidates may use the following ideas:

Mark A (What happened)

- Was asleep – woken by damage to plane
- Storm outside – lightning
- Woke up – still in seat – upside down
- Floated downstream
- Entertained self
- Sometimes rested on banks

N.B. Look for overview (had to keep going) and good development

Worksheet 10.2b (2) Practice Paper 2 Marking Guidance

Mark B (How she coped)

- Her Dad's positive mentality inspired her
- She had useful prior knowledge
- She didn't think too much
- She conserved her energies
- She entertained herself
- She looked forward to things at home
- She dreamed of the future
- She bribed herself

Mark C (Advice to the young people)

- Think positive
- Use the things you know/Use your common sense
- Don't be over analytical
- Don't let negatives overwhelm you – think of the good things
- Motivate yourself with small treats
- Distract yourself if something is hard

Some students may also infer less obvious points:

- Have faith – miracles do happen
- Family is important
- We all have hidden strengths

Make sure that you can discern some relation to the content of the passage before rewarding.

A: CONTENT (Extended tier)

Use the following table to give a mark out of 15.

Band	Marks	Description
Band 1	13–15 marks	The answer reveals a **thorough** reading of the passage, applying a wide range of ideas. There is an appropriate amount of supporting detail, which is well integrated into the speech, contributing to a strong sense of purpose and message. Candidates create a consistent attitude for the girl and make a range of sound inferences based on her behavior, taking on the role/character of the writer. Original ideas are consistently well related to the passage.
Band 2	10–12 marks	There is evidence of a **competent** reading of the passage. The candidate does well to represent the girl's attitude and some character, and to integrate some of the material with occasional effectiveness, and without repeating the passage. There is some development, but the ability to sustain may not be consistent. There is frequent supporting detail throughout.
Band 3	7–9 marks	The passage has been read **reasonably well**, but the response may not reflect range or complexity in assimilating material. There may be some mechanical use of the passage. Supporting detail is used occasionally. Opportunities for development are rarely taken and ideas are simply expressed.
Band 4	4–6 marks	Some reference to the passage is made without much inference or more than brief, factual development. Answers may be thin, lack originality or in places, lack focus on the text, but there is some evidence of **general understanding** of the main points of the passage.
Band 5	1–3 marks	Answers are either very general with little specific reference to the text OR **copy** sections of the original. Content is insubstantial and there is little realisation of the need to modify material from the passage.
Band 6	0 marks	There is little or no relevance to the question or to the passage, or the response copies unselectively or directly from the passage.

© HarperCollins Publishers 2013

Worksheet 10.2b (3) Practice Paper 2 Marking Guidance

B: QUALITY OF WRITING: Structure and order, style & language

Use the following table to give a mark out of 5.

Band 1	5 marks	The language of the speech has character and sounds real, as the girl might speak. Comments are very clearly expressed and enhanced by a wide range of effective and/or interesting language. Structure is sound throughout.
Band 2	4 marks	Language is mainly fluent and there is clarity of explanation. There is a sufficient range of vocabulary to express thoughts and feelings with some precision. There are occasional hints of character or appropriate voice. The speech is mainly well structured.
Band 3	3 marks	Language is clear and appropriate, but comparatively plain, expressing little character. Individual points are rarely extended, but explanations are adequate. There may be flaws in structural presentation, such as very plain beginnings and ends.
Band 4	2 marks	There may be some awkwardness of expression and inconsistency of style and language is too limited to express shades of meaning. Look for structural weakness in presentation of material, or some copying from the passage.
Band 5	1 mark	There are problems of expression and structure. Language is weak and undeveloped. There is little attempt to explain ideas, and may have frequent copying.
Band 6	0 marks	Sentence structures and language are unclear and the work cannot be understood.

Question 2

Reread the descriptions of:

(a) the plane journey and crash in paragraph 1, beginning 'One minute I was asleep...'

(b) waking up after the crash in the tree canopy in paragraph 2, beginning 'It must have been hours later...'

Select four powerful words and phrases from each paragraph. Your choices should include imagery. Explain how each word or phrase selected is used effectively in the context.

Write about 200 to 300 words, allowing for the size of your handwriting.

Up to 10 marks are available for the content of your answer. [Total: 10]

For this question, 10 marks are allocated to assessment of Reading Objective R4 (see syllabus).

General notes on likely content:

This question is marked for the candidate's ability to select effective or unusual words and for an understanding of ways in which the language is effective. Expect candidates to select words that carry specific meaning, including implications, additional to general and to ordinary vocabulary.

Alternative acceptable choices and explanations should be credited. Mark for the overall quality of the answer, not for the number of words chosen.

Worksheet 10.2b (4): Practice Paper 2 Marking Guidance

The following notes are a guide to what good candidates might say about the words they have chosen. They are free to make any sensible comment, but only credit those that are relevant to the correct meanings of the words and that have some viability.

Candidates could score full marks for excellent comments on three words from each part of the question. Mark and credit what is positive.

Paragraph 1

- Sense of fear, shock, horror, very sensory – noise, speed
- The contrast of being asleep and then awake
- The contrast of the pleasant dream and the rude awakening
- The content of the dream – the smile of the sloth versus the awful situation when she wakes up
- The word 'wrenched' – implying rough, unwilling and painful
- 'Scream of metal' – to describe the loud harsh noise of the metal tearing but also personifying the plane and implying pain
- 'Trembling' – meaning the wings are breaking but also personifying them and implying fear
- 'Stark white skeletal fingers of lightning' – personification suggests malice on the part of the lightning. Associations with skeletons are frightening and suggest death.

Paragraph 2

Odd mixture of pleasant and unpleasant

- 'still strapped in' implies safety and security
- 'haven' suggests a place of safety and refuge
- 'safe, almost warm' suggests that she is content and comfortable
- 'which had opened to embrace me...' sounds friendly and protective
- 'my dad's voice – loud and jolly' – reminder that she has parents – suggests safety and that someone will look for her
- 'cloud-strangled' sun – personification suggests menace. Sun is usually positive and a life force. That it isn't able to work properly suggests she is under threat
- 'shivered' suggests that she is ill/cold/scared, all of which implies that she is vulnerable
- 'sodden clothes' – wet through, which is not very healthy and suggests she may get ill
- 'upside down' suggests that she may fall – is unable to escape – and is therefore vulnerable
- 'snapped branches' and 'stretched' creepers imply damage and unnatural events which suggest that something bad has happened and could happen again
- 'which had opened and embraced me and then resealed itself...' suggests that the jungle wanted her and will not let her go, which is intimidating.

Marking criteria for Question 2: Reading

Your teacher will give you a copy of the **Paper 2, Question 2** Reading mark scheme which awards up to 10 marks for this question.

Worksheet 10.2b (5): Practice Paper 2 Marking Guidance

Question 3

Answer the questions in the order set.

(a) Notes

What are the hardships faced by the trapped miners in **Passage B**?

Write your answer using short **notes**.

You do not need to use your own words.

Up to 15 marks are available for the content of your answer. [15]

(b) Summary

Now use your notes to write a summary of what **Passage B** tells you about the hardships faced by the trapped miners.

You must use **continuous writing** (not note form) and **use your own words** as far as possible.

Your summary should include all 15 of your points in **Question 3(a)** and must be 200 to 250 words.

Up to 5 marks are available for the quality of your writing. [5]

[Total: 20]

For this question, 15 marks are allocated to assessment of Reading Objectives R1, R2 and R5 (see syllabus); 5 marks are allocated to assessment of Writing Objectives W1–W3 (see syllabus).

A: Reading content for Question 3(a)

Give one mark per point up to a maximum of 15.

(a) The hardships faced by the trapped miners in Passage B:

1. Trapped (44 days)
2. Little contact with outside – only through tubes
3. No natural day or night
4. Poor artificial light
5. Slow delivery of food
6. (Public) toilet/waste areas
7. Mud
8. Arduous journey to shower
9. Have to do chores
10. Told what to do
11. Possible lack of oxygen
12. Heat
13. Danger from walls caving in
14. Water seeping in
15. Skin issues
16. Toothache
17. Constipation
18. Withdrawal from tobacco

Note: Although lifting of words and phrases from the passage is acceptable, it is important that in such cases candidates show evidence of understanding by clearly focusing on the key details; over-lengthy lifting which does not identify specific points should not be rewarded. Credit responses which attempt to use own words and convey the essence of the point.

B: Marking criteria for Question 3(b)

Your teacher will give you a copy of the **Paper 2, Question 3** Writing mark scheme which awards up to 5 marks for the quality of your writing.

Worksheet 10.2c (1): Sample responses to Paper 2, Q1 (Extended response task)

Read the three sample student responses to Practice Paper 2, Question 1 (the extended response task). Identify the different types of content that are included in each response, as outlined in the first part of the mark scheme (see **Worksheet 10.2b**):

- A (What happened)
- B (How she coped)
- C (Advice to the young people).

Highlight the relevant phrases in each response with either A, B or C.

Then decide how many marks you would award for Content (i.e. reading) (out of 15) and Quality of writing (out of 5).

	Reading	Writing	Total
Sample student response A			
Sample student response B			
Sample student response C			

Sample student response A

Good morning one and all. Such a wonderful sight to see young, brilliant faces, taking another great step in the race of life. Students probably might have heard elders giving pieces of advice on how to tackle the great difficulties of life. Now, I shall too, through a very interesting example provide you with the same advice. However, I can vouch that it won't be as boring as others tend to explain.

Now, where to begin from... As you might have heard from the teachers, I had been involved in a brutal plane crash. Practically, hanging upside down for hours and hours, by a great canopy. Alone. No news from my fellow passengers. I was completely isolated and stranded. There was one moment where I thought of staying put. Warm, safe and comfortable. If I had done so, I wouldn't have been speaking to you, in one piece.

In such cases it's better not to think much. It's best not to be pessimistic and keep up your will power all the time. Think of something that motivates you, something that keeps your mind away from all the negative thoughts. So, there I was hanging alone with the world upside down, in the middle of nowhere. I decided to get down. Part of my basic swimming training, pursued years ago, I recollected the very first thing to get away – find water and follow it. It is easiest to float on water and periodically wave your heavily bruised and scratched arms.

(incomplete)

© HarperCollins Publishers 2013

Worksheet 10.2c (2): Sample responses to Paper 2, Q1 (Extended response task)

Sample student response B

Hello everybody. Now some of you will recognise me from the news: 'The one that got away!' Others of you won't. I am here to talk to you about my experiences and to encourage you to be the kind of person that always 'gets away' in future! You've already come a long way – but I think that my story might just help you to go even further in the next stage of your lives…

It all started with the usual hair brained hectic idea: a three week adventure holiday; lots of stories to bring home to friends and family et cetera…and this is what it almost was. That is up until the return flight where one minute I was happily asleep and the next I was hearing the death cries of the plane as it went down, frazzled by lightning.

The next thing I knew, I had glass cutting into my wrist from my broken watch and a heavy pressure on my neck and shoulders. I was upside down – not zip-wiring down a ravine laughing my head off, but hanging from my very pricey airplane seat – with not a survivor around me. Okay – lesson one – don't let the unexpected throw you! I could've just sat there – I was woozy and a bit stunned. It would have been easy to take the easy path. It'll happen to you often enough; stay in bed or get up and go to that interview? Keep doing the same old boring job or break away and re-train for something else? I released my belt – and crash…my journey to safety had begun! In truth – and here's a word of praise for the olds – it was my Dad who inspired me; he was always so positive – getting us kids up on winter's mornings, and hanging there I swear it was his voice which I heard telling me not to be a slacker!

Lesson two came quickly: don't think you have nothing to offer in a new situation. Hey guess what? I'd never been stranded in a rain forest before. You might never have had to change a tyre or give CPR – but I'm betting you know something useful that you could bring to the table. I racked my brains – and do you know, I did know some useful stuff. 'Always follow water' was probably the best bit of advice my teenage brain had managed to store, but I also had some pretty good ideas about what to steer clear of after all those guided walks around national parks – and a nifty way of sterilising my wounds courtesy of Bobby the retriever's nasty case of maggot infestation!

So – I floated down the river. Yes I'm abbreviating…lots of tears, lots of fears (Oh the crocodiles!) but basically I broke it down into little bits and just focused on getting to the end of the next thing. Then I'd reward myself with break. It's a skill you can use every day; when you're facing a mountain of paperwork at Uni just think of it as 3 pages an hour and then you can have a milkshake!

Obviously I eventually found people – and was rescued – or I wouldn't be up here boring you now…but it changed my live anyway…I know that I am strong – stronger than I ever imagined. I know that my family is everything to me – they were there when I needed them and they are still there now. And, finally I know that even a bad situation can be turned around with determination and self belief. These are the final lessons I'd love for you to take from school today. Believe in yourselves. You can do anything!

Worksheet 10.2c (3): Sample responses to Paper 2, Q1 (Extended response task)

Sample student response C

Good morning everyone! Today is a joyous day for all of you students. Congratulations to all of you on successfully graduating from high school. And every day is joyous for me, as I am thankful to be alive! I had a near death experience just a week ago...

Me and my friends were tired after three weeks of a hectic adventure. We were on a plane going back home finally. Naturally, after suffering from extreme exhaustion, I dozed off instantly. However, I was awakened by an awful noise and was given a rude shock. The lightning had severely damaged the wings of our plane and the plane was falling down! I was terrified and didn't know what to do. The plane crashed into a concrete jungle-like area and the plane was destroyed.

I unbuckled the seat and fell on to the ground. My eyes were bloodshot (probably due to the change in air pressure) and my head was aching as if it was a football being kicked by enthusiastic kids, and I had cuts and scratches all over from head to toe. It wasn't easy – half my bones were fractured, but I had to get out of there – I had no other choice.

My mind was telling me to rest but I had to get out of there – my life depended on it! I explored around, and soon enough, I found water – a river. I floated in the water – it wasn't easy at all. But, I went on; one step at a time. It wasn't easy, but it was my only chance! I went on and on, slowly but surely, and after a few hours, I did come across a human habitat...an island. I was relieved and decided to go for it. With the help of some locals I contacted a few people... and reached home that day itself!

This was an invaluable experience in my life...and you can learn from it too... if I would have given up and remained in the jungle, I may not have been here today talking to you. We should never give up hope, and never lose faith in ourselves. My dad always said, 'Up and at 'em. Slackers never get anywhere!' Where there's a will, there is a way. The mind is stronger than the body. You can achieve what you wish to, as long as you believe that you can do it. Nothing is impossible!

I hope that you have learnt a lot from this speech and use the lessons to help you and bring out the best in you. Nothing is impossible! Never give up. Treasure your families.

Worksheet 10.2d (1): Sample responses to Paper 2, Q2 (Writer's effects question)

Read the two sample student responses to Practice Paper 2, Question 2 (the writer's effects question). Decide which band of the mark scheme each answer would fall into (see **Worksheet 10.2b**):

- Which band would each response fall into?
- How many marks would you award each response?

	Band	Suggested mark
Sample student response A		
Sample student response B		

Hint: focus on Bands 1 and 2 for Student Response A, and Bands 2 and 3 for Student Response B.

Sample student response A

The writer has used words and phrases in paragraph one which very clearly describe a sense of shock and horror and create a real sense of fear. The phrase, 'wrenched awake', suggests that her eyes opened with a shock and she was awake roughly because wrenching is a sharp sudden pull – often painful. 'Scream of metal tearing from metal' gives us a feeling that there was friction between the parts of the plane and the tree, a loud sound was created as a result of this, almost like a woman screaming for help, which suggests fear and is horrible. Also, they use personification; 'white skeletal fingers of lightning', which signifies that the lightning was almost malevolent. Finally the phrase, 'trembling wings', gives us a vivid image of the plane and a sense that it is vulnerable and abused as it is shivering in fear.

In the second paragraph the writer has given us an opportunity to visualise the mixed condition of the survivor. She has given the effect successfully by words like, 'shivered' and 'irritably', which give us a clear visual description that she wasn't in comfort because both are negative words. Also the phrases, 'snapped branches' and 'stretched creepers', suggest that the trees are in bad condition after the plane crashed – everything is damaged. On the other hand, 'almost warm', tells us that she was comforted as heat is usually a good thing; life giver. Moreover, 'embrace me' signifies that she felt someone was comforting her by putting arms around her and haven is like a haven – it's a place of retreat and restoration. She's both comfortable and uncomfortable – because she wants to stay – but has to go.

Worksheet 10.2d (2): Sample responses to Paper 2, Q2 (Writer's effects question)

Sample student response B

The plane was moving at high speeds when it crashed into the tree canopy. It also shows that it happened suddenly when he was sleeping. The phrase 'wrenched awake' gives an apt description about how the writer woke up suddenly and forcefully because that is what wrenched means. There is an onomatopoeia used by the writer to show that the plane was breaking apart, the tearing of the metal was sounding as if someone was screaming. The lightning that is breaking the plane is compared to white skeletal fingers – a symbol of death? – which are reaching the wings of the plane.

In the second paragraph the writer was feeling scared when he saw 'shadows being cast on the jungle floor' and he felt as if some animal was coming closer to him but then he got to know it was the sun which was hidden behind the clouds. It looked as if the clouds were killing the sun. As the plane logged into the trees, the writer could see 'snapped branches' and 'stretched creepers' all around the plane making it look wrecked. When he woke up he was upside down strapped to the 'triangular haven seats' of the plane. The seats are considered safe, as a place of refuge. The writer was feeling very comfortable as the 'high tree canopy…opened to embrace me'.

Worksheet 10.2e: Sample responses to Paper 2, Q3 (Summary question)

Read the two sample student responses to Practice Paper 2, Question 3 (the summary question). Identify which of the content points from the mark scheme are covered in each answer (see **Worksheet 10.2b**). Mark the relevant numbers on the responses below.

- How many marks do you think would they earn for Content (Reading)?
- How many marks would they earn for Quality of writing?

	Reading	Writing	Total
Sample student response A			
Sample student response B			

Sample student response A

1. Trapped
2. Safe
3. Muddy
4. Wet
5. Dark
6. Hot

The miners

The men are trapped men but safe. They live in lots of mud which wouldn't be very nice but I would really dislike the water that seeps in and the fact that it's really hot and dark.

Sample student response B

(a) long day
trapped
heat
humidity
water on floor
mud
rock falls
food comes slowly
missing contact with outside

(b) The life of the unfortunately trapped miners is not easy as they have to face innumerable difficulties to survive. The miners spend ten to twelve hours down in the heat and humidity to work. The drilling and communication tube which connects the miners to the outer world uses water as a lubricant. Thus, water usually streams down into the mines and there is mud which is awful too. Moreover, a small rock fall in the mine can suddenly trigger a full scale collapse which can prove disastrous for the workers. Additionally, it takes a lot of time to deliver food to the miners. They are even suffering from loneliness because they just get messages down a tube.

Worksheet 10.2f — Paper 2 Self-review

Task Now that you have marked your own responses to Practice Paper 2, you should be able to identify your strengths and weaknesses and set targets for improvement. Complete the table below in order to record your findings and conclusions.

Question	Mark	At my target level?	Could be improved	Specific weakness(es)
1				
2				
3				

Targets (try to set one for each question type)
1 Extended response
2 Writer's effects
3 Summary

Worksheet 10.3a (1): Practice Paper 3: Directed writing and composition

Directed Writing and Composition **2 hours**

Answer **two** questions: **Question 1 (Section 1)** and **one** question from **Section 2**.
Dictionaries are **not** permitted.
All questions in this paper carry equal marks.

Section 1: Directed Writing

Question 1

Write a letter to your grandparents in which you should:

- evaluate the arguments for and against the purchase of a console
- explain the reasons behind your wish to have one.

Base your letter on the fact file and the article, but be careful to use your own words. Address each of the two bullets.

Begin your letter:

'Dear Nan and Grandad…'

You should write about 250 to 350 words, allowing for the size of your handwriting.

Up to 10 marks are available for the content of your answer, and up to 15 marks for the quality of your writing.

[Total 25]

- Parents should take more responsibility. Use locks? Go shopping with kids?
- Violent games account for one in 2000 new games produced every year.
- Children know the difference between reality and fantasy. Think of the fairy tales they read!
- Too much violence on screen can make children less sensitive to it in real life.
- Games are rated as films, e.g. 18/12/PG, etc.
- Adult content videos can be kept behind the counter.
- Laws regarding adult content apply to games?
- Do children copy what they see?

Worksheet 10.3a (2): Practice Paper 3: Directed writing and composition

This article from *The Times* was written as a reaction to a report, called The Byron Review, which proposed tighter controls on computer games and raised concerns about their effects.

Not all gaming is bad – it can be as engrossing as a novel or chess

Nigel Kendall

Times games reviewer

IF THERE was a time when the market for video games in this country truly came of age, it was the run-up to last Christmas. Spurred on by the launch of three new home consoles in the space of 12 months, sales of video game titles hit £332.6 million in the final quarter, of last year, up 19 per cent, by volume and 36 per cent by revenue from the year before, according to figures released by the industry body ELSPA. Over the full year, 78 million video games were sold in Britain. So who is playing them all?

The Byron review comes at a time when more families than ever are playing video games, thanks largely to the motion sensitive Nintendo Wii console, which allows players to mimic the movements of real sport. For the first time since Space Invaders arrived in arcades 30 years ago, gaming is becoming a social and sociable activity. The Wii excels at on-screen sports such as table tennis and golf, and the reason for its popularity with both parents and children is that it brings the fun back into playing. Playing it is enjoyable and watching someone else flailing around with a remote controller is hilarious.

Yet the Wii is technically a primitive machine compared with its competitors, the Microsoft Xbox 360 and Sony PlayStation 3 (PS3). These two consoles, dubbed 'next-generation' because they can display high definition images on modern flat-screen televisions, retain an undeniably masculine bias. These are the gorillas of gaming and many of the games are designed to get players beating their chests in an artificial world, to the exclusion of the real one.

Many of the early releases for these consoles were squarely aimed at young males, with a heavy emphasis on shooting, driving and sports. Both consoles are also capable of connecting to the internet, opening up the possibility of playing against hundreds of opponents online. It is this aspect of gaming, and the perceived target market, that has caused the most concern. If, as expected, the Byron review comes out in favour of statutory certification, one option open to the makers of the consoles is to make the parental lock feature (currently installed as an option) the default setting. Adults would then need to key in a secret code to play the game of their choice.

But to label all gaming as 'bad' is to do the industry a disservice. As with novels, films and internet websites, there are good and bad games, and the process of becoming engrossed in a well-told story is similar, whether it unfolds digitally or on the pages of a book. Many games, notably the 77-million-selling Japanese *Final Fantasy* series, tap into the market for modem myth, marrying storylines and are as satisfying to play – and as demanding – as chess.

Faced with the success of the Wii, Sony and Microsoft have recently changed marketing tack to get themselves out of the spare room and into the living room, re-positioning themselves as home entertainment hubs.

Both machines can play DVDs. The Sony PS3 also plays high-definition Blu-ray discs and comes with a built-in hard disc that can be used to store photos, videos, music or content downloaded from the internet via the built-in wi-fi capability.

Worksheet 10.3a (3): Practice Paper 3: Directed writing and composition

Section 2: Composition

Questions 2 and 3

Write about 350 to 450 words, allowing for the size of your handwriting, on **one** of the following questions.

Up to 13 marks are available for the content and structure of your answer, and up to 12 marks for the style and accuracy of your writing.

Descriptive writing

2 (a) 'The Forgotten Corner'. Write a detailed description of this place, paying particular attention to the sights and sounds that can be experienced there. [25]

OR

2 (b) 'The Threat'. Use this title to create a description of a person who creates a menacing atmosphere around them. [25]

Narrative writing

3 (a) Write the dramatic moments of a story that involve the escape of an animal. [25]

OR

3 (b) 'Abandoned'. Write the opening chapter of an account of being lost when you or a character that you can invent accidently get left behind. [25]

Worksheet 10.3b: Which type of composition?

Task Sort the following characteristics into two columns in the table below to show whether they belong to *descriptive* writing or *narrative* writing.

1. Everything builds to a crisis
2. Vivid sensory details
3. Structure could be sense by sense
4. Atmosphere is created
5. A chronological progression
6. Strong opening such as a flashback
7. Imagery and use of sophisticated vocabulary are very important
8. Characters are revealed by their actions and words
9. Various 'seeds' are planted in the first third that build up tension
10. Structure can follow physical movement

Descriptive	Narrative

Worksheet 10.3c (1): Practice Paper 3 Marking guidance

Paper 3, maximum raw mark 50

Note: all examiners are instructed that alternative correct answers and unexpected approaches in candidates' scripts must be given marks that fairly reflect the relevant knowledge and skills demonstrated.

Section 1: Directed writing

Question 1

Write a letter to your grandparents in which you should:

- evaluate the arguments for and against the purchase of a console
- explain the reasons behind your wish to have one.

Base your letter on the fact file and the article, but be careful to use your own words. Address each of the two bullets.

Begin your letter:

'Dear Nan and Grandad…'

You should write about 250 to 350 words, allowing for the size of your handwriting.

Up to 10 marks are available for the content of your answer, and up to 15 marks for the quality of your writing.

[Total: 25]

This question tests Writing objectives W1–W5:

- articulate experience and express what is thought, felt and imagined
- sequence facts, ideas and opinions
- use a range of appropriate vocabulary
- use register appropriate to audience and context
- make accurate use of spelling, punctuation and grammar.

AND aspects of Reading objectives R1–R3:

- demonstrate an understanding of explicit meanings
- demonstrate an understanding of implicit meanings and attitudes
- analyse, evaluate and develop facts, idea and opinions.

Worksheet 10.3c (2): Practice Paper 3 Marking guidance

General notes on possible content

A thorough reading of both texts would result in the following possible pros and cons.

Pros

- They can be locked/rated/kept hidden so nothing inappropriate need be seen.
- There are lots of games and hardly any are violent.
- Games are subject to the same laws as any other media – so they are no worse than a film.
- Violent games do no harm anyway – children can tell what is real and what isn't
- Not all children copy what they see.
- Families can play on them together.
- It's fun!
- Can access the internet through it – can play online, can be as complex and demanding as chess.
- A modern art form.
- Can play DVDs/store photos/music, etc.

Cons

- Kids copy bad behaviour.
- They can be addictive.
- Many games are high adrenaline/highly masculine.
- Can access the internet.
- Can play online.

Additional content

In addition, more subtle points that can be inferred from the texts might be:

- Gaming is good for families – brings them closer.
- Gaming is a way of expanding learning via the internet.
- Gaming can be mentally stimulating and culturally of value.
- A console could save money in the long run.
- A console may cause yet more time wasting/less studying.
- Problems only occur when there are already behavioural issues.

Look particularly for the responses where points have been clearly re-ordered to offer point and rebuttal and where the student has sequenced ideas to build a developing argument.

This question is marked out of 15 for Writing and 10 for Reading.

Worksheet 10.3c (3) Practice Paper 3 Marking guidance

Use the following table to give a mark out of 10 for Reading.

Band 1	9–10 marks	Most aspects of the pros and cons of consoles are thorough, perceptive and convincing – the links between these and the text above are strong and logically made. Ideas grow out of the pros and cons and are developed to suggest a sound rationale for purchase and the opposite view. Effective reading between the lines.
Band 2	7–8 marks	Many of the aspects of consoles, good and bad are discussed and there is evidence of linking them to the texts above. Pros and cons are well linked to the text and ideas are developed. Good overall use of material.
Band 3	5–6 marks	Acceptable coverage of pros and cons but not many implicit points are developed/mentioned. Comments are linked to the text but are more stated than developed.
Band 4	3–4 marks	Some coverage of pros and cons is noted, but the answer consists chiefly of a retelling/outlining with occasional/slight linking. Points should be connected.
Band 5	1–2 marks	The answer as a whole is occasionally, though slightly, related to the text. The aim of the linking is partially clear but use of material is erratic.
Band 6	0 marks	Answer does not relate to question and/or too much unselective copying directly from the material to gain a mark in Band 5.

Your teacher will give you a copy of the generic Paper 3, Section 1 mark scheme to enable you to give a mark out of 15 for Writing.

Section 2: Composition

Questions 2(a), 2(b), 3(a) and 3(b)

Your teacher will give you a copy of the generic **Paper 3, Section 2** mark scheme, which awards up to 25 marks for your chosen question.

Give two marks:

- the first mark is out of 13 for content and structure: see Table A
- the second mark is out of 12 for style and accuracy: see Table B

Remember that these marks will not necessarily match and one mark may well be (much) higher than the other.

The maximum overall mark for the composition is 25. Write the total clearly at the end as follows (e.g.) C7 + S10 = 17 (C standing for 'Content', S standing for 'Style').

It is important that marking is not 'bunched': do not be reticent about awarding marks in the top and bottom bands.

Worksheet 10.3d (1): Sample responses to Paper 3, Q1 (Directed writing task)

Read the two student responses to Question 1 on Paper 3 (directed writing task).

1. Identify the different types of content included in each response ('Pros', 'Cons' and 'Additional content'), as listed in the marking guidance (see **Worksheet 10.3c**). Mark these on the two student responses in this worksheet.

2. Then decide how many marks you would award for Reading (out of 10) and Writing (out of 15), using **Worksheet 10.3c** and a copy of the generic Paper 3, Section 1 mark scheme which your teacher will give you.

	Reading	Writing	Total
Sample student response A			
Sample student response B			

Sample student response A

Dear Nan and Grandad

Mum told me that you rang up last night and asked what I wanted for my Birthday. I'm hoping she said a games console – but she says that she told you I want a new bike. As I'm not sure whether she's teasing or not I thought I'd drop you a line.

The thing is a console would change my life. It's a blue ray player, a way of getting on the net and a source of hours of fun-all in one. (That would save money in the long run as I could give Kelly my old DVD player.) I'd even be able to put all your old photo's on there Nan...

I know that Mum is worried that I'll spend too long on a console and become a couch potato but actually the games I've been looking at are quite active. In fact Mum and dad could get involved too. There's a brilliant workout on there and even a golf game for Dad. I've got a friend whose whole family play on theirs together. We could even get you two over for a table tennis tournament- on screen of course Nan, I know you've got a bad knee.

Dad reckons I only want a console to play what he calls 'death and destruction' games. I am quite keen on some of those but they do have age ratings on the boxes and he could check that I haven't got any that are over 15s. He can put a parent lock or a timer on it too so that I can't stay up too late or pay all day when they're out shopping.

I'm a bit offended that everyone thinks I'm going to turn into some violent hooligan just because I play games on a console. I do know what's real you know. I've been reading fairy tales since I was tiny but I don't expect pumpkins to turn into carriages do I? The game I'm really after is amazing- it's called Final fantasy and it's a strategy game. My teacher plays it online and he reckons it's actually good for the brain- and as hard as chess.

So-there are three new consoles just out. I'd be happy with any of them to be honest- but if you like we could go down and have a look together? I could show you how to play cards online and then you could play even when you have to rest your bad leg.

See you soon I hope

John

Worksheet 10.3d (2): Sample responses to Paper 3, Q1 (Directed writing task)

Sample student response B

Dear Nan

I really want a games console for Christmas and Mum said I should ask u because she won't get me one.

Everyone at school's got one and they all play online for hours and I feel left out. I get really bored at the weekend but if I had one of these I could play loads of different games with my friends without even having to get out of bed.

There are loads of great games out-and I really like all of them but Mum says I cant have anything rated 18 because Jordan might hear swearing and copy it. How pathetic is that? Think of the fairy tales she reads him. They aren't all bad though. Violent games account for 1 in 2000 games sold. If they give me a chance I can show her some great games.

If I got one then we could watch films on it when you come over because you can plug it into the telly and watch dvds.

Please get me one. I promise I'll wash your car every week Grandad.

Jeff

Worksheet 10.3e (1): Sample responses to Paper 3, Q2 (Descriptive writing)

Read the two student responses to Question 2 of Paper 3 (composition – descriptive). Your teacher will give you a copy of the generic Paper 3, Section 2 mark scheme to help you decide which band each response belongs in for:

- content and structure (Table A, 1st column) – mark out of 13
- style and accuracy (Table B) – mark out of 12.

	Content and structure	Style and accuracy
Sample student response A		
Sample student response B		

Sample student response A

The Threat

Thud! Thud! Thud! The ground shaked as his heavy footsteps slammed it, causing everyone around to shiver in fear, running a chill down their spine, him giving an angry stare at anyone he set his eyes on. He had a very fair complexion, and his dark black eyes were a great contrast to his skin colour. He had a big thick beard completely covering the outline of his face. His long hair was also jet black, falling slightly below his hair – it looked as if it hadn't been washed in weeks.

He wore a white sleeveless vest, which exposed his extra-bulging biceps. It seemed as if he hit the gym all night every day. The mere sight of his biceps would intimidate even the greatest of gangsters. His nerves could be clearly traced as his skin above the nerves rose at an elevated height. He had a big giant tattoo of a black eagle, almost completely covering his upper left arm. On his other arm, there was a tattoo of a skeleton with a sword going through his face! It probably signified his attitude towards his victims: no one knows for sure as no one has the guts to even speak to him. Also, on his right hand is a black bracelet with the word 'KILL' written on it. He wore a brass knuckle on his right hand, reason enough to fear him!

He wore dark-green military pants, just the type that soldiers wear. Rumour has it that he is a trained army officer. Also, there are rumours that there is a gun – a Desert Hawk, and a melee – safely kept in his pockets, along with a steel chain too, for added armour!

Once, he was crossing the road, and a car, on the road, rang the horn to tell him to hurry up. This made him so angry that he opened the door of the car, and threw the driver on the road, and then he sat in the car, and ran him over! He ran him over in his own car!

Black Eagle, as he is referred to by everyone (due to his tattoo) strikes fear in every soul he sets his eyes on. He isn't someone you'd want to mess with that's for sure. Beware, the Black Eagle might just be in your locality, right now! Beware!

Worksheet 10.3e (2): Sample responses to Paper 3, Q2 (Descriptive writing)

Sample student response B

The Forgotten Corner

I was six; and a young and naïve age it was. The sultry days of the summer of 1996 seemed never ending as I visited my ancestral home accompanied by my parents and a parade of suitcases and steamer trunks. It is all a haze of sun filled days and indulgent adults, until the day I lost my lucky blue ball, the one that my frail, dear old, grandmother had gifted me. My blood boiled at their indifference; every time I heard, 'I don't know Tom, ask Ms Smith (the house keeper) or Mr Eustace (the butler) or Willa (the cook) or Mr Wade (the gardener)!' from my cousins when I asked them to find it. I even asked Sarah, the girl with the 'cooties', and she replied, 'Forget it Tommy, it's only a stupid ball!' I could not stand an insult to my precious possession and almost thumped her. Only the forbidding presence of my tall, glowering grandfather stopped me from doing so.

However, I was not to be thwarted – searching high and low in the airy old house, until one day I reached a place that I can only call the 'forgotten corner'. It seemed a place everyone had forsaken. It was a corner unlike any other, standing quietly in the shadows at the far end of the extraordinarily enormous nursery. We children had never realized or even noticed it. I knew instantly that it was the 'mysterious land' where Ms Smith had hidden all the merit candies. My eyes glistened with glee; surely this was where all treasure ended up?

It smelt different though, not the sweet smell of licorice lollies or gummy bears we normally associated with the Amahs, but the fresh, strong smell of Aloe Vera, I used my, then, sharp young eyes to hunt for the source and within no time felt myself craning upwards in awe at a looming, marble window sill, crammed with infinite pots of deep green rubbery shards that gracefully danced in the soothing breeze.

My face was stroked with the cool air and the sweet smell of lavender from Grandma's gardens overwhelmed me incredibly. I peered downward, yearning to catch a blue flash and know that my quest was over but instead was treated to a feast of smooth wood, all the colours of the chocolates Mama kept in her sitting room, which stretched away in front of me. No dusty rugs with faded patterns telling me stories of olden days – just smooth boards inviting me to slide, slide, slide.

I tip-toed backwards, anxiously checking the thick, dusty curtains which were clumped in grey pillars around the window – just in case one of my horrid cousins was lurking, ready to tell. My pupils dilated suddenly as I took flight, launching myself across the shiny expanse and then skimming, effortlessly and unexpectedly towards… a towering bookcase – full of treasures!

As I collided with the heavy wood it rocked, a beast shaking off a small assailant, and one by one its content started to spill. A shower of books in all possible colours and shades lured me towards them even as they fluttered – musty pages rustling – past my head. I ducked gingerly as small tin cars, red and green where the paint was still visible, rained down – and then the real trouble began as the plop of hard hail told me that a jar of ancient marbles had finally tipped and was on it's way towards me. Each hit the floor solid and sharp making crack-crack noises like the bullets Mr Wade used to scare off the herons when they try to spear Grandma's fish. My heart thumped like a drum as I waited for the inevitable…

'Tommy! What are you doing now?' The cry of indignant cousins hung in the air – but I was oblivious. There, nestled, like a precious egg, in amongst the scattered gravel carpet of marbles was my ball. I lunged, triumphant, and then smoothed it lovingly feeling its gentle pressure return my embrace.

Worksheet 10.3f (1): Sample responses to Paper 3, Q3 (Narrative writing)

Read the two student responses to Question 3 of Paper 3 (Composition – narrative). Your teacher will give you a copy of the generic Paper 3, Section 2 mark scheme to help you decide which band each response belongs in for:

- content and structure (Table A, 1st column) – mark out of 13
- style and accuracy (Table B) – mark out of 12.

	Content and structure	Style and accuracy
Sample student response A		
Sample student response B		

Sample student response A

Abandoned

Abandoned. That's how I found you. You want to know how I felt at that moment? It was with sheer horror that I looked at you – you were a day old baby, covered in nothing but a flimsy cloth, lying on top of a heap of filth by the roadside. But when you looked at me, it was almost a miracle. You stopped crying and I felt a connection so strong that everything else paled in significance.

What was I doing there? It was one of the poorest areas of our city where the lowest strata of people eked out their living and subsisted on nothing but the leftovers thrown by the poor quality eateries, the muddy water supplied by leaking pipes that were centuries old and the rancid air that pervaded the entire place. As a newly recruited journalist of 'The Daily Times', it was my very first assignment to do a feature on the place teeming as it was with poor immigrants, the homeless and beggars.

That's how I came to be on that particular street looking at a motley crowd that had gathered around you. You were bawling your lungs out – even then you were a fighter, I could see it. No one wanted to touch you. It took me a good ten minutes to decide what I was going to do…

Now, you are with me. Sixteen years have elapsed. Sixteen years of love, laughter and happiness mingled with acrimony, tears and pain. There have been good times with all their highs and then there have also been those moments of despair when you have tried me to the utmost and have tested my patience and understanding. My family thought I would have to sacrifice my life and career for you. They were dead set against my adoption of you. But still, I went ahead – firm in my decision, knowing that raising you as a single parent would not be an easy task.

Why am I telling you all this? Well, it's your sixteenth birthday today. And you are a grown up girl now. And I want you to know the truth of your birth.

Would you like me to continue? Yes? I can see your face, so beautiful and innocent with your questioning eyes looking into mine…Yes, I will tell you all.

Worksheet 10.3f (2): Sample responses to Paper 3, Q3 (Narrative writing)

Sample student response B

Abandoned

Me and my hiking group had been on the move for 6 hours. We were on our way to Mount Red Rock, 120 km from Sandy Shades, the town we had started at.

It was my second hike since March, I had enlisted on a program with some friends. I agreed to hike in the moutinous regions of Australia.

'How you holding up Kev?' asked my friend Jack. 'better than you for sure' I replied. We smiled at each other, we had been friends since pre nursery. 'Well let's just see if you can say that when that storm comes!' Jack said. 'Oh I am not worried about that. I'm more worried about that big butt of yours falling on me!' I said. The entire group was chuckling encluding Jack. Then the guide reminded us that we have been hiking for 6 hours and in another 3 we would stop for dinner.

The entire group was relieved but Jack being witty as he is answered 'Oh come on! Just three hours? We can hike till the next day!' The guide smiled and answered 'Sure if you were to fancy to death. Plus with that storm coming you wouldn't stand a chance.' Again everyone laughed but not for long since we were all tired.

An hour passed without a sound. We were all tired. By now I had fallen to the back and Jack, like always was at the front. 'Ouch!' cried a girl, breaking the silence. 'Are you alright? What happened?' asked the guide. 'I'm, fine, just have a cramp' she replied. The guide thought for a while before informing. 'OK, let's all take a break.' Everyone cheered as they sat on their bags and started eating everything.

I sat down behind a rock, out of sight, at the back. I noticed just how tired I was. Slowly my eyes closed and I fell asleep as the sun set.

When I woke the first thing I noticed was the darkness, then I noticed something a little more frightening – everyone was gone. 'Hello?' I asked the night. 'Guys!' I shouted, but got no replie. I didn't know which way the group had gone, but I started walking forward. It was dark and that must be why I didn't see the drop and as I fell and hit the bottom, I fell asleep for a second time.

This time when I woke the first thing I noticed was the pain in my leg, it was broken. I looked around but saw nothing above me is the cliff I fell off of.

I've tried calling for help but the thunder in the distance covers my noise. It is getting cold, I just hope I get through the night. For now however all I can do is write.

Its October 5th and I believe I am truly abandoned.

Worksheet 10.3g — Paper 3 Self-review

Task Now that you have marked your own response to Practice Paper 3, you should be able to identify your strengths and weaknesses and set targets for improvement. Complete the table below in order to record your findings and conclusions.

Question	Mark	At my target level?	Could be improved	Specific weakness(es)
1 Reading				
1 Writing				
2 Content and structure				
2 Style and accuracy				

Targets (try to set several for each question type)

1 Directed writing

   a) Reading

   b) Writing

2 Composition

   a) Content and structure

   b) Style and accuracy

Appendix 1 — Summary questions: exam focus

Summary questions test your ability to:

- understand texts
- make clear, brief notes
- select, order and collate information and present it in your own words
- write concisely and fluently.

Core: Paper 1, Question 3 (15 marks)

You will be given one question following Reading Passage B. Question 3 is a two-part summary question, for which you will have 25–30 minutes. For part (a) of this question, you will need to make notes on key points from the passage. In part (b), you will be asked to summarise information on a particular aspect of the passage in 100–150 words using your notes from part (a).

This question is worth 15 marks, 5 marks of which are for the quality of your writing.

This question tests Assessment objectives R1, R2 and R5, and W1, W2 and W3.

Extended: Paper 2, Question 3 (20 marks)

You will be given one question following Reading Passage B. Question 3 is a two-part summary question, for which you will have about 40–45 minutes. For part (a) of this question, you will need to make notes on key points from the passage. In part (b), you will then be asked to write a summary about a particular aspect of the passage in 200–250 words using your notes from part (a).

The question is worth 20 marks, 5 marks of which are for the quality of your writing.

This question tests Assessment objectives R1, R2 and R5, and W1, W2 and W3.

Checklist for success

Understanding the question:

- ✓ Read the question carefully.
- ✓ Focus on what the question asks.
- ✓ Underline the main points in the passage(s) relating to the question.

Preparing to answer the question:

- ✓ Locate: find key points from the text, using skimming and scanning.
- ✓ Select: choose the most relevant points from those you've found and list these as notes.
- ✓ Order: put these points in the best order to answer the question, using your own words.

Answering the question:

- ✓ Make sure you provide the information the question asks for.
- ✓ Cover all the main relevant points and structure your summary logically.
- ✓ Try to use some complex sentences, combining points that are well punctuated and fluent.
- ✓ Write tightly and succinctly.
- ✓ Do not include introductory or concluding sentences, but get straight into the summary.
- ✓ Avoid including any quotations or examples.

Appendix 2: Writer's effects questions: exam focus

Writer's effects questions test your ability to understand how writers achieve effects.

Writer's effects questions appear on both Paper 1 (Core) and Paper 2 (Extended). They will ask you to respond to a passage by answering questions about the effect of particular words, phrases or other techniques the writer uses to make an impact on the reader.

Core: Paper 1, Question 1

You will be given two questions following Passage A, which will be 500–600 words long. Question 1 is a multi-part comprehension question, for which you will have about 35 minutes. As part of this, you will have two specific tasks on writer's effects. These should take you 15–20 minutes in total.

Answer in full sentences where you can, but keep to the point and focus on the task. The writer's effect questions are worth 9 marks in total.

Extended: Paper 2, Question 2

You will read Passage A of about 650–750 words. After you have answered an extended response question on Passage A, the second question (called the 'language question' in the IGCSE syllabus) will focus on writer's effects. Question 2 is worth 10 marks and you will have about 20 minutes to respond to it. It will be broken into two parts and ask you to:

- reread specified paragraphs or sections of the passage
- make your own choice of a specified number of words and phrases that create effects from these sections and write about them.

Checklist for success

Understanding the question:

- ✓ Read the question carefully.
- ✓ Make sure you understand what the question is asking of you.
- ✓ To understand what effects the writer might be seeking to achieve, work out what sensory or emotive appeals the writer is making to the reader. Ask yourself:
  - How does the writer/narrator seem to feel?
  - How does he or she want us to feel or think?
  - What words, phrases or techniques have been chosen to achieve this?
  - What mood or atmosphere do these choices create?

Answering the question:

- ✓ To answer the question, follow a clear process:
  - Locate the words and phrases or section referred to.
  - For Paper 2, select the words or phrases needed or referred to.
  - Explain or analyse what is being suggested.
- ✓ Make sure you can understand and explain the meaning of particular words and phrases.
- ✓ Draw conclusions and inferences about the atmosphere and tone created.
- ✓ You choose words and phrases carefully to answer the question.

For higher grades:

- ✓ Read between the lines for implied or suggested meanings.
- ✓ Aim to not only explain, but also interpret meaning, using your own words.
- ✓ Think about how effects work together so you can comment on combined effects.

Appendix 3: Extended response and directed writing questions: exam focus

Extended response questions appear in Question 2 of Paper 1 (Core) and Question 1 of Paper 2 (Extended), and directed writing appears in Section 1 of Paper 3 (Core and Extended).

Extended response/directed writing questions test your **reading** ability – that you can:
- demonstrate understanding of explicit meanings
- demonstrate understanding of implicit meanings and attitudes
- analyse, evaluate and develop facts, ideas and opinions.

These questions also test your **writing** ability – that you can:
- articulate experience and express what is thought, felt and imagined
- sequence facts, ideas and opinions
- use a range of appropriate vocabulary
- use register appropriate to audience and context
- make accurate use of spelling, punctuation and grammar (Paper 3 only).

Core: Paper 1, Question 2, extended response (15 marks)

You read Passage A on the question paper and respond to it as directed with a piece of extended writing (200–300 words). You will have about 25 minutes for this. You will be marked out of 5 for your writing skills and out of 10 for your reading skills.

Extended: Paper 2, Question 1, extended response (20 marks)

This question refers to Passage A. You are asked to use and develop the information there in another form as a piece of extended writing (250–350 words), e.g. a letter, an article, a report, a speech or a dialogue. You will have about 40 minutes for this. You will be marked out of 15 for your reading skills and out of 5 for your writing skills.

Paper 3, Section 1, directed writing (25 marks)

You read one or more texts on the question paper. You are then directed to use and develop the given information in another form, e.g. a discursive or argumentative letter or article of 250–350 words. You will have about 60 minutes for this. You will be marked out of 15 for your writing skills and out of 10 for your reading skills.

Checklist for success

Decode the question:
- ✓ Make sure you are clear what the question is asking you to do. For example:
  - **what role/voice** you need to take on to write the text
  - **why** you are writing (main purpose)
  - the **type or form** of writing you must do, if provided
  - **who** it is for (the audience)
  - **what to include** (information from the texts provided and your own ideas).

Match your content to what the question asks:

For example:
- ✓ Make your 'voice' convincing – if the role/voice is of a young reporter, for example, make sure your style matches how he or she would write.
- ✓ Maintain your focus on the purpose; if it is to persuade someone rather than analyse a situation, use appropriate persuasive language.
- ✓ If the form is an article, do not write in the form of a letter! This may seem obvious, but these things can be easily missed.
- ✓ Get the content right. If the question asks you to give the reasons or evidence, make sure you do just that.
- ✓ Use the information you have been given, but make sure you add your own ideas as long as they are linked back to what is in the text.
- ✓ Organise your answer carefully. Points from the text should be reused in an order that suits the task.

Appendix 4: Composition questions: exam focus

Composition is the focus of Section 2 of Paper 3 (Core and Extended). This question allows you to write more freely without the need to draw information from a specific passage or text. It offers a real opportunity to 'show off' your writing skills in original, yet appropriate ways.

The composition question tests your ability to:

- articulate experience and express what is thought, felt and imagined
- sequence facts, ideas and opinions
- use a range of appropriate vocabulary
- use register appropriate to audience and context
- make accurate use of spelling, punctuation and grammar.

Paper 3, Section 2 (25 marks)

Section 2 makes up 50% of Paper 3 and is worth 50% of the marks, i.e. 25 marks.

You have about an hour to write a 350–450 word composition, choosing one title out of a choice of:

- two descriptive titles
- two narrative titles.

For the composition response, up to 13 marks are awarded for content and structure and up to 12 marks are awarded for style and accuracy.

Checklist for success

Choose your task carefully:

- ✓ Read all tasks/titles – do not just choose the first task you find in the list that you like.
- ✓ Choose the task that will allow you to shine and 'show off' your skills.

Draw on what you know:

- ✓ You will have spent a great deal of time learning how to write in each of these two different styles. Remember the specific ideas about content, structure and style which your teacher will have discussed with you.

For descriptive or narrative tasks:

- ✓ Use ambitious and well-chosen vocabulary.
- ✓ Create vivid images in the reader's mind through simile, metaphor, use of the senses and varied sentences.
- ✓ Consider and take an original 'angle' on the story or description, particularly when considering its structure, where experimentation and conscious use of structural techniques is rewarded.
- ✓ Maintain a focus on correct grammar, punctuation, paragraphing, spelling, etc.

Appendix 5: Written coursework focus

You have to write three coursework assignments to complete your portfolio, which will be assessed by an external moderator. There are a total of **50 marks** available.

Component 4: Coursework portfolio (50 marks)

You submit a portfolio of three assignments, each of about 500 to 800 words. You can do the assignments in any order. The assignments are:

- **Assignment 1**: informative, analytical and/or argumentative
- **Assignment 2**: descriptive and/or narrative
- **Assignment 3**: a response to a text or texts chosen by your teachers – the text(s) will contain facts, ideas, opinions and arguments, and you should respond to them by selecting, analysing and evaluating points from the material. You can write in any appropriate form that you wish.

Your work may be handwritten or word-processed, and you may use dictionaries.

You must include the **first draft** for **one** of the three assignments submitted. This first draft will not contribute to your mark.

Your Coursework portfolio primarily tests your **writing** ability – i.e. that you can:

- articulate experience and express what is thought, felt and imagined
- sequence facts, ideas and opinions
- use a range of appropriate vocabulary
- use register appropriate to audience and context
- make accurate use of spelling, punctuation and grammar.

Assignment 3 also tests your **reading** ability – i.e. that you can:

- demonstrate understanding of explicit meanings
- demonstrate understanding of implicit meanings and attitudes
- analyse, evaluate and develop facts, ideas and opinions.

You will be marked out of a total of 40 for your writing skills across the assignments and (for Assignment 3 only) out of 10 for your reading skills.

Checklist for success

For Assignment 1:
- ✓ Focus on the purpose: how are you going to inform, analyse or argue? Draw on all the skills and techniques you know about writing in this way.
- ✓ Choose a topic or issue that really interests you and which can be sustained.
- ✓ Try to choose an interesting form of writing rather than a straightforward essay.

For Assignment 2:
- ✓ Ensure you are clear about the distinctive stylistic requirements of narrative and descriptive writing.
- ✓ Generate a range of inventive, ambitious and original ideas by trying out multiple ideas and story-lines at the planning stage.
- ✓ When considering which of your ideas to develop, think about whether your idea has enough depth and potential to show off your language skills.
- ✓ Plan the structure of your piece with care.
- ✓ Use ambitious vocabulary, imagery, compelling characters, plot twists, sentence variety, as required by the task you choose.

For Assignment 3:
- ✓ Ensure you refer selectively to the facts, data and opinions from the text or texts you have chosen to write about and evaluate them in your own response.
- ✓ Add your own ideas to those provided in the chosen text.
- ✓ Make sure your response is logical, well sequenced, argued or explained coherently and clearly with language that matches the purpose.

For **all assignments**: check your work thoroughly for correct spelling, punctuation and grammar usage.

Appendix 6: Speaking and listening: exam focus

You have to give an individual presentation, which will be assessed by an examiner. You will then discuss the topic with the examiner (or your teacher). There are a total of **30 marks** available.

Part 1: **Individual task (3–4 minutes)** **(10 marks)**

You will give a presentation, a talk, a speech or a monologue. For example, you might talk about a recent film you have seen, suggesting why others might also like it.

The **individual task** tests your ability to:

- articulate experience and express what is thought, felt and imagined
- present facts, ideas and opinions in a sustained, cohesive order
- communicate clearly and fluently and purposefully as an individual and in dialogue with other speakers
- use register appropriate to audience and context.

Part 2: **Discussion (6–7 minutes)** **(20 marks)**

The **individual task** leads into a conversation with the teacher or examiner about your chosen topic. So, for example, you could develop a talk about a film into discussion of wider issues such as censorship, popular culture and the film industry.

The **discussion** tests your ability to:

- articulate experience and express what is thought, felt and imagined
- present facts, ideas and opinions in a sustained, cohesive order
- communicate clearly and fluently and purposefully as an individual and in dialogue with other speakers
- use register appropriate to audience and context
- listen to and respond appropriately to the contributions of others.

Checklist for success

First be sure of your priorities:

- ✓ Choose a topic about which you have genuine knowledge.
- ✓ Research, so that basic understanding is well supported by background details. For example, if talking about a film: *information about the actors and the director, whether the film is a re-make, the critics' views.*
- ✓ Plan, so that the presentation moves smoothly through its different sections.
- ✓ Prepare an impressive opening and ending.

To deal with the discussion:

- ✓ Make a list of further questions the teacher/examiner might ask. For example: *Why is this sort of movie popular? Is it justifiable to spend so much time and money on a movie?*
- ✓ Prepare some ideas about how to reply to these.

Use these techniques to impress during the discussion:

- ✓ Sustain the use of standard English.
- ✓ Use rhetorical language, where appropriate: *I'm sure you would agree that...; Isn't it fair to say...?*
- ✓ Demonstrate the ability to organise thoughts, even in discussion: *Could I offer three thoughts in response...? First, it is fair to say that... Secondly...*
- ✓ Recognise the need to respond to original ideas: *That is an interesting idea. I had never thought of that before. However, when you think that...*
- ✓ Have the confidence to challenge, where appropriate: *I'm sorry, but I don't think that is correct. Most movie lovers are perceptive and make judgments based on...*
- ✓ Talk confidently with the examiner, rather than just answer questions: *Yes. And so, have you yourself ever thought: 'That scene could have been directed better by...?'*
- ✓ Be calm and thoughtful.

Finally, stay focused...

... so you don't forget what the other speaker has said. Stick to the point you are supposed to be talking about.

Appendix 7: Speaking and listening: coursework focus

You will be assessed by your teacher or an external moderator on your performance during the course in three different speaking and listening tasks (see examples below). There are a total of **30 marks** available, divided equally between the three tasks. These tasks test your ability to:

- articulate experience and express what is thought, felt and imagined
- present facts, ideas and opinions in a sustained, cohesive order
- communicate clearly, fluently and purposefully as an individual and in dialogue with other speakers
- use register appropriate to audience and context.
- listen to and respond appropriately to the contributions of others (Tasks 2 and 3).

Task 1: An individual activity (10 marks)

This could be a presentation, a talk, a speech or a monologue (in character). For example, you talk about your favourite hobby or describe a place that enjoyed visiting.

Task 2: A pair-based activity (10 marks)

For example, you and another student role-play an argument between two neighbours; or your teacher will interview you and another student about how something at school could be improved.

Task 3: A group activity (10 marks)

For example, you and other students discuss in a group who to invite (and why) to open the new local shopping centre; in a parole board scenario, your teacher presents cases for prisoners, and you and other students discuss in a group whether or not each case merits early release.

Checklist for success

Individual activity:

- ✓ Choose a topic about which you have genuine knowledge and interest.
- ✓ Research the topic thoroughly. Include essential factual details and important attitudes or views others may have, as background: *a place you have visited may have tourist leaflets; a book on its history, pointing out its good and bad features.*
- ✓ Plan the activity carefully. Consider who your audience will be and structure your activity so that the audience can follow your line of thought or argument throughout.
- ✓ Prepare an opening that immediately engages your audience, and an ending that they will remember.

Pair and group activities:

- ✓ Prepare thoroughly, by researching factual details, alternative arguments and views.
- ✓ Have extra detail, to support, develop or modify your ideas as necessary.
- ✓ In discussion, put your case or view firmly and confidently: *I must point out, though, that...*
- ✓ If you are leading a group activity, research the topic as much as possible. Be prepared to introduce new detail or ideas into the discussion.
- ✓ Show you are listening to the other person or persons. Ask pertinent questions: for extra detail or clarification; to challenge views; to summarise another viewpoint or argument. This will clearly demonstrate that you have heard and understood what has been said: *Yes, I see your point, but have you thought of these consequences...?*
- ✓ If using role play, develop sufficient background to the role to make the character believable.
- ✓ When a role play is prepared, ensure you make an equal contribution to that of your partner(s).
- ✓ If you are taking a role, balance being a believable character with putting forward the character's views clearly. Don't concentrate on one and ignore the other.

Use these techniques to impress:

- ✓ Sustain the use of standard English in most circumstances.
- ✓ Use rhetorical language, where appropriate: *I'm sure you would agree that...; Isn't it fair to say...?*
- ✓ Demonstrate that you can think clearly, even under pressure in a discussion.
- ✓ Stay calm and be thoughtful.
- ✓ Don't digress: stick to the topic.

Appendix 8 (1) — Two-year scheme of work: Year 1

The tables on these two pages suggest a structure for using the materials in the Student Book and Teacher Guide over a two-year course. Each year is divided into six 'units', with each unit equating to approximately 18 to 24 hours of teaching time.

Year 1

Unit 1	Unit 2	Unit 3
Skills focus: An introduction to Reading skills: • skimming • scanning • selecting • recognising explicit meaning • recognising implicit meaning • synthesis. *Student Book Chapter 1*	**Skills focus:** An introduction to Reading skills: • skimming • scanning • selecting • recognising explicit meaning • recognising implicit meaning • synthesis. *Student Book Chapter 1*	**Skills focus:** An introduction to Writing skills: The conventions of forms *Student Book Chapter 3: Lessons 1–6* Key technical skills *Student Book Chapter 2*
Exam focus: Summary questions *Student Book Chapter 4* *Chapter 5: Lessons 1 and 2*	**Exam focus:** Summary questions *Student Book Chapter 4*	**Exam focus:** Extended and directed writing *Student Book Chapter 6*
Speaking and listening: Group activity: opportunity 1 *Student Book Chapter 9:* *Lessons 1–3, 6–12*	**Speaking and listening:** Paired activity: opportunity 1 *Student Book Chapter 9:* *Lessons 1–3, 6–8, 10–12*	**Speaking and listening:** Paired activity: opportunity 2 *Student Book Chapter 9:* *Lessons 1–3, 6–8, 10–12*

Unit 4	Unit 5	Unit 6
Skills focus: Writing for a purpose *Student Book Chapter 3:* *Lessons 7–15*	**Skills focus:** Recap on recognising implicit meaning Recognising words that stimulate the senses Recognising words that stimulate the emotions *Student Book Chapter 1: Lessons 4–9*	**Skills focus:** Descriptive writing (One task could be used as Coursework piece 2*.) *Student Book Chapter 7:* *Lessons 1, 2, 3, 4, 7* *Chapter 8, Lessons 1, 3, 6*
Exam focus: Extended and directed writing *Student Book Chapter 6*	**Exam focus:** Writer's effects questions *Student Book Chapter 5: Lessons 3–6*	**Exam focus:** Descriptive writing *Student Book Chapter 7:* *Lessons 1, 2, 3, 4, 7*
Speaking and listening: Individual activity: opportunity 1 (This activity could be developed to offer an opportunity to cover skills ready for the Speaking and listening examination if being taken.) *Student Book Chapter 9:* *Lessons 1–5, 10–12*	**Speaking and listening:** Group activity: opportunity 2 *Student Book Chapter 9:* *Lessons 1–3, 6–12*	**Speaking and listening:** Paired activity: opportunity 3 *Student Book Chapter 9:* *Lessons 1–3, 6–8, 10–12*

* Students taking Component 4, Coursework, rather than the Paper 3 examination could utilise a piece of formative assessment from this Unit for their portfolio, as long as the level of independent work involved was appropriate.

Appendix 8 (2) Two-year scheme of work: Year 2

Year 2

Unit 1	Unit 2	Unit 3
Exam focus: Narrative writing (One task could be used as Coursework piece 2*.) *Student Book Chapter 7: Lessons 1–2, 5–6* *Chapter 8: Lessons 1, 3, 6*	**Exam focus:** Discursive/argumentative writing (One extended and developed task could be used as Coursework piece 1*.) *Student Book Chapter 6: Lesson 4* *Chapter 8: Lessons 1, 2, 6*	**Exam focus:** Extended and directed writing recap (One task could be developed into a Coursework piece 3*, but additional preparation would be required.) *Student Book Chapter 6* *Chapter 8: Lessons 1, 4–6*
Speaking and listening: Group activity: opportunity 3 *Student Book Chapter 9: Lessons 1–3, 6–12*	**Speaking and listening:** Individual activity: opportunity 2 (This activity could be developed to offer an opportunity to cover skills ready for the Speaking and listening examination if being taken.) *Student Book Chapter 9: Lessons 1–5, 10–12*	
Unit 4	**Unit 5**	**Unit 6**
Examination practice Chapter 10	Examination practice Chapter 10	Examination practice Chapter 10

* Students taking Component 4, Coursework, rather than the Paper 3 examination could utilise a piece of formative assessment from this Unit for their portfolio, as long as the level of independent work involved was appropriate.